Schooling Internationally

The number of schools that call themselves international is growing expo-nentially. In addition, many other schools are exploring the concept of international-mindedness and what that might mean in the contemporary world of globalisation.

This book sets out to provide a critical perspective on current issues facing 'international schooling', particularly the conflict between 'internationalising' and 'globalising' tendencies and to explore these as they affect teaching and learning, curriculum, pedagogy and assessment as well as to explore the contribution international schools might make to the achievement of global citizenship. It is the first book to critically analyse the ambiguities, tensions and conflicts that face those involved with, and researching, international schools and their role in global networking. Issues addressed include:

- the political economy of international schools;
- their relations to global and local cultures, global markets and civil society;
- the role of international schools in global networking;
- the micropolitics of such schools;
- the growth, complexity and challenges facing the International Bacca-laureate;
- the future demands for and of teachers in international schools;
- the nature of teaching and learning in international schools;
- the problematic idea of an international curriculum;
- issues facing international assessment;
- the challenge of education for global citizenship.

This provocative book will be essential reading for those teaching in, leading and governing international schools in countries around the world, as well as those who are contemplating entering the rapidly expanding world of international schooling.

Richard Bates is Professor of Social and Administrative Studies in the Faculty of Education at Deakin University, Australia.

Schooling Internationally

Globalisation, internationalisation and the future for international schools

**Edited by
Richard Bates**

Routledge
Taylor & Francis Group

LONDON AND NEW YORK

First edition published 2011
by Routledge
2 Park Square, Milton Park, Abingdon, Oxon, OX14 4RN

Simultaneously published in the USA and Canada
by Routledge
270 Madison Avenue, New York, NY 10016

Routledge is an imprint of the Taylor & Francis Group, an informa business

Typeset in Garamond Three by
Florence Production Ltd, Stoodleigh, Devon
Printed and bound in Great Britain by
CPI Antony Rowe, Chippenham, Wiltshire

British Library Cataloguing in Publication Data
A catalogue record for this book is available from the British Library

Library of Congress Cataloging-in-Publication Data
Schooling internationally : globalisation, internationalisation, and the
future for international schools / [edited by] Richard Bates.
    p. cm.
    1. International education. 2. International schools. 3. Education and
    globalization. I. Bates, Richard J.
    LC1090.S423 2011
    370.116—dc22   2010025863

ISBN13: 978-0-415-58927-7 (hbk)
ISBN13: 978-0-415-58928-4 (pbk)
ISBN13: 978-0-203-83480-0 (ebk)

Contents

Notes on contributors   vii

1 Introduction   1
   RICHARD BATES

2 Global networking and the world of international
   education   21
   MICHAEL WYLIE

3 The political economy of international schools
   and social class formation   39
   CERI BROWN AND HUGH LAUDER

4 International schools and micropolitics: fear,
   vulnerability and identity in fragmented space   59
   RICHARD CAFFYN

5 Teachers for the international school of the future   83
   MARY HAYDEN AND JEFF THOMPSON

6 Teaching and learning in international schools:
   a consideration of the stakeholders and their
   expectations   101
   HELEN FAIL

7 International curriculum   121
   JAMES CAMBRIDGE

8 Assessment and international schools   148
   RICHARD BATES

9   The International Baccalaureate: its growth and
     complexity of challenges   165
     TRISTAN BUNNELL

10 Education for global citizenship: reflecting upon the
     instrumentalist agendas at play   182
     HARRIET MARSHALL

     Name index   201
     Subject index   207

Contributors

Richard Bates is Professor of Education (Social and Administrative Studies) in the School of Education at Deakin University. His scholarly work has been concerned with the Sociology of Education (where he contributed to the debate over the 'new' sociology of education in Britain in the 1970s) and Educational Administration (where he contributed to the emergence of an alternative 'critical' theory during the 1980s). His work as Dean (1986–2000) drew him into debates over teacher education and his Presidency of the Victorian and Australian Councils of Deans of Education led him to contest official views regarding teacher supply and demand and to challenge the marginalisation of teacher education programmes. He is past President of the Australian Teacher Education Association, a past President of the Australian Association for Researchers in Education and a Fellow of the Australian College of Education, the Australian Council for Educational Administration and the Australia Teacher Education Association. He has recently written about morals and markets, public education, ethics and administration, the impact of educational research, and social justice and the aesthetics and emotions of educational administration as well as teacher education. His current preoccupation is with the development of international schools.

Ceri Brown currently holds an ESRC Ph.D. studentship at the University of Bath, into the schooling experiences of turbulent children from low-income backgrounds. She was previously a teaching fellow on the early childhood studies top BA programme at Bath and has six years' experience conducting qualitative and ethnographic research with children and young people. Her research interests include: the effects on pupils of moving schools and transition, international schooling, social capital theory, the role and function of friendship, children's learner identities, early childhood care and education and children in poverty.

Tristan Bunnell has taught IB Diploma Economics for twenty years. He worked at the International School of London for fourteen years, and has been at the Copenhagen International School since 2004. He obtained his doctorate, entitled *A study of public relations activity in international schools* *and its use as an indicator of their unique character*, from the University of Southampton in 2003. His research interests include the organisational culture of international schools, and current developments in international schooling. He has published over twenty academic papers, including many about the growth and development of the International Baccalaureate.

Richard Caffyn is a Visiting Research Fellow at the University of Bath and works currently as the Elementary Director and both an IB and international schools consultant at the International School of Milan. He was, until recently, Head of Research Support and Development for the International Baccalaureate. He is a leading researcher and presenter on international school micropolitics and has worked as a teacher, divisional head and administrator in schools throughout Europe. His research interests and publications focus on international school management, leadership and cultures, as well as power and conflict in schools. He is currently undertaking post-doctoral work into the reasons why micropolitics occur in international schools and organisational psychodynamics.

James Cambridge is an independent international education consultant. He was formerly Head of Research Projects with the International Baccalaureate Research Unit at the University of Bath. Dr Cambridge has worked in Britain, the Middle East and Southern Africa in a variety of educational contexts including science teaching, assessment, curriculum development, initial teacher education and continuing professional development. His research interests include inquiry into international curriculum, international schools, evaluation of institutions and educational programmes, and intergenerational service learning. Publications include chapters in edited books and articles in peer-reviewed journals.

Helen Fail was course leader for the MA in Education: International Schools at Oxford Brookes University from 2002 to 2008 where she taught courses relating to cross-cultural issues and a multilingual and multicultural education. Her doctoral research was on the life histories of former international school students examining the long-term effects of an internationally mobile and cross-cultural childhood. Prior to this she taught French and English in national and international schools in the UK, France, Nigeria, Israel, Switzerland and the US and worked as a cross-cultural consultant focusing on cross-cultural transition and the characteristics of third culture kids (TCKs). She currently works as a freelance educational consultant specialising in cross-cultural issues.

Mary Hayden is Director of the Centre for the study of Education in an International Context (CEIC) at the University of Bath, and has directed the Masters and Doctorate programmes in Education offered by that university to large numbers of teachers working in international schools worldwide. Her postgraduate teaching and research supervision focus particularly on international schools and international education, an area in which she has researched and published widely. She has examined Masters and Doctoral level work for universities worldwide and has also directed a number of research projects. She is a member of the International Primary Curriculum (IPC) Advisory Board, academic advisor to the International Leadership Management Programme (ILMP), and Editor of the Journal of Research in International Education. She is a founding Trustee of the Alliance for International Education.

Hugh Lauder is Professor of Education and Political Economy at the University of Bath (1996 to present). He was formerly Dean of Education at Victoria University of Wellington, New Zealand. He specialises in the relationship of education to the economy and has for over ten years worked on national skill strategies and more recently on the global skill strategies of multinational companies. His books include Brown, P., Lauder, H. and Ashton, D. (2010) *The Global Auction: The Broken Promises of Opportunities, Jobs and Rewards*, Lauder, H., Brown, P., Dillabough J.-A. and Halsey, A. H. (eds) (2006) *Education, Globalization and Social Change*, Brown, P., Green, A. and Lauder, H., (2001) *High Skills: Globalisation, Competitiveness and Skill Formation*, Brown, P. and Lauder, H. (2001) *Capitalism and Social Progress: The Future of Society in a Global Economy*, (reprinted in Chinese, 2007). He has published many academic papers including on international education and globalisation, and is editor of the *Journal of Education and Work*.

Harriet Marshall is a Lecturer in International Education at the Centre for the Study of Education in an International Context, Department of Education, University of Bath. Her interests are broad and include the following: global and cosmopolitan learning; citizenship education; globalisation, education and the curriculum; and gender and global citizenship education. She has written on all of these themes in publications such as the *Journal of Curriculum Studies,* the *Cambridge Journal of Education, World Studies in Education, Gender Education and Equality in a Global Context* (Fennell and Arnot (eds) 2008, Routledge) and *The SAGE Handbook of Research in International Education* (Hayden, Thompson and Levy (eds) 2008). Prior to being a lecturer Harriet was a full-time teacher of Politics, Sociology and History at a London comprehensive school.

Jeff Thompson teaches, supervises and researches through the Centre for the study of Education in an International Context (CEIC) of the University of Bath, in areas relating to international schools and international education. He has worked closely for many years with curriculum, evaluation and assessment/examinations systems both nationally and internationally – including holding senior examination appointments for the International Baccalaureate Organization and for many universities throughout the world at undergraduate, Master's and Doctoral levels. Professor Thompson has published widely in the field of international education, is Chair of the Advisory Board for the International Primary Curriculum (IPC), and was Founding Editor of the Journal of Research in International Education. He holds Board chairmanship and membership of a number of international schools, and is a Director of the International Board for the United World Colleges. He was Founding Chair of the Alliance for International Education and continues as a Trustee.

Michael Wylie is the Director of the International School of Nice in France. He is also a member of the ECIS Heads Committee. Michael has worked as teacher, senior administrator and researcher in Vanuatu, France, Venezuela and Australia. He has worked with the International Baccalaureate Organization as an examiner and has implemented IB programmes into four schools. He has also worked with a variety of curricula models from the UK, France, the US, Fiji and Australia. Michael has completed research studying the effects of Western curricula models on indigenous students in Vanuatu from a post-colonial perspective and completed a Ph.D. exploring the relationships between theory and practice in international schools.

1 Introduction

Richard Bates

Global education: global industry

The number of identifiable international schools seems to be growing at a
very rapid rate, now standing at over 5,000, with the most rapid growth
occurring in Asia (especially China), Europe and Africa (Brummitt 2007, 2009).
As Macdonald (2006) and Bunnell (2007) suggest, there is now an 'international school industry'. That there should be such an industry should be no
surprise in view of two factors. First, as a result of globalisation, the growth
of the middle class in many developing countries has reached the point where
it is now sufficient to support the expansion of such an industry from an elite
to a more general status. As the World Bank reports:

> Globalization is likely to bring benefits to many. By 2030, 1.2 billion
> people in developing countries – 15 per cent of world population – will
> belong to the 'global middle class', up from 4000 million today. This
> group will . . . enjoy access to international travel, purchase automobiles
> and other advanced consumer durables, *attain international levels of education*
> and play a major role in shaping policies and institutions in their own
> countries and the world economy.
>
> (World Bank 2007, emphasis added)

Second, there is growing recognition that education at all levels is now a global
service industry worth billions of dollars. In 2007–8 USA overseas revenue
from international education was US$15.54 billion; UK revenue was US$ 6.34
billion; Australian revenue was US$6.9 billion and Canadian revenue US$6.5
billion (Maslen 2009). While much of this revenue concerns tertiary level study
an increasing percentage of it applies to pre-tertiary study. Clearly, as Carrie
Lips suggested (somewhat tendentiously) to the CATO Institute as far back
as 2000, 'Increasingly entrepreneurs recognise that the public's dissatisfaction
with one-size-fits all schools is more than just fodder for political debates. It
is a tremendous business opportunity' (Lips 2000).

So the context for the development of international schools is provided by
a significant growth in middle class demand for education and a recognition,

especially by English speaking countries, of the value of the international market for education services and the prospects for its privatisation and commercialisation (see also Dale and Robertson 2002; Robertson 2003; Tamatea 2005; Lauder 2007; Bhanji 2008).

But the context for the expansion of international schooling is not simply numerical. It is also ideological, for this growth in numbers has coincided with the globalisation of neo-liberal ideologies committed to the reorganisation of societies and social relations. In particular, as Robertson argues, neo-liberalism has three main aims:

> (1) the redistribution of wealth upward to the ruling elites through new structures of governance, (2) the transformation of education systems so that the production of workers for the economy is the primary mandate and (3) the breaking down of education as a public sector monopoly, opening it up for strategic investment by for-profit firms.
>
> (Robertson 2008: 12)

If such objectives seem a world away from the hopes of Kurt Hahn and his colleagues it seems important to ask just how international schools are located structurally and ideologically in this pattern of globalisation.

Both Sylvester (2005) and Wylie (2008) have attempted to locate international schools within matrices that indicate the diversity of international schools and their educational provision. The dimensions of Sylvester's matrix range from Politically Sensitive to Politically Neutral on one axis and from Education for International Understanding to Education for World Citizenship on the other. Wylie's, somewhat more complex, matrix includes Colonialism through Post-colonialism, Global Economy, Global Ideology and Global Civil Society on one axis and school Message Systems (Curriculum, Pedagogy and Assessment) and Mechanisms of Learning and Control (Teachers and ICT) on the other. Both point to the very considerable diversity of purpose and provision in international schools and the difficulty of making generalisations about such diversity.

The purpose of this volume is not to add further to these attempts to organise our understanding of the diversity of international schools and international schooling, but rather to critically address the major issues that shape the contexts and practices of international schools, especially those that arise from tensions between global cultures and local cultures and between the demands of global markets and calls for global citizenship. In particular, we examine the implications for *schools* in terms of curricula, pedagogies and assessment regimes, and for *teachers* in terms of their work and careers.

Global cultures and local cultures

Contemporary discussions of globalisation pay considerable attention to issues of culture. On the one hand, theorists such as Fukuyama suggest that the world is converging on a single (Western liberal-democratic-capitalist) culture that presages 'the end of history'.

> What we are witnessing is not just the end of the Cold War, or a passing of a particular period of post-war history, but the end of history as such: that is, the end point of mans' ideological evolution and the universalisation of western liberal democracy as the final form of human government.
>
> (Fukuyama 1992: 13).

On the other hand, theorists such as Huntington claim that we are entering a period in which historically divergent cultures will lead to an intensification of conflict and a 'clash of civilizations'.

> [T]he post-Cold War world is a world of seven or eight major civilizations. Cultural commonalities and differences shape the interests, antagonisms, and associations of states. The most important countries in the world come overwhelmingly from different civilizations. The local conflicts most likely to escalate into broader wars are those between groups and states from different civilizations.
>
> (Huntington 2002: 27)

So where does this leave us? It would seem that Fukuyama's claim has already been invalidated by the very history whose end he celebrated. Huntington's thesis has come under major attack (Sen 2006), although there is a general consensus that there are irreducible and unresolvable differences in values and commitments between cultures. Moreover, there is growing criticism of the idea that a global cultural/moral/political consensus can be achieved through the imposition of particular Utopian visions by military or economic means (Gray 2008).

Recognition of this reality is put forcefully by Gray in his analysis of the history of millenarian movements driven by apocalyptic religion and militarised politics. In order to escape the appalling consequences of such regimes, Gray suggests that we need to recognise that

> There is no prospect of a morally homogeneous society, still less a homogenized world. In the future, as in the past, there will be authoritarian states and liberal republics, theocratic democracies and secular tyrannies, city-states and many mixed regimes. No one type of government or economy will be accepted everywhere, nor will any single version of civilization be embraced by all of humanity.
>
> (Gray 2008: 294–5)

Moreover, he argues, the existence of a variety of religious commitments needs to be recognised and the attempt to resolve religious differences through the attempt to impose secular solutions abandoned.

It is time the diversity of religions was accepted and the attempt to build a secular monolith abandoned. Accepting that we have moved into a post-secular era does not mean religions can be freed of the restraints that are necessary for civilized coexistence. A central task of government is to work out and enforce a framework whereby they can live together. A framework of this kind cannot be the same for every society, or fixed forever. It embodies a type of tolerance whose goal is not truth but peace.

(Gray 2008: 295)

Whatever position one takes with regard to Gray's analysis of religion, his advocacy of attempts to reach a *modus vivendi* across religious differences and his acknowledgement that attempts to impose solutions based upon claims to unique insights into the truth of particular apocalyptic and utopian beliefs have led to extraordinary, increasing and unacceptable violence are surely insights worth pursuing.

But religious differences are not the only source of cultural difference in the modern world. Differences of nationality, ethnicity, gender and class, for instance, constitute 'publics' that all have claim to equality of treatment, or as Fraser (2003) puts it, claims to justice involving redistribution, recognition and representation. This does not mean, however, that cultural norms of particular groups are to be allowed free reign, for, as Olssen argues

cultural minorities whose practices are based on deeply illiberal oppressive relations based on gender, or sex, or any other basis of difference, cannot be tolerated and neither can group practices that fail to respect the fundamentally important principles of democratic politics, such as respect for the other, a willingness to negotiate, tolerance, or the institutional basis of deliberation or the rule of law.

(Olssen 2004: 187)

Moreover, as Sen (2006) points out, individuals always have multiple identities that often span cultural as well as other forms of affiliation and membership.[1] In this sense we are all cosmopolitan and we all cross various boundaries.

The attempt to establish a global culture must, therefore, be based on the search for principles underpinning the idea of cosmopolitanism that are neither coercive nor relativist and that search for accommodations between incommensurable 'truths' (see also Pieterse 2006; Bates 2008).

This is a particular issue for those organisations that are working to promote curriculum and assessment practices across cultures, for cultural diversity provides the context within which the search for an educationally appropriate notion of global culture is conducted and as a multitude of 'publics' emerge and lay claim to particular visions of culture and those educational practices that sustain them.

Intercultural education: international education

Much contemporary discussion of multicultural or intercultural education is framed in terms of response to the increasing cultural diversity within *national* systems under pressure of recognition of historically subjugated minorities and the influx of migrants from developing countries. This perspective can be differentiated from the idea of *international* education which is characterised more by the internationalist ideals of international schools. As Hill (2007) suggests

> Multicultural education is usually equated with intercultural education and manifests itself in national settings via such terms . . . and activities as migrant education, bilingual education, immersion programmes, minority education, and community education . . . [and appeals to] 'the concept that all students regardless of their gender, social class and their ethnic, racial or social characteristics, should have an equal opportunity to learn'.
>
> (Troutman 1998: 166 in Hill 2007: 248)

On the other hand, international education, such as that stated as the aim of international schools,

> pays little attention to the issues of a pluralist society within a national system. It emphasises a supra-national view where the interdependence of nations is fundamental to global cooperation; it proposes a curriculum of international understanding necessary to achieve world peace.
>
> (Hill 2007: 248)

Despite the 'overlap' that Hill looks for between multicultural and international education, this is a significant difference in orientation for, as he acknowledges,

> [Multicultural education] attempts to integrate immigrants into a national system and at the same time to mould that system so that it 'does not distinguish between natives and foreigners' (Portera 1998: 217). International education, on the other hand, seeks to integrate students into an international system where differences in culture are the norm. It places an emphasis on a curriculum and teaching approach which will develop skills, knowledge and attitudes necessary to function effectively as citizens of the world.
>
> (Hill 2007: 257–8)

Hill's commitment to international education is quite consistent with the ideals of those who founded the international schools movement such as Kurt Hahn whose establishment of the United World Colleges is described as a 'project in education which combined internationalism and peace with the martial virtues of disciplined service to others, together with exposure to the formative benefits of residential life' (Sutcliffe 1991: 33). As a response to the second European war this was admirable, but, as Sutcliffe also recognises, it was an ideal that, while it sustained the United World Colleges, was not, by itself, a sufficient response to the needs of a growing body of international diplomats, politicians, bureaucrats and businessmen that emerged in the 1970s. Indeed, '[b]y the 1970s, the problems of the mobile and expatriate families were sand, not oil in the wheels of international trade. An international academic passport was required' (Sutcliffe 1991: 34).

One response was the establishment of the International Schools Association and, subsequently, the International Baccalaureate. However, as Renaud makes clear, the ISA and IB were distinctly class related and responsive to only one of two distinct patterns of international migration.

> This phenomenon of mobility had developed considerably since the Second World War, not only numerically but also in terms of social classes. . . . [T]wo main categories of internationally mobile groups existed: one at either end of the socio-economic scale. On the one hand were diplomats, servicemen and senior level commercial or business executives. On the other hand were the migrant workers, but in a proportion considerably less than that of today.
>
> (Renaud 1991: 6)

It seems, therefore, that international schools were established in response to a particular segment of the internationally mobile population, that which Sklair (2001, 2002) later called 'the transnational capitalist class'.

Whether the values, behaviours, customs, attitudes, beliefs and artefacts of this group of internationally mobile individuals constitute a 'culture' is a matter for debate for, while they share the experience of impermanence, transience and constant readjustment to 'other cultures' they are also determinedly focused on maintaining their original cultural identity which they anticipate resuming at various points in the future.

It is also a moot point as to whether the members of this group are particularly 'internationally minded' in that their engagement with other cultures is often both limited and determinedly instrumental and seldom more than superficially 'intercultural'. This is reflected in the experience of students in international schools who constantly form and reform friendships as they and their [temporary] friends are continually on the move (Fail *et al.* 2004; Zilber 2004). Moreover, the 'intercultural' experience of students may well be limited to the cultural composition of their particular school with little reference to the cultures and geography within which the school is situated and would probably not involve more than superficial contact with members of local cultures who were not also members of the 'transnational capitalist class'.

Indeed, it may well be that international schools exist mainly in a sort of bubble, floating free of the local cultural context within which they are geographically situated (Lautrette 2008).

This does not mean that attempts to develop generalised cultural values for international schools (Pearce 2001, 2003; Lewis 2001) are not worthwhile. Indeed such efforts are consistent with the ideological commitments of international schools. But it does indicate that both the definition of consistent international values and their transmission may be quite problematic and restricted to a particular class identity (Allan 2002; Jackson 2002; Jalaluddin 2002).

However, the expansion of international schools into a greater variety of countries, the increasing involvement of nationals as well as expatriates in such schools and the increasing demand from members of emerging middle classes with localised cultural identities may intensify the issues facing the process of cultural formation in international schools.

The need to address such an accommodation to local cultures is put strongly and persuasively by Paul Poore of Harare International School in Zimbabwe. While endorsing the role of international schools in promoting international (and intercultural) education and encouraging the tolerance of difference, he also observes that

> all we have to do is look at the leaders of international education to see that our schools themselves are culturally loaded: they are often founded with the assistance of Western governments for the purpose of educating the children of their employees (not to spread multiculturalism); they are largely headed by white educators from the first world who are trained in leadership theories which are culturally biased . . . ; they are staffed largely out of necessity by native English speakers; they operate from western liberal humanist curricula often packaged as international; they are more often than not accredited by western agencies which have no real concern with the issue of culture other than the superficial inclusion of the host culture in the curriculum; and they pride themselves on the 'third culture' of the school which is generally rarely more than a variation of the dominant (usually American or British) culture.
>
> (Poore 2005: 352–3)

If this is so, then there would seem to be some quite practical impediments to the development of an international education that is truly located within the idea of a 'global culture'.

But above and beyond this difficulty lies an even more substantial issue for, as Van Oord (2005) suggests, cultural differences are not simply a matter of content, or superficial similarities and differences, but of deep structures which determine culture-specific ways of learning. Following Balagangadhara, Van Oord argues that

A culture is a tradition that can be identified in terms of a specific configuration of learning and meta-learning. In each configuration, one particular kind of learning activity will be dominant: it will subordinate other kinds of learning activities to itself. Such configurations of learning processes can be seen as 'culture specific ways of learning'.

(Van Oord 2005: 181)

This being the case, Van Oord suggests, it is important to resist 'the enticement to interpret other cultures as varieties of the West . . . [If] we presume that cultures differ, we should be aware that they will differ differently and that their experience of difference will also be different' (Van Oord 2005: 186). Such an argument echoes that of Poore when he suggests that

effective cross-cultural engagement is dependent upon possessing the understandings and competencies, attitudes and identities which comprise intercultural literacy. And while intercultural literacy is at the very heart of our reason for being, it seems that this most important element is largely taken for granted in shaping the culture of our [international] schools.

(Poore 2005: 353)

This is not simply an issue for international schools, although it is perhaps writ large in such schools because of the claims they make to foster international understanding, but an issue of more general importance in education as more and more national schools are caught up in the process of globalisation. What is at stake here are the very definitions and organisations of knowledge that are to prevail in a globalised world.

Global modernity represents . . . the economic, political, social and cultural reconfiguration of the world. Conflicts now are both between and within societies, between those groups that are integrated into global capitalism and those who are increasingly marginalised by it – the vast majority of the world's populations facing questions of everyday survival. Second, as the empire of capital goes global, it internalises political and cultural conflicts between competing systems, or seriously 'alternative' modernities, . . . as conflicts over supremacy in global capitalism and for the loyalties of a 'transnational capitalist class'.

(Dirlik 2006: 4)

These conflicts are apparent in the ways of knowing pursued by different multinational groupings such as the differences between the USA and Europe and ASEAN in social, political, economic and military affairs. They are also apparent in the differences between countries within each bloc and in the differences between groups within each nation state. The concatenation of local, national, regional and would-be global cultures provides, then, an increasingly complex context within which not only superficial cultural differences, but fundamentally different ways of seeing and understanding the world compete for our attention and loyalty (Anderson-Levitt 2003; Coulby and Zambeta 2005; Bates 2008).

Some of this complexity is conveyed by Dirlik:

> As Eurocentrism has come under scrutiny, so have the ways of under-standing the world that are hopelessly entangled in modern capitalism, colonialism and the universalization of values of parochial, regional or civilizational values that were rendered into universal truths with Euro/American domination of the world. At the same time, the assertion of claims to alternative modernities has been accompanied by the reassertion of value or knowledge systems once relegated to 'traditions' doomed to disappear with the global advent of modernity. Likewise with conflicts within societies, where received ways of knowing have come under scrutiny and criticism from class, gender, ethnic, and indigenous perspectives, which are empowered not only by the increasing visibility of those constituencies, but also by accumulating evidence of the destructiveness of ways of knowing that have brought as great harm to certain portions of humanity as it has brought benefits to the privileged, and which may now have become obstacles to confronting crucial questions of human survival.
>
> (Dirlik 2006: 4)

There is some evidence of the difficulties that international schools face in dealing with these complexities. Sato suggests that 'even though a "global" culture may someday exist, we are far from that moment' (2007: 452) and that 'it is not very productive to place too much emphasis on universal values, while completely ignoring minor [sic] cultural differences' (2007: 452). On the other hand 'the more teachers discuss culture in terms of "national culture", the greater the risk of reinforcing more stereotyped images of cultures' (2007: 452).

One response to such issues is for international schools to differentiate themselves in terms of the treatment of particular global or local cultures. Yamato and Bray (2006) in their study of international schools in Shanghai suggest that on the one hand, the particular concerns of French, German, Japanese and Korean schools were the maintenance of their 'home' languages and cultures for expatriate children. On the other hand, the English/Chinese schools showed a complex division of response to demands for particular types of English or Chinese language international education. In particular, international schools and the international divisions of Chinese schools catered respectively for a) internationally mobile English language families, b) returning expatriate Chinese whose Chinese language skills were limited and whose children found total Chinese immersion too stressful and c) overseas Chinese students seeking a Chinese international education (Yamato and Bray 2006: 72).

In a study of international schools in Hong Kong, Bray and Yamato (2003) describe the complexity of local and wider forces that act on such schools.

> Locally, such forces include the dynamic of Hong Kong's multiracial society, dissatisfaction among many local families with the Hong Kong education system, growing prosperity which has permitted many families to consider sending their children to fee-charging schools outside the Hong Kong education system, the labour market which continues to attract overseas professionals and their families to Hong Kong, and the political environment which tolerates plurality in educational provision. Wider forces include the growing mobility of labour which is associated with globalisation, and the international trend towards decentralisation and diversification in educational provision.
>
> (Bray and Yamato 2003: 67)

Cadell, in a study of national schools and English-medium (private) schools in Nepal, shows how 'English-medium instruction emerged as a key dimension of the selling of dreams [and as] a way to mediate the risks of an unknowable modern future' (2006: 468). The intensity of cultural loyalties aroused by such differences is shown by the demand of Maoist (nationalist) military groups for 'the prevention of "western influence" in teaching; and, ultimately the nationalisation of schooling' (2006: 471). The violence associated with such tensions is displayed through her description of the fate of some teachers and principals.

> [T]he extent to which Maoists have been able to enforce their demands through the use of violence and intimidation does set their activities apart. Teachers and school owners who do not comply have been faced with humiliation in front of their students, such as having shoes tied around their necks. Other responses have been considerably more violent in nature, involving the dousing of school principals in kerosene, physical abuse and the bombing of premises.
>
> (Cadell 2006: 471)

So the tensions between global and local cultures can produce quite uncivilised outcomes that display the intensity of competing objectives and interests.

Global markets: global education

If the tension between global and local cultures is a significant source of difficulty in schools, and international schools in particular, then so is the tension between attempts to establish global markets on the one hand, and global civil society on the other.

We are all aware of the global nature of the products and services we buy as well as the media through which we recognise them and the financial structures through which we buy and sell. But we are aware only vaguely of the nature and effects of the structures through which all this happens. For most of us globalisation of markets is epiphenomenal, a sort of *deus ex machina* that operates above and beyond our consciousness while it facilitates our everyday behaviour. But, as Robertson, Bonal and Dale point out 'globalization is the outcome of processes that involve real actors – economic and political – with real interests' (2002: 472).

Increasingly these actors are transnational corporations (TNCs) through which the market is transacted and extended. Bhanji points out that in 2003–4 the scale of these transnational corporations was formidable.

> TNCs now comprise of some roughly 64,000 firms, with more than 866,000 affiliates including subsidiaries and millions of suppliers and distributors connected through global value chains (UNCTAD, 2004). Of the 100 largest economies in the world, only 49 are countries – the majority are TNCs (Love & Love, 2003). In 2003, combined revenue of the global 500 companies was over $14 trillion and these companies employed over 47 million people
>
> (Bhanji 2008: 55)

Until recently such TNCs have exhibited little direct interest in education, confining their interests to the sale of products to governments, but in the last few years they have begun to involve themselves in two major ways. Firstly, the size of global educational expenditure by both governments and individuals is regarded as creating a global business opportunity provided that it can be marketised (that is either freed from the hands of governments or restructured to constitute a government sponsored and paid-for system of independent schools). Secondly, education is seen as a necessary vehicle for the transformation of societies and their education systems so as to produce both the skills and the disciplines required by the TNC's global expansion.

> In the field of education, corporations have traditionally sold their services or products directly to governments (e.g. the textbook industry) or have donated products directly through corporate foundations in support of schools. This is changing. New forms of private authority in education are emerging as a result of globalisation that differ from previous forms of private sector engagement. These new forms of private authority are transnational in scope and mobilise GCSE [global corporate social engagement] norms to legitimise their influence over the broad frame and direction of their activities in education. *They require the extra-economic benefits of engaging social sectors like education in order to reproduce themselves globally*
>
> (Bhanji 2008: 55–6, emphasis added)

As far as direct marketisation is concerned, the focus of international actors that mobilise action in support of TNCs (such as WTO and OECD) has been on trade liberalisation and the breaking down of barriers to the operations of transnational corporations in service industries generally and education in particular (Dale and Robertson 2002; Robertson *et al.* 2002; Robertson 2003; Sidhu 2007).

The breaking down of trade barriers in education, however, leads, as in other spheres, to market segmentation and stratification, often at the expense of social needs. As Robertson, among others, points out, the effect of such negotiations as those over the General Agreement over Trade in Services (GATS) is to privilege those countries with a 'competitive advantage' in the provision of education services while opening up third world and developing nations to commercial exploitation. Specifically, the new neo-liberal provisions of the GATS were sponsored by the USA and Australia, supported by the EU, Japan and New Zealand, all exporters of education services (Robertson 2003).

While the primary target of such liberalisation is the emerging middle class in the developing world, the secondary target is the vast number of children in the third world that have little or no access to education. The numbers here are staggering.

> Over 100 million children around the world have no access to education: of which 60% are girls. The vast majority (96%) are in developing countries, particularly Asia and sub-Saharan Africa. Among children who do enrol, many drop out before completing primary schools. In sub-Saharan Africa, primary school enrolment is 58% and the completion rate is just 33%. An estimated $10 billion (US) is needed globally per year to reach UPI (Universal Primary Education) by 2015. In 2005 only $3 billion was committed, resulting in a significant financial shortfall.
>
> (Bhanji 2008: 57)

Moreover, international organisations such as the OECD and WTO have shifted their emphasis from development aid towards trade in educational services: '... trade in education (is) now regarded as the means towards successful capacity building of educational institutions in the majority (developing) world, where previously international aid and nation building were seen as the solution to building institutional capacity' (Sidhu 2007: 221–2). Private provision of basic education is clearly on the agenda as pressure is exerted on governments and international agencies to expand provision to these 100 million children. Increasingly, claims are made that private provision is better than state provision and that the solution to the problem is Education Without the State (Tooley 1996).

At the same time, TNCs are seeing the expansion of corporate global education as a means for ensuring that there is a supply of labour appropriate to their changing needs, conversant with the required technologies, disciplined in its commitment to lifelong skilling, re-skilling and multi-tasking, compliant with continual corporate organisation and reorganisation, and committed to continuous consumption of ever changing corporate products. Moreover, education is also seen as a testing ground for new modalities of production and incorporation especially through the trialling of information technologies as low-cost, universal-reach mechanisms that can potentially be expanded at low unit cost into a mass market (Bhanji 2008). In addition, schools are seen as open to the development of a 'corporate sponsored curriculum' through which new consumer markets can be developed via sponsorship of technology (with advertising strings attached) and curricular materials that present corporate interests as disinterested and that involve continual product placement (McLaren and Farahmandpur 2005).

The World Economic Forum is a strong advocate for such developments in, for instance, its 2007 Report, summarised by Bhanji, arguing that

> improving education benefits the private sector by: building a skilled workforce; increasing purchasing power; and improving productivity. The report further highlights that individual firms can benefit from engaging in the education sector by enhancing skills for workers; developing new markets by collaborating with local partners, testing new business models or products and gaining access to new markets; enhancing brand reputation through long-term investments in education that can solidify a firm's presence in the community and lastly engaging in education can bolster employee motivation, morale and retention.
>
> (Bhanji 2008: 68)

What is happening here, under the pressure from TNCs and their international organisations such as the World Economic Forum, supported by multi-government organisations such as the World Bank and the International Monetary Fund, as well as by a plethora of regional organisations, is the detachment of education from its local and national roots and the transformation of its historical purpose in consolidating national identity and citizenship. Global agreements such as GATS have the potential to undermine national governments' capacity to regulate the provision of education and curricular and assessment processes within their borders as the adjudication of such matters passes to TNCs through the development of 'international' curricular and 'international' assessment through mechanisms such as PISA (Brown 2003).

What is being sought is the detachment of education from national governments in ways that the TNCs have themselves become detached from national jurisdiction, creating their own quasi-legal framework for operating globally outside the restrictions of nation states.

> [T]hrough GATS, the conditions are being created for disembedding education activity from its fixed institutionalised location as a nationally regulated redistributional and legitimatory commodified public good, forcing into motion and into the global marketplace to be fixed through

processes of successive liberalization as part of the built-in GATS agenda. In essence, the WTO, through the GATS process, has the potential to establish a new set of global rules of the game for the governance of education within national territories, in the process transforming states' power and therefore the processes of development within and across nation-states.

(Robertson *et al.* 2002: 489)

As well as threatening the powers of nation states, this process of 'rescaling the governance of education to the global level' (Robertson *et al.* 2002: 489) is focused upon the disembedding of individuals from their local identity as citizens and the embedding of their identities as workers and consumers in a dynamic and unpredictable international market.

Global education: global citizen?

Ironically, the move of global capital to free itself from the nation state has quite significant limits because of its dependence on local and relatively immobile infrastructure and also, in situations of market collapse such as the 1930s and 2000s, on the economic powers and resources of states and their citizens. As Brenner suggests, following Marx and Harvey:

> On the one hand, in its drive to accumulate surplus value, capital strives 'to annihilate space through time' and therefore to overcome all geographical barriers in its circulation process. Yet, to pursue this continual dynamic of deterritorialization and 'time–space' compression, capital necessarily depends upon relatively fixed and immobile territorial infrastructures, such as urban, regional agglomerations and territorial states.
>
> (Brenner 1998 in Robertson *et al.* 2002: 474).

Such 'immobile territorial infrastructures' are not only resources for capital but also resources for identity formation – that is they are cultural complexes that are almost always associated with national and local identities articulated in part through schools and education systems. Indeed, the central purpose of schooling during the nineteenth and early twentieth century was that of creating citizens loyal to the nation state. This purpose demanded that children be detached from immediate family loyalties and that they embrace commitments to the broader community represented by the state.

Neo-liberal doctrines saw the relationship between 'individuals and their families' on the one hand, and the state on the other as being direct and unmediated: as Margaret Thatcher famously remarked 'there is no such thing as society, only individuals and their families'. And indeed, the notion of society, and more particularly civil society, as a mediating structure standing between the individual and the state fell into disuse in political science to the point where Hobsbawm (1994: 139) could describe it as 'nostalgic rhetoric'.

However, during the past two decades the idea of civil society has re-emerged as a crucial concept in social, political and economic controversies (Comaroff and Comaroff 1999; Kaldor 2003; Kocka 2004; Bates 2008). These debates about the nature of civil society arise between those, on the one hand, who see civil society as an arena, a public sphere, within which self-governing communities articulate particular interests, values and norms which may then become incorporated into the administrative/political system; and those, on the other hand, who see civil society as a system of shared norms, values and interests deriving from particular national, religious and ethnic traditions that encourage social cohesion and support the nation state in its pursuit of advantage in global competition (McLeneghan 2000; Bates 2008).

The idea of civil society as a middle ground between the individual and the state is an idea of growing importance, as a strong civil society is seen increasingly as a protection both against the untrammelled power of the state and against the capriciousness of the individual. As Havel insists, the public and the private are necessarily closely related but neither should be allowed to have primacy over the other. It follows therefore that within civil society the relationship should be constructed so that 'the public is not allowed to destroy the private (totalitarianism), nor the private allowed to destroy the public (atomising liberal-individualism)' (in Baker 2002: 149).

Such a conception of civil society implies ideas of equity and democracy without which civil society is impossible, particularly in conditions of pluralism within increasingly complex societies. Here, issues of communication across different groups become a central concern for

> No multi-cultural society is possible unless we can turn to a universalist principle that allows socially and culturally different individuals and groups to communicate with one another. But neither is a multi-cultural society possible if that universalist principle defines one conception of social organisation and personal life that is judged both to be normal and better than others. The call for freedom to build a personal life is the only universalist principle that does not impose one form of social organisation and cultural practices. It is not reducible to laissez-faire economics or to pure tolerance, first, because it demands respect for the freedom of all individuals and therefore a rejection of exclusion, and secondly because it demands that any reference to cultural identity be legitimised in terms of the freedom and equality of all, and not by appeal to a social order, a tradition or the requirements of public order.
>
> (Touraine 2000: 167)

Implicit in these discussions of civil society is the idea of citizenship of a nation state, for most of the legal frameworks that codify the ideas emerging from civil society are constructed within such states. However, it is possible to see such ideas as pertinent to the construction of a global civil society where norms of behaviour are not left simply to the demands of the market, but are governed by notions of the public good articulated on a foundation of equity and participation through global forums and agencies other than TNCs.

Much of the work in constructing such agencies is undertaken by transnational social movements (TSMs) or by transnational advocacy networks (TANs) that are committed to the development of cooperative and democratic global institutions with influence on the politics of global organisations (Keck and Sikkink 1998; Boli and Thomas 1999). Such work is related to education by Mundy and Murphy (2001), in their discussion of the role of education in the construction of global civil society through which they identify five key trends:

> Development and relief organizations are becoming more interested in education, and in advocacy, and they increasingly link these two together. Virtual nongovernmental coalitions have increasingly taken up the theme of education as a component of their agendas for global governance, linking it to the issue of debt relief, and to an interlocking frame of international and national responsibilities for social security and solidarity. Teacher unions around the globe have committed themselves to a renewed inter-nationalism, and through their newly formed organ, Education International, they are launching a campaign in support of public education for all. There are clear signs of new forms of cross-organisational collaboration and of unprecedented levels of interaction between INGOs and intergovernmental bodies around the theme of education.
>
> (Mundy and Murphy 2001: 125)

While, as noted above, international schools tend to operate at an elite level of transnational corporate society, there are those within such schools who are committed to the idea of global citizenship within some notion of global civil society. Roberts, for instance, is a strong advocate of an education for active citizenship based upon knowledge, skills, attitudes and values and experience centred around global issues that might lead to 'awareness of and a sense of responsibility in one's everyday life, that one is influenced by, and influences things beyond one's country, on a global scale. And acting accordingly . . .' (Roberts 2003: 77). Bohler, following Kubow *et al.*, argues the need to develop citizenship through allegiance to 'overlapping communities' – local, regional, national and multinational (2008: 25) along with the need 'to provide citizens with the means of interpreting and negotiating the nature of the public good within structures unaccustomed to political dialogue and consensus building' (2008: 27). Lewis (2005) develops criteria and priorities that would guide a curriculum for global citizenship and advocates the development of assessment criteria that would encourage civic responsibility. A note of caution is introduced, however, by Matthews and Sidhu (2005) in their assessment of Australian ideas of international education that tend to be informed by the requirements of global markets rather than by notions of global citizenship. As they observe,

Markets do not nurture a concern for social justice nor solve pressing global problems such as environmental degradation, growing inequality, unsustainable economic development and instability. Marketised expressions of international education are ultimately disengaged from notions of a global public good.

(Matthews and Sidhu 2005: 63)

They go on to argue that a strong alternative is required, one that

Crucially . . . requires teachers to understand international education as something more than the means to competitive advantage in international trade markets . . . Intercultural sensitivities, including identification with a global community are important preconditions for effective participation in 21st century civic life.

(Matthews and Sidhu, 2005: 63)

Conclusion

The emergence of international schools in significant numbers across the globe demands analysis of their purposes, practices and outcomes and an examination of their connections to global economic, social and cultural movements. Such schools, as well as those that call themselves 'internationally minded', have both pragmatic and idealistic agendas as do those that send their children to them and those that teach and study within them. How the tensions between these agendas work out in practice has important economic, social and cultural consequences and will contribute to the forms that globalisation/internationalisation take.

Consequently, what the chapters of this book attempt to do is to set such schools in context and to critically analyse the role of international schools in global networking (Wylie) and class formation (Brown and Lauder); outline an approach to the micropolitics of international schools (Caffyn); examine the nature of international teachers (Hayden and Thompson) and international teaching (Fail); discuss issues of international curriculum (Cambridge) and international assessment (Bates); look carefully at the complexity and challenges facing the International Baccalaureate Organisation as a major player in international schooling (Bunnell); and discuss the prospects for and impediments to international education for global citizenship (Marshall).

We attempt to move beyond description and to suggest ways in which the complex and contradictory tensions within the world of international schooling and its global context might be examined critically. We also hope that this volume may serve as an invitation to others to extend and further develop analyses of the important and increasingly widespread activity of schooling internationally.

Notes

1   As Sen points out with regard to his own identity 'I can be, at the same time, an Asian, an Indian citizen, a Bengali with Bangladeshi ancestry, an American or British resident, an economist, a dabbler in philosophy, an author in Sanskrit, a strong believer in secularism and democracy, a man, a feminist, a heterosexual, a strong defender of gay and lesbian rights, with a non-religious lifestyle, from a Hindu background, a non-Brahmin, and a non-believer in an afterlife (and also, in case the question is asked, a non-believer in a "before-life" as well' (Sen, 2006: 19).

References

Allan, M. (2002) Cultural borderlands: cultural dissonance in the international school, *International Schools Journal* XXI(2): 42–53.

Anderson-Levitt, K. (2003) The schoolyard gates: schooling and childhood in global perspective, *Journal of Social History* Summer: 987–1006.

Baker, G. (2002) *Civil Society and Democratic Theory*, London: Routledge.

Bates, R. (2008) The politics of civil society and the possibility of change: a speculation on leadership in education. In E. Samier (ed.) *Political Approaches to Educational Leadership*, New York: Routledge, 173–88.

Bhanji, Z. (2008) Transnational corporations in education: filling the gap through new social norms and market unilateralism? *Globalisation, Societies and Education* 6(1): 55–73.

Bohler, T. (2008) The broadening compass of Education for Democratic Citizenship, *International Schools Journal* XXVII(2): 23–8.

Boli, J. and Thomas, G. (eds) (1999) *Constructing World Culture: Non-government Organizations*, Stanford, CA: Stanford University Press.

Bray, M. and Yamato, Y. (2003) Comparative education in microcosm: methodological insights from the international schools sector in Hong Kong, *International Review of Education* 49(1/2): 51–73.

Brown, P. (2003) The opportunity trap: education and employment in a global economy, *European Educational Research Journal* 2(1) 142–180; reprinted in Lauder, H., Brown, P., Dillabough, J. and Halsey, A. *Education, Globalization and Social Change*, Oxford: Oxford University Press.

Brummitt, N. (2007) International schools: exponential growth and future implications, *International Schools Journal* XXVII(1): 35–40.

Brummitt, N. (2009) Facing up to global recession, *International School Magazine* 12(1): 13–14.

Bunnell, T. (2007) The international education industry, *Journal of Research in International Education* 6(3): 349–67.

Cadell, M. (2006) Private schools as battlefields: contested visions of learning in Nepal, *Compare* 36(4): 463–79.

Comaroff, J. and Comaroff, J. (1999) *Civil Society and the Political Imagination in Africa: Critical Perspectives*, Paris: Lavoisier.

Coulby, D. and Zambeta, E. (eds) (2005) *Globalisation and Nationalism in Education*, London: Routledge.

Dale, R. and Robertson, S. (2002) The varying effects of regional organizations as subjects of globalization of education, *Comparative Education Review* 46(1): 10–36.

Dirlik, A. (2006) Representation. In N. Gentz and S. Kramer (eds) *Globalization, Cultural Identities, and Media Representations*, Buffalo, NY: SUNY Press.

Fail, H., Thompson, J. and Walker, G. (2004) Belonging, identity and third culture kids, *Journal of Research in International Education* 3(3): 319–38.

Fraser, N. (2003) *Redistribution or Recognition*, trans J. Golb, J. Ingram and C. Wilke, London: Verso.

Fukuyama, F. (1992) *The End of History and the Last Man*, New York: Free Press.

Gray, J. (2008) *Black Mass: Apocalyptic Religion and the Death of Utopia*, London: Penguin.

Hill, I. (2007) Multicultural and international education: never the twain shall meet? *Review of Education* 53(3): 245–64.

Hobsbawm, E. (1994) *The Age of Extremes*, London: Michael Joseph.

Huntington, S. (2002) *The Clash of Civilizations and the Remaking of World Order*, New York: Free Press.

Jackson, K. (2002) Making the reality match the mission statement: infusing diversity in the life of your school, *International Schools Journal* XXI(2): 60–8.

Jalaluddin, A. (2002) Education in a culturally diverse world, *International Schools Journal* XXI(2): 54–9.

Kaldor, M. (2003) Civil society and accountability, *Journal of Human Development* 4(1): 5–23.

Keck, M. and Sikkink, K. (1998) Activists beyond borders. In D. Meyer and S. Tarrow (eds) *The Social Movement Society*, Langham, MD: Rowman and Littlefield.

Kocka, J. (2004) Civil society from a historical perspective, *European Review* 12(1): 65–79.

Lauder, H. (2007) International schools, education and globalization: towards a research agenda. In M. Hayden, J. Levy and J. Thompson (eds) *The SAGE Handbook of Research in International Education*, Los Angeles: SAGE, 441–9.

Lautrette, A. (2008) The message systems of Desert School, unpublished thesis, Deakin University, Australia.

Lewis, C. (2001) Internationalism: towards a higher standard, *International Schools Journal* XX(2): 23–38.

Lewis, C. (2005) What must a school do to be globally responsible? *International Schools Journal* XXIV(2): 17–23.

Lips, C. (2000) Edupreneurs: a survey of for-profit education, *Policy Analysis* 386: 1–29.

McCleneghan, M. (2000) Social capital: exploring the theoretical foundations of community development education, *British Educational Research Journal* 26(5): 556–82.

Macdonald, J. (2006) The international school industry: examining schools through an economic lens, *Journal for Research in International Education* 5(2): 191–213.

McLaren, P. and Farahmandpur, R. (2005) *Teaching against Global Capitalism and the New Imperialism: A Critical Pedagogy*, Lanham, MD: Rowman & Littlefield.

Maslen, J. (2009) The real economic returns from foreign students, *Global Higher Education* 9 August: 17.

Matthews, J. and Sidhu, R. (2005) Desperately seeking the global subject: international education, citizenship and cosmopolitanism, *Globalisation, Societies and Education* 3(1): 49–66.

Mundy, K. and Murphy, L. (2001) Transnational advocacy, global civil society? Emerging evidence from the field, *Comparative Education Review* 45(1): 85–126.

Olssen, M. (2004) Neoliberalism, globalisation, democracy: challenges for education, *Globalisation, Societies and Education* 2(2): 231–7.

Pearce, R. (2001) Plural vision for plural schools: how we can disagree yet both be right, *International Schools Journal* XX(2): 39–45.

Pearce, R. (2003) Cultural values for international schools, *International Schools Journal* XXII(2): 59–65.

Pieterse, N. (2006) *Globalization or Empire?* New York: Routledge.

Poore, P. (2005) School culture: the space between the bars; the silence between the notes, *Journal of Research in International Education* 4(3): 351–61.

Renaud, G. (1991) The International Schools Association (ISA): historical and philosophical background. In P. Jonietz (ed.) *International Schools and International Education*, London: Kogan Page, 6–14.

Roberts, B. (2003) What should international education be? From emergent theory to practice, *International Schools Journal* XXII(2): 69–79.

Robertson, S. (2003) WTO/GATS and the global education services industry, *Globalisation, Societies and Education* 1(3): 259–66.

Robertson, S. (2008) Globalisation, education governance and citizenship regimes: new democratic deficits and social injustices. In W. Ayers, T. Quinn and D. Stovall (eds) *Handbook of Social Justice in Education*, London and New York: Routledge.

Robertson, S., Bonal, X. and Dale, R. (2002) GATS and the education service industry: the politics of scale and global reterritorialization, *Comparative Education Review* 46(4): 472–96.

Sato, C. (2007) Learning from weaknesses in teaching about culture: the case study of a Japanese school abroad, *Intercultural Education* 18(5): 445–53.

Sen, A. (2006) *Development as Freedom*, Oxford: Oxford University Press.

Sidhu, R. (2007) GATS and the new developmentalism: governing transnational education, *Comparative Education Review* 51(2): 203–27.

Sklair, L. (2001) *The Transnational Capitalist Class*, Oxford: Blackwell.

Sklair, L. (2002) Democracy and the transnational capitalist class, *Annals of the American Academy of Political and Social Science* 581: 144–57.

Sutcliffe, D. (1991) The United World Colleges. In L. Jonietz (ed.) *International Schools and International Education*, London: Kogan Page.

Sylvester, R. (2005) Framing the map of international education, *Journal of Research in International Education* 4(2): 123–51.

Tamatea, L. (2005) The Dakar framework: constructing and deconstructing the global neo-liberal matrix, *Globalisation, Societies and Education* 3(3): 311–34.

Tooley, J. (1996) *The Global Education Industry*, London: Institute of Economic Affairs.

Touraine, A. (2000) *Can we live together?* Stanford, CA: Stanford University Press.

Van Oord, L. (2005) Culture as a configuration of learning, *Journal of Research in International Education* 4(2): 173–91.

World Bank (2007) *World Bank Development Report 2007: Development and the Next Generation*, Washington: World Bank.

Wylie, M. (2008) Internationalizing curriculum: framing theory and practice in international schools, *Journal of Research in International Education* 7(1): 5–19.

Yamato, Y. and Bray, M. (2006) Economic development and the market place for education, *Journal for Research in International Education* 5(1): 57–82.

Zilber, E. (2004) Mobility in metaphor: colourful descriptions of third culture kids, *International Schools Journal* XXIV(2): 17–21.

2 Global networking and the world of international education

Michael Wylie

NASA satellites watch the earth at night. While it is impossible to see the whole globe in darkness as the earth rotates endlessly, orbiting the sun, NASA scientists have been able to piece together a night image of the earth. It is an amazing image to see. Through this image we see brightness and darkness, we see connection and disconnection and flows of information and capital. We see an incongruent world. Yet throughout the light and dark areas international schools are located, connected through curriculum, pedagogy and assessment, networked through organisations such as the International Baccalaureate Organization and the Council of International Schools. This chapter explores global networking and then through three vignettes demonstrates how international education can be enacted in contrasting contexts and how, within these contexts, dynamic ideological tensions exist.

Figure 2.1 Earth at Night, Astronomy Picture of the Day, 11 August 2002.

Source: C. Mayhew and R. Simmon (NASA/GSFC), NOAA/NGDC, DMSP Digital Archive, http://antwrp.gsfc.nasa.gov/apod/astropix.html

A networked global society?

> Networks are appropriate instruments for capitalist economy based on innovation, globalization, and decentralized concentration . . . for a culture of endless deconstruction and reconstruction . . .
>
> (Castells 2001: 502)

Castells sees Information and Communication Technologies (ICT) as a vehicle forging a network society that has dominated global economies, capital flow, commerce, information and power and as making possible new sources of change and domination in social and cultural discourses.

According to Castells,

> industrialised countries with about 15 percent of the population of the planet account for 88 percent of Internet users. There was considerable regional disparity in the diffusion of the internet. While only 2.4 percent of the world population had access to the internet, the percentage was 28 percent in Finland (the most Internet oriented society in the world at the turn of the century), 26.3 percent in the US, and 6.9 percent in OECD countries excluding the United States. Within countries, social, racial, gender, age, and spatial inequality in Internet access was substantial.
>
> (Castells 2001: 377)

Thus connectivity cannot be taken for granted, to the point where 'households with incomes of greater than $75,000 US and higher were 20 times more likely to have internet access than those at the lowest levels of income' (Castells 2001: 377). This empirical data leads to a conclusion that being connected to the information society is a privilege for an emerging global middle class, both locally and globally. The democratisation of knowledge across the World Wide Web is accessible only to a limited global class.

In his opening address to a conference on interpreting international education, Sir John Daniel stated that in the 1900s there was by proportion much freer movement of capital and trade as well as in principle freer movement of people. He continued to say, 'The point remains, however, that today's globalization is the globalization of money, images and products rather than the globalization of people. In fact governments are going to greater lengths to prevent the movement of people' (Daniel 2002: 2). It is with the aid of ICT that globalisation has taken on a whole new meaning. Access to ICT and the associated literacies has emerged as a necessity to access economic advantage.

So, does thinking globally imply that one must have access to the information highway? In developing countries, constraints in keeping up with computer and telecommunication technology can be insurmountable. The cost to access the internet in a developing country in an internet café often equates to a significant price for people who are living on a few dollars a day. Schools in sub-Saharan Africa often have no access to electricity and limited access to water. The struggle for developing countries to keep up with modernisation can be considered as a new form of colonialism.

> From an instrumental perspective, new technologies can empower or dis-empower social actors – states, groups, classes, and institutions. On a more fundamental, but perhaps less visible level, technologies can influence the self-understandings and identities of social actors and perhaps even the very nature of power itself.
>
> (Litfin 2002: 65)

Information technology is having an impact on global politics and how people live. As Litfin (2002) suggests, the advantages of information technology cannot be seen simply as tangibles, such as increased profitability and greater efficiency but more so as changes in the way we think and live.

International education involves communication between students, teachers and curriculum writers in all parts of the developing and developed world. Evans (1997) explores the impact of communications and transportation on the shifting borders. An example of this eloquently stated is that 'it is a shorter cultural journey from Melbourne to London, than it is from Darwin to Jakarta' (Evans 1997: 8). The ability to communicate, share information and travel with such ease has resulted in a preferred cultural connection which is from West to West.

Said argues that technological advancement, along with its vocabulary, condemns the third world to subordination:

> Around the colonized there has grown a whole vocabulary of phrases, each in its own way reinforcing the dreadful secondariness of people who, in V.S. Naipaul's derisive characterization, are condemned only to use the telephone, never to invent it. Thus the status of colonized people has been fixed in zones of dependency and peripherality, stigmatised in the desig-nation of underdeveloped ruled by superior, developed, or metropolitan colonizer who was theoretically posited as a categorically antithetical overlord.
>
> (Said 2000: 295)

The unpredictable reaction of societies to the rapid developments and changes in information and communication technology is central to education's role in a new global economy. Education is being exploited by governments as a way forward to economical advantage in developing knowledge based economies. There is a perpetual epistemological shift due to the influences of ICT. Pedagogies are constantly changing as society is continually adopting ICT and adapting to the influence of ICT. Pedagogies are emerging which are becoming global in nature. The ability to locate and obtain vast amounts of information and the free movement of information across national borders is impacting the nature of 'international schooling'. The emergence of ICT as an essential literacy contributes to a new form of colonialism, serving hegemonic economic interests.

Connected by the movement of information, the movement of capital and the movement of people exists a network of schools. These schools are instrumental in the processes of globalisation. By structuring social relationships and through institutional practices, ideologies are transmitted, along with the transfer of power and control.

Globalisation and social control within international schools

Schools structure social relationships, resulting in a discursive transmission of power and control. The structure of these social relationships controls the message systems within schools such as curriculum, pedagogy and evaluation as well as the transmission of ideology. Bernstein, looking for an approach which discerns between these message systems and transmission, explains: 'I wanted to develop a different approach which placed at the centre of the analysis the principles of transmission and their embodiment in structures of social relationships' (1975: 3).

Globalisation is frequently argued to be both politically and economically motivated by the hegemonic interests of the West, or 'developed world'. Schools are a major instrument in maintaining this hegemony, through mechanisms such as those suggested by Bernstein

> Inasmuch as the school is a major instrument of the division of labour through its control over the occupational fate of its pupils, it has taken on a pronounced bureaucratic function. Here it subordinates pupils' needs to the requirements of the division of labour through the examination system . . . knowledge is rationally organised by the teacher and transmitted in terms of its examination efficiency. Control over such pupils stems from control over their occupational or higher educational fate. Such control is bureaucratic. The instrumental order of the school is likely to be transmitted through bureaucratic procedures which affect curriculum, the transmission of knowledge and the quality of the pupil-teacher relation.
>
> (Bernstein 1975: 63)

Herein lays a dilemma. Bernstein writes from a Western industrial perspective, relevant to the period of his work. But he recognises that his work on the transmission of knowledge and the message systems of schools can be applied to different schools, countries and cultures.

Bernstein considers that schools are agents of cultural change and that all schools irrespective of their context are engaged in the socialisation of their pupils.

The major factors affecting the behaviour of pupils in school are four: the family setting and social origins of the child, the age group or friendship patterns of the child, the school itself, and the pupils' occupational fate. The analysis should hold irrespective of the type of secondary school – grammar, secondary modern or comprehensive – and in principle, should be capable of extension to other countries, in fact whereever a school is an agent of cultural change.

(Bernstein 1975: 37–8)

Societies have developed new rules of distribution of power and control that are closely linked to globalisation. ICT has developed at an unforeseeable rate and continues to do so, influencing the message systems articulated by Bernstein. Teachers' roles have changed as they merge with these technologies. Much has changed, yet much has stayed the same. Society still acts to divide people, and schools are the agents that introduce pupils to their position in this division of labour. Yet society can be broadened on a global scale. The hierarchy resulting from the division of labour now includes those in all places of the world, from sub-Saharan Africa, China, the US, the UK, India . . . The distribution of knowledge is currency of globalisation.

The new concept is a truly secular concept. Knowledge should flow like money to wherever it can create advantage and profit. Indeed knowledge is not like money, it is money. Knowledge is divorced from persons, their commitments, their personal dedications. These become impediments, restrictions on the flow of knowledge, and introduce deformations in the working of the symbolic market.

(Bernstein 2000: 86)

Ideologically the domination of most of the world has occurred through processes of the West maintaining colonial discourse in colonised countries, and through post-colonial discourses in countries that have gained independence despite the expansion of Western capitalism. As against such expansionary practices of global capitalism an alternative humanistic possibility is recognised through a new global ideology that proposes global civil values in a global civil society.

Schools and their message systems, as defined by Bernstein, are central to a global society's distribution of power and principles of control. Schools are unique yet 'their selective organisation, transmission and evaluation of knowledge is ultimately bound up with patterns of authority and control' (Bernstein 1975: 81) and their knowledge is realised through the message systems of curriculum, pedagogy and evaluation and through redefined notions of teachers' work and the use of ICT. Colonial, post-colonial, global economy and global civil ideologies are competing mechanisms of social control that imply differing forms of curriculum, pedagogy and assessment and different utilisation of ICT and structuring teachers' work (Wylie 2008).

The following sections demonstrate how international education exists in a variety of contexts, relying on networks and mechanisms for maintaining networks. International schools can be viewed through a theoretical lens relating colonial, post-colonial, global economic and global civil ideologies to the practice within these schools.

Three case studies

By exploring three personal experiences, my writing privileges an historical and autobiographical approach to narrating. Each school chosen as part of this narrative and its context and problematic illustrate examples in the field of international education. The three schools are in completely different areas of the NASA night map, Matevulu College, Santo, Vanuatu; Kardinia International College (KIC), Geelong, Australia and the International School of Nice (ISN), Cote d'Azur, France. Each school and its community engages in international schooling in a variety of ways, and holds different notions of internationalism.

I begin by describing Matevulu College, a secondary school for indigenous Ni-Vanuatu students in which I worked from 1989 to 1993. While this experience is rather distant, the discourses described at Matevulu College are still present in local schools around the so called 'developing world'.

Matevulu College, Santo, Vanuatu

Matevulu College is a Vanuatu Government Agricultural Secondary College with 500 secondary students. The College is fully residential and students are indigenous Ni-Vanuatu. It is located on 820 hectares and includes a cattle stud and tropical agricultural gardens. The College is co-educational and during my time there, a large number of students came from distant, isolated villages. The students live in dormitories forming their house identity. The College utilised a 12 million dollar Australian Government grant to establish the school and the curriculum. When Matevulu opened in 1983, the original intent of the curriculum was that the college should be an 'Academic Secondary School with an Agricultural Emphasis' (ADAB 1980). My position was funded by the Australian Government to help establish the college and implement the curriculum from years 7 to 13. During this period much debate took place on what curriculum was to be implemented. Matevulu had implemented the International General Certificate of Secondary Education (IGCSE) into years 11 and 12, but this was to change.

Vanuatu is one of the world's most complex nations linguistically. It has an average of 1,000 speakers for each of its 105 languages. Each village speaks its own vernacular. Bislama has developed as the national language. Bislama (a pidgin language) has a developed and documented grammar, structure and spelling. It is the government, urban and inter-village language. However, many isolated village dwellers can only speak their vernacular. English and French are promoted in the constitution as being the academic, commercial and international languages (Crowley and Lynch 1985 in Wylie 1993a). The curriculum from year 7 to 10 is national and uniform between French and English schools. The system had to be unified, complete to matriculation level if standards were to improve (Mathews 1990). The curriculum was Eurocentric in its content and delivery.

A year 10 external leaving certificate is taken by students across Vanuatu to decide whether they are able to continue onto years 11, 12 and 13. During my posting in Vanuatu, only two other schools had education past year 10, Malapoa College and Lycee Bougainville. Malapoa offered the IGCSE and Lycee Bouganville, a modified version of the French Baccalaureate. At Matevulu College, initially the IGCSE was implemented, as the college was primarily Australian funded and was taking a lead from the English school. The debate was, however, what would be the best curriculum in preparing students for university or future post secondary study?

My position as the Head of Studies included the search and pursuit of a curriculum model that would both suit the perceived needs of the local people as well as having the rigour to equip students entering university. The International Baccalaureate (IB) was considered and researched, due to its benefits of being bilingual French and English and its relationship with the IGCSE, which was in the process of being phased out. A Pacific certificate, based in Suva, Fiji, was then seriously considered, called the Pacific Senior Secondary Certificate (PSSC). The curriculum content was based around the national curriculum in New Zealand. At this stage there was an injection of interest from the Ministry of Education (MOE), National Planning and various donor governments who had a vested interest in the education sector. As a result, an autocratic evaluation of the PSSC in the context of post year 10 education in Vanuatu was undertaken by the MOE. The recommendation of the evaluation was that Matevulu College should adopt the PSSC (Beveridge 1991). The tension between the needs of Ni-Vanuatu society and cultural identity and the motives and intentions of the curriculum at Matevulu College gave rise to a contradiction that questioned the role and purpose of education in Vanuatu in a post-colonial context.

I produced a case study describing a period of radical curriculum change at Matevulu College. The study was based on the implementation of a second cycle curriculum for years 11, 12 and 13 and its broader impact. The study of the year 11 programme, in light of the developing second cycle curriculum, illuminated concerns relating to the effects of the programme. Discussion began to be framed by deeper conceptual and ideological concerns revealing an underlying Westernisation of the curriculum failing to communicate and relate to the uniqueness, the pluralism and historic diversity of Vanuatu custom and culture.

In Vanuatu, cultural pluralism is embedded in language, in art and in dance. Culture depends on these media for reproduction and like an endangered species will be lost forever once the reproductive methods have been disturbed. Multiple realities are illustrated in story, song and art. Verification is obtained by consensus. In determining historic record, truth is determined by what is believed to be just in particular circumstances. All the discoveries of the Case Study (Wylie 1993b) were radiating out from the school into the wider society being realised in the process of social evolution. When children have forgotten their language, have lost the ability to carve, are ashamed of dance and wearing custom dress, culture is lost and forgotten as we forget a dream, without record or substance.

> My culture and custom are very important and I think that I had better not lose them because every time I return home my parents often say to me that my behaviours are changing. In the first place they told me I had no respect for others, secondly I forget how to weave such things as mats and baskets, which I very much knew before.
> (C. H. – Vanua-Lava Year 11 student, 1993 Case Study)

> I could speak and write my language but now I am bored at speaking because I mix up some language words with English words (S. A. – Year 11 student, 1993 Case Study).
> (Wylie 1993b)

The results of the case study illuminated a number of concerns. In the context of that study, it became apparent that as a result of the national education schooling system a continued process of colonisation of the Ni-Vanuatu was occurring. The 1993 case study inspired in me a great interest in the wonders and harmony of the lives of indigenous people and just how much Western people can learn and gain by relating to and appreciating their knowledge systems. This led me to wonder how Western educated students might learn and understand the richness of the lives of indigenous people:

> in the long run it could prove that whites have more to learn from the original inhabitants than the other way around, not only for giving aboriginal people a fairer deal at least but for coming better to terms with ourselves and our environment.
> (Lloyd 1986, quoted in Gunew and Rizvi 1994: 78)

The colonising influences of education in the Vanuatu context are relevant to international education. Fifteen years after, neo-colonialism is still a reality in Vanuatu as it is in much else of the so-called 'developing' world. The relevance of the Vanuatu Case Study is to illuminate education's colonising influence and ask whether international education is part of a new global imperialism.

On the surface, relating the complex issues of post-colonialism and the effects of Western imperialism on indigenous peoples to international education may not seem completely relevant. Yet, by finding a reference external to Western epistemology, it becomes possible to consider international education through different eyes, from the margins. From this distance it becomes possible to review the intent, philosophical development, and the effects of international education, not just in a local school or community, but also in a broader educational context.

Through the writing of Smith (1999), Thiong'o (1986) and Achebe (1988) globalisation and Western imperialism have been ideologically fore-grounded when exploring the trends and motives of international education. This literature tells how indigenous peoples have lost their identity and become dehumanised and culturally impoverished by an insidious process of Western domination. Smith (1999) considers the quest for Western knowledge and learning as a new form of colonialism. She develops an historical and philosophical background to imperialism beginning during the enlightenment period. Smith provides an ideological background to Western curricula, socially, epistemologically and philosophically. She considers Western philosophies as fragmenting society through an emphasis on individuality in stark contrast to indigenous epistemology which has developed to complement nature and shared communal identity. According to Smith, indigenous peoples have been systematically dehumanised and historically disqualified by a colonial devaluation of their knowledge. Globalisation has become a new form of imperialism and post-colonialism has become a more refined form of colonialism.

Thiong'o (1986) explores this in far greater depth. He considers international education as devaluing indigenous culture, beliefs and identity, where the loss of language results in the disruption of cultural reproduction. 'The effect of a cultural bomb is to annihilate a people's belief in their names, in their languages, in their environment, in their heritage of struggle, in their unity, in their capacities and eventually themselves' (Thiong'o 1986: 3).

Thiong'o (1986) considers the relationship between a child's language, schooling and family as being in perfect harmony for the pre-colonial child. The disassociation of the natural and social environment through colonisation leads to a process of alienation. Often the language of instruction is not the language of the indigenous community and the curriculum has a Western or Eurocentric nature, particularly in regard to history, art, literature, food technology and geography. 'For colonialism this involved two aspects of the same process: the destruction or deliberate devaluing of a people's culture, their art, dances, religions, history, geography, education, orature and literature, and the conscious elevation of the language of the coloniser' (Thiong'o 1986: 16).

As colonial powers relinquish their rule and governance, countries find a new independence based on post-colonial discourse. In many cases, the colonial elite are replaced by a new hegemonic indigenous class reproducing the same colonial discourses and serving the same imperialist objective. Thiong'o (1986) explores the role colonial languages (as the languages of instruction in schools) have played in maintaining the colonial past.

However, according to Said (2000), the 'colonized' has gone beyond being a category synonymous with the third world and has expanded to include women, subjugated and oppressed classes and national minorities. Said, by deconstructing the imperialist and post-colonial contexts of writers such as Joseph Conrad and T.S. Eliot, reveals discourses that underlie imperialistic relations present in today's world. Said (1993) explores culture's relationship to the broader political and ideological context and suggests that globalisation is the result of modern imperialism:

> thanks to the globalised process set in motion by modern imperialism; to ignore or otherwise discount the overlapping experience of Westerners and Orientals, the interdependence of cultural terrains in which the colonizer and colonized co-exist and battle each other through projection as well as rival geographies, narratives, and histories, is to miss what is essential about the world in the past century.
>
> (Said 1993: xx)

In reflecting on Foucault's influence on Said, Cambridge explores imperialism and the effects of Western societies on other cultures. He interprets the influences of imperialism from not only a materialistic perspective but also from the perspective of the 'colonisation of the mind' (Cambridge 2007: 421).

Thaman (1997) continues this argument by claiming that education in developing countries is a tool of imperialism, designed to transmit the accumulated knowledge, skills and values of foreign cultures, which results in the alienation of many Pacific Islanders from their cultural knowledge, understanding and values. If Western ideology is embedded into curriculum, practitioners, educators, teachers unavoidably will continue to fall into the traps of the colonial past and their predecessors. Thaman builds an argument that recognises the influences of globalisation on the peoples of the Pacific Islands and draws attention to the practices and pedagogy of teacher educators.

> In my view, education is inevitably about culture because it is the values of a culture that must underpin its education system . . . Today Pacific peoples share world view that comprises intricate webs of inter-relations which provide meaning to and frameworks for daily life and cultural survival.
>
> (Thaman 2006: 5)

In a broader context, is the role international education plays in the process of globalisation contributing to and reinforcing post-colonial discourses? This question is answered by Quist:

I think of the nature of current discourse on international education. This is often discourse characterized in the main by the Western (developed) world talking to itself and demonstrating an unwillingness or inability to fully engage with the relevant perspectives and demands of colonial/postcolonial discourse. The end result is a conversation in which the much larger majority world (described variously as 'underdeveloped' or 'developing' or 'The Third World') is, at worst, largely absent or, at best hanging rather perilously on the periphery.

(Quist 2005: 5)

Most of the world, as described by Quist, is grappling with colonial/post-colonial struggles and is now being marginalised by a new wave of globalisation. Yet Quist through his argument assumes colonial and post-colonial discourses need to be understood and included in emerging global discourse rather than suggesting that globalisation is but a manifestation of imperialism and colonisation.

Post-colonialism discourses have made way for the globalisation of the smallest and isolated communities and cultures. Globalisation, with ideology grounded in consumerism, expansionism and Westernisation, indoctrinates and engulfs peoples and cultures more efficiently and clinically than post-colonisation. Globalisation is shrouded in the misconception that cultural identity is no longer owned by the imperialists (as was the case in colonial times and thereafter) but rather a matter of worldwide cultural identity. As articulated by Pieterse 'Empires come and go, globalisation continues' (2004: v). This identity is, however, dominated by the economic and cultural forces of the West and spread through the advancement of media and communications.

Contemporary globalisation, though multidimensional, has been primarily economically driven. From the 1980s the dominant project has been neo-liberal globalisation . . . Neo-liberal globalisation hinges on economics and finance, while empire prioritises geopolitics and military and political power. Neo-liberal globalisation and hegemony are intrusive, but empire is intrusive to a much greater degree.

(Pieterse 2004: 32)

As globalisation changes our world, international education can be viewed as another franchised commodity to be sold in ever-expanding markets. The motives of international education from a post-colonial perspective can be seen as a complex social tool for maintaining colonial discourse and propagating economic imperialism to an emerging global middle class of citizens. Has the activity of international schooling become instrumental in the stratification of peoples, culturally, ethnically, religiously and economically or does it provide a pathway to freedom and development?

After four years in Vanuatu and the end of my project, my family and I decided to live and work in France. We spent one year at L'Ecole Active Bilingue Jeannine Manuel, a bi-lingual French–English international school in Lille, the Flanders region, teaching the International Baccalaureate Diploma, and then moved to Caracas, Venezuela, to teach the International Baccalaureate Diploma at Escuela Campo Alegre (ECA) an American style international school. After two years in Venezuela we decided to return to Australia. Each of these schools has their own stories. The world of international education was becoming apparent to me as a network transcending the globe and opening an educational field that was yet to be theorised and explored.

After my experiences with international schools and international education models such as those offered by the IBO, I was keen to find a similar school in Australia. During August 1996, a small advertisement appeared searching for teachers and administrators at a newly opened international school named Kardinia International College (KIC). This seemed to be what I was looking for.

I was recruited at the school and started there in January 1997. The school commenced with a population of thirty-six students in 1996 and was to grow to 1,700 during an eleven-year period. Nearly all students come from the local Geelong region. KIC is a Kindergarten to year 12 (K–12) College located in Geelong, Victoria, Australia and is privately owned by a Japanese educator, Mr. Yoshi Katsumata. Yet KIC was not the type of international school I expected. It was yet again a different experience of what I thought international education might be. KIC was a contrast to my previous ideas and experiences and left me bewildered.

Kardinia International College, Geelong, Australia

Kardinia International College is a newly developed school, established in the buildings of a previous Presbyterian girls' school. The school was opened in 1996 with little more than thirty students and now enrols some 1,700 students from kindergarten to year 12.

KIC may have had an advantage in starting from scratch, relatively unencumbered by heritage, tradition and history. Katsumata, the Director of the Board, had a vision for the college to build an international school. The management and board structure of the college was based on a Japanese traditional style giving the Principal autonomy in decision and policy making. Japanese heritage, tradition and culture have gradually and subtly influenced the various discourses at KIC, through exchanges, celebrations and language.

Kardinia International College began with a conceptual foundation of 'four cornerstones' and a number of fundamental philosophies. The four cornerstones are:

- internationalism
- technology
- living the school motto
- each student is an individual learner.

The motto of the college is 'Wisdom leads to Respect and Friendship' and its symbol is a bridge representing a meeting place for all cultures and peoples (Kardinia International College 2007).

One of the greatest dilemmas Kardinia International College faces is what makes it 'international'. Parents, students, teachers and various members of the community have asked this question. 'International' is emblazoned in the name of the school, present as one of the cornerstones and symbolised in the College icon. Yet what makes Kardinia International College any more international than any other school in the immediate area?

There are roughly sixty students from overseas, coming from countries such as China, Vietnam, Korea, Argentina, Japan, Nauru and Thailand. Written into the philosophy of KIC is that all students are 'international students'. This rhetorical claim is realised in many ways. There are, for example, several student exchanges: every year a group of twenty students from year 10 travels to a home stay exchange at Katsumata's school in Japan. Students from Japan also visit Kardinia in a reciprocal arrangement. Commencing in 2003, groups of year 9 students travelled to Chang Mai, Thailand, at the Prem Centre, for one term. Four groups of year 9 students spend one term at Chang Mai during any one year. The Prem Centre is an international school with approximately 300 students from the expatriate community and wealthy locals. The staff is recruited from mainly Australia, the UK, the US and New Zealand. The Prem Centre offers exchanges for visiting schools as an economic venture. As a part of this trip, students visit villages, orphanages, Buddhist temples and are based in the luxury of the Prem Centre. As well as the exchanges there is a bi-annual exchange trip to France for six or eight weeks where year 10 and 11 students stay with French families and attend French Lycées. At KIC the International Baccalaureate Diploma (IBD) has been introduced into years 11 and 12 and the IB Primary Years Programme (PYP) been implemented in the Junior School, from Kindergarten to Grade 6.

A major research project took place during 2006–7. Students, teachers and parents were interviewed and questionnaires were distributed. It was possible to map the responses of the participants of the study using the International Education Matrix (Wylie 2008). By exploring the message systems curriculum, pedagogy and evaluation and the mechanisms for power and control, teachers work and the use of ICT, participants were able to be located through a theoretical trajectory from colonialism, post-colonialism, global economics, global ideology and global civil society. Reponses were able to be mapped. It was possible to make comparisons and contrasts between the members of the KIC community and the associated discourses. In general, the activity of KIC is mapped around the global economy ideology and merges into global ideology and global civil society. Teachers were positioned ideologically around global civil society values, yet were constrained by instrumental factors that control curriculum and assessment. Local students and parents ideologically shift between global economy ideology and the desire for economic advantage but hope for a global civil society and incorporate ways of achieving both. Overseas students are motivated by global economy ideology but are discursively shifted to global ideology and global civil society by the message systems at KIC. Overseas students are Westernised through the globalisation of education and the domination of Western discourse on capitalist global markets. Through this Westernisation, overseas students are exposed to post-colonial ideologies. Through exchange programmes, the matrix is further explored. Post-colonialism is present in the Chiang Mai experience as well as global civil society ideology. Post-colonialism is associated with, but external to the discourses at KIC.

Intercultural understanding was often conflated with international education. Culture is ideologically and politically constructed and maps out social activity. The way individuals understand and relate to other cultures is relational and interpreted through the ideological dimension of the International Education Matrix. Intercultural understanding is functional and underpinned by theories of power and control. Students at KIC adopted a global economy understanding of cultural differences yet shifted in a trajectory between global economy and global civil society. Complex functional discourses result through these intercultural understandings.

The contrast between the ideological positioning of the discourses presented through the research demonstrated that complex tensions and conversations can exist in the enactment of international education in a single institute such as KIC. These conversations are ideologically positioned and often the ideological intent is not realised practically. What is apparent is that complex ideological differences can coexist in social activity. The tensions between discourses result in continual ideological movement and shifting, subtle relationships between power, privilege and knowledge.

After nearly eleven years working at Kardinia International College, I was appointed as Director to the International School of Nice, on the Cote D'Azur on the French Riviera. This was to be yet another experience and another major move for my family.

The International School of Nice

Located on the French Riviera, serving the international community is the International School of Nice (ISN). There are thirty-seven different nationalities among students and teachers. There are no dominating cultural groups; however, the three main nationalities are English, French and American. It is not uncommon to find a class group with every student coming from a different nationality. ISN is a K to 12 school offering the International Baccalaureate Diploma in years 11 and 12 and is in the process of implementing the International Baccalaureate Primary Years Programme (PYP) into years K to 5. Nearly all students are multilingual and are able to switch seamlessly between languages. The language of instruction is English.

The origin of ISN was an American-style school called the American International School of Nice (AIS). Many of the original staff are present at the school and help maintain the character of an American style of education. Much of the language and structure is still present, such as Lower School, Middle School and Upper School sections, American style graduation, Halloween celebrations . . . mixed with multicultural celebrations and French language and discourse.

Students from ISN come from economically elite families. The cost of the education is expensive. Some parents do stretch to afford to pay the school fees. However, many families are from among the wealthiest capitalist class in the world. Some families relocate to the French Riviera as it is an attractive location. However, these families can also move after a few years in search of another lifestyle. ISN is managed by the Chamber of Commerce and Industry (CCI). The mission and motive behind CCI involvement in ISN is clear. According to the ISN prospectus:

> The International School of Nice is one of the educational institutions directed by the Chamber of Commerce and Industry of Nice Cote d'Azur (CCINCA) which provides support and guarantees the financial stability of the school . . .
> Overseas studies indicate the need for international educational institutions to accommodate the needs of families who move from their home countries. For this reason the CCINCA is enthusiastic to take an active role in the development of the International School of Nice.
>
> (ISN 2008)

Being the Director at ISN and having my children at the school can lead to interesting moments. It is not unusual for parents to own luxury yachts, extravagant cars and properties. It is in fact another world. As a part of the creativity, action and service (CAS) component of the IBD programme, IB students travel to Tanzania and take part in a service project with the International School of Moshi (ISM). Students work in a local primary school, helping to build new classrooms and painting the building. The school has no electricity, one tap and an average of seventy students per class. Students taking part in this trip were exposed to a new scale of economy, from one extreme to another. I took part in this trip and it was amazing to see the impact that was made on the ISN students. Even after their return, students reflected on their experiences through reflective writing and writing their extended essays. The International Baccalaureate is able to transcend an incongruent world.

Ideologically, the motives of CCINCA are purely economic. In order to stimulate economic growth in the region an International School is necessary. Parents' desires are for their children to go to the best universities in the United Kingdom, the United States, Europe and Canada and to forge networks with other students and families from a similar transnational capitalist class.

Transnational defines groups, institutions, discourses that cross borders and identify with no one country or state. Transnational has emerged as a class that propagates Western capitalist ideology. 'Global system theory proposes that the most important transnational forces are the transnational corporations (TNC), the transnational capital class, and the culture-ideology of consumerism' (Sklair 2001: 2). Cambridge argues that international education is fast becoming:

> a globally branded product with schools as the local distributors of this franchised brand, essentially dedicated to serving the values of a transnational capitalist class . . . and local socio-economic elites who are looking for a lever in positional competition with the national education system.
>
> (Cambridge 2002: 4)

The International Baccalaureate Diploma is well recognised by universities throughout the world. Yet the institutional practices through the message systems (curriculum, pedagogy and evaluation) and the mechanisms for power and control (teachers and ICT) are providing the means for students to succeed in their IBD yet shifting students ideologically towards an understanding of global civil values. These students, who are likely to be the financial leaders of the next generation, will have an understanding of the complexities of the global issues that maintain injustices, poverty and extreme inequalities and may be positioned to make a difference for a new future. The aim is to instill global civil society values in students that allow for ethical globalisation such as those outlined by Clark:

- The eradication of poverty (spiritual as well as economic);
- Inclusion, that is, a voice in decision-making, and economic equity;
- Social justice, that is gender equity, labour and human rights, the rights of speech and association, and a fair and independent judicial system;
- Respect for nature and culture; and
- Citizens' involvement in governance; in other words, greater public disclosure and accountability for all public office and institutionalized popular participation.

(Clark 2001: 25)

Conclusion

International schools exist in a variety of contexts. International schools are located in developing countries, developed countries with a colonial history, or colonial countries, and can be examined from a colonial or post-colonial perspective. As a result of globalisation in the developing and developed worlds a new form of imperialism has emerged focused on global economy ideologies. As a result of the rapid development and deployment of information and communication technologies new literacies are emerging. ICT and teachers are merging to transmit knowledge that has become essential to the membership of the transnational capitalist class.

Through three stories abstract ideas of international education emerge. One of the strongest common themes between these cases has been the introduction of the IB programmes as an alternative curriculum model (or in the case of Matevulu College, a Western-style curriculum, the PSSC). At ISN, in Nice, the transnational capitalist class, elite students from France and expatriates, are given access to a privileged knowledge, in the form of the IB and American-style curriculum models and therefore power.

By employing a theoretical trajectory from colonialism, through post-colonialism, global economic theory to global civil society the practical activities of these international schools are explored through the message systems (curriculum, pedagogy, assessment) and the mechanisms of learning and control (teachers and information and communication technologies). Even within a single institution, such as in each of the cases explored, no one static definition of 'international education' or ideological location for the activity exists. Rather there is a constant struggle between ideological perspectives among constituents framed by the institutional discourse of international schools, international educational organisations and curriculum authorities.

References

Achebe, C. (1988) *Hopes and Impediments: Selected Essays*, New York: Doubleday.

ADAB (1980) *Santo Secondary School Appraisal Study*, Canberra: Australian Development Assistance Bureau.

Bernstein, B. (1975) *Class, Codes and Control: Towards a Theory of Educational Transmissions*, London: Routledge and Kegan Paul.

Bernstein, B. (2000) *Pedagogy, Symbolic Control and Identity: Theory, Research, Critique* (revised edn), Lanham, MD: Rowan & Littlefield.

Beveridge, P. (1991) *Full-time Foundation Studies Programme in the Context of Post Year Ten Education in Vanuatu*, Vanuatu Government.

Cambridge, J. (2002) Globalising and internationalising tensions in international education. Paper presented at the Interpreting International Education Conference, Geneva: 11–13 September 2002.

Cambridge, J. (2007) Realism and anti-realism in international education research. In M. Hayden, J. Levy and J. Thompson (eds), *The SAGE Handbook of Research in International Education*, London: Sage, pp. 412–4 .

Castells, M. (2001) *The Rise of the Network Society* (2nd edn), Cambridge, MA: Blackwell.

Clark, J. (2001) Ethical globalization: the dilemmas and challenges of internationalizing civil society. In M. Edwards and J. Gaventa (eds), *Global Citizen Action*, Boulder, CO: Lynne Reinner, pp. 17–28.

Daniel, J. (2002) International education in an era of globalisation: what's new? Paper presented at the Interpreting International Education Conference, Geneva: 11–13 September 2002.

Evans, T. D. (1997) (En)countering globalisation: issues for open and distance education. In L. Rowan, L. Bartlett and T. D. Evans (eds) *Shifting Borders: Globalisation, Localisation and Open and Distance Education*, Geelong: Deakin University Press, pp. 11–23.

38   *Michael Wylie*

Gunew, S. and Rizvi, F. (1994) Aboriginal arts in relation to multi-culturalism. In F. Rizvi and S. Gunew (eds) *Culture, Difference and the Arts*, St. Leonard: Allen & Unwin, pp. 69–85.

International School of Nice Prospectus (2008) The Chamber of Commerce and Industry, Nice, Côte D'Azur.

Kardinia International College (2007) Kardinia International College Website: www.kardinia.vic.edu.au (accessed 10 February 2007).

Litfin, K. (2002) Public eyes: satellite imagery, the globalization of transparency, and new networks of surveillance. In J. Rosenau and J. Singh (eds) *Information Technologies and Global Politics*, New York: State University of New York Press, pp. 65–89.

Mathews, P. (1990). Opening address of the Secondary Principals' and Teachers' conference. Paper presented at the Secondary Principals' and Teachers' conference, Port Vila, Vanuatu.

Pieterse, N. J. (2004) *Globalisation or Empire?* London: Routledge.

Quist, I. (2005) The Language of International Education: a Critique. *IB Research Notes*, 5(1): 2–6.

Said, E. W. (1993) *Culture and Imperialism*, London: Alfred A. Knopf.

Said, E. W. (2000) *Reflections on Exile and Other Essays*, Cambridge, MA: Harvard University Press.

Sklair, L. (2001) *The Transnational Capitalist Class*, London: Blackwell.

Smith, L. (1999) *Decolonizing Methodologies, Research and Indigenous Peoples*, London; New York: Zed Books.

Thaman, K. H. (1997) Considerations of culture in distance education in the Pacific Islands. In L. Rowan, L. Bartlett and T. D. Evans (eds), *Shifting Borders: Globalisation, Localisation and Open and Distance Education*, Geelong: Deakin University Press, pp. 23–37.

Thaman, K. H. (2006) Partnership for progressing cultural democracy in teacher education in Pacific Island countries. In R. Bates and T. Townsend (eds) *Globalisation, Standards and Professionalism: Teacher Education in Times of Change*, Dordrecht: Springer-Verlag, pp. 4–6.

Thiong'o, N. W. (1986) *Decolonizing the Mind: The Politics of Language in African Literature*, London: James Currie.

Wylie, M. (1993a) A Description of the Curriculum in Practice at Matevulu College, Santo, Vanuatu. *ECS 803 Curriculum Evaluation and Case Study*, Geelong: Deakin University.

Wylie, M. (1993b) Matevulu College Case Study. Unpublished Case Study, Geelong: Deakin University.

Wylie, M. (2008) Internationalising curriculum: framing theory and practice in schools. *Journal of Research in International Education* 7(1): 5–19.

3 The political economy of international schools and social class formation

Ceri Brown and Hugh Lauder

Introduction

One of the major aims of sociological analysis is to understand the unintended consequences of actions that appear laudable but that may be overtaken by events. The original development of international schools was inspired by a set of ideals about the fostering of fellow feeling and cooperation. This set of ideals was given a specific educational form by the introduction of curricula such as the International Baccalaureate (IB) which provides a broad and sophisticated education. However, the current round of economic globalisation has placed the ideals associated with international schools and their programmes in a different light with respect to issues of who wins and loses in education. The place of international schools within this global competition for credentials is not just about winners and losers but whether through the agency of the winners they are implicated in the creation of a transnational ruling class (Lauder 2006). At stake, therefore, are two issues: are there groups who gain an unfair advantage in the competition for credentials by attending international schools and, do the latter act as a key route to positions of power within the global economy? If so, do they have a common view of the world that enables them to act as a class in rationalising their economic and political interests?

This chapter attempts to situate international schools within this context of economic and cultural globalisation. It raises questions about the privileged nature of elite international schools and how they relate to issues of the global positional competition for credentials and access to the world's elite universities. In turn, this discussion leads into a consideration of a debate that was present throughout much of the early twentieth century and that is now germane again, albeit in a different form, between neo-Marxists who argued that social class is key to understanding global economic and social development, especially the formation of a global class structure, and those who considered nationalism to provide a better account of political interests and motivations. While this is a rather stark distinction, especially in relation to the early twentieth-century Marxist debates, which saw nationalism as central to a particular form of globalisation (Callinicos 2009), we shall see that the question of the relationship between nationalism and globalisation has remerged, albeit in a different form, between neo-Marxists (Wood 2002; Robinson 2007) as well as between them and their 'nationalist' protagonists (e.g. Gellner 1983).

If the context for international schools is one in which they can be seen as implicated in the formation of a transnational ruling class, this is quite different from a context that sees global economic development as informed by a competition between nation states for economic power. In the latter case international schools may have a role to play in national class formation but if this was so, the consequences would be quite different for understanding the role of international education and its relationship to questions of global power and decision-making.

In order to pursue these questions we adopt the following strategy. In the first section we discuss the nature and social background of the students who attend different kinds of international schools and discuss the advantage created by such schools in providing the possibility of access to the world's leading universities through the credentials they offer. In the second, we discuss two issues in relation to the culture and consciousness that they may foster. The privileged nature of these schools has been recognised at least since the mid 1990s. The questions then are a) what are the implications of this privilege for both the sense of global and/or national citizenship that such schools may foster and b) do they produce the personal qualities that leading transnational companies and other global organisations such as NGOs may find desirable when recruiting?

This discussion raises two key elements in social class formation: the way that students in a position of privilege relate to the world in terms of their understanding of global change and problems and their rights and duties in relation to them, and how they gain access to positions that will enable them to become part of either a transnational or national ruling class. In the third section we move to a discussion of the claims of neo-Marxists and their 'nationalist' opponents. Here we outline the theories that have been advanced with respect to the formation of a global ruling class. In the fourth we 'test' them against recent developments in global political economy to illuminate the claims of the two positions. There are two considerations. It can be argued that in terms of a ruling ideology, neo-liberalism may fit the bill in that, at least until the recent economic recession, it seemed to guide policy with respect to the creation of global markets. The question is: are its fundamental assumptions shared by all key decision makers across the globe? If not, then what, if any, shared political and economic interests serve to unite these key decision makers? Finally, in the context of the debate over the nature of social class formation, global or national, we return to examine the relationship between international schools, national school systems and the role of the state. Do all nations allow their students access to these schools and even if they do, does that provide a route through to the creation of either a global or national ruling class? In both cases the role of the nation state can be seen as crucial.

In some countries there are prohibitions on either international schools or international qualifications such as the IB with respect to the national school system. In others, the state appears to be in tension between the principles of equity that should enable all children within the nation state to an open competition with respect to school achievement and upward social mobility, and that of enabling some to become part of the elite that can have an impact on the nature and direction of globalisation.

In addressing these issues, this paper draws upon original data from interviews with top HR managers within transnational corporations across a range of diverse industries, as well as with leading policymakers in key nations, as part of a research study exploring the effects of the global labour and education markets (Brown *et al.* 2010).

The argument advanced in this monograph is that while the possibility of the creation of a transnational ruling class appeared plausible at the turn of this century or even in its first few years, this is now in doubt with the rise of China and India. Here there are two positions that can be taken. The first is that while there are historical factors that may inhibit the rise of a global ruling class, it is, in the long term, inevitable. The alternative is that this position was plausible when globalisation was being driven by a Western neo-liberal agenda but that the shape of globalisation now appears quite different; rather than the emergence of a global ruling class, what we are witnessing is a new form of imperialist competition. It is on a consideration of the merits of these positions that we conclude the chapter. It should be stressed that this is a preliminary attempt at developing some of the key questions on this issue. The data we bring to bear should not be considered definitive in any way but rather indicative and worthy of further exploration.

The nature of elite international schools

In the introduction to this chapter we stressed that international schools had been established with high ideals. For example, in 1910 the International School of Peace was established in Boston by Edwin Ginn. The mission statement was given as the need to:

> educate the peoples of all nations to a full knowledge of the waste and destruction of war and of preparation for war, its evil effects on present social conditions and the well-being of future generations and promote international justice and the brotherhood of man.
>
> (Scott 1912: 380 in Sylvester 2007: 16)

While more recently A.D.C. Peterson (1987), who inspired the development of the IB wrote: 'We sought not to produce a generation of rootless "world citizens" but one of Americans, English, French, Germans, Mexicans, Russians and others who understood each other better, sought to cooperate with each other and had friends across frontiers' (in Wilkinson 1998: 228). It is clear then that from the outset those involved in developing international schooling models emphasised the foundational values of peace, respect and equality as underpinning an ethos of international schooling. However, international schools are neither uniform in the curriculum they provide nor in the students they attract and this has occasioned a major debate on their nature. Hayden and Thompson have argued that:

> While one cannot state with any certainty exactly how many schools exist, or what precisely their characteristics might be, what can be asserted with confidence is that the body of institutions which would describe themselves as international schools is extremely diverse.
>
> (Hayden and Thompson 2000: 48)

There are three points in relationship to this debate that we would draw attention to. The first is that there has been an exponential rise in the numbers of such schools. In 2003, Canterford (2003) estimated that if the current rate of growth was to continue, then by 2010 there could be as many as 2,000. That figure has more than doubled with most recent reports indicating 5,187 international schools registered (Brummitt 2009). There is little doubt that two related factors have fuelled the rise of the international school sector. The first is globalisation. As transnational companies, NGOs and diplomatic missions have increased in global range and number so the children of these expatriate communities have required educating. However, alongside this development has been the polarisation of wealth in Western and developing countries which has provided emerging elites or ruling classes with the resources to enrol their children in international schools with the hope that they will achieve the credentials and networks to gain access to their parents' class and/or the global labour market for professional workers. MacDonald has estimated that the total tuition revenues created by these schools could be in excess of 5.3 billion US dollars per annum (2006: 198). He has also shown that the average international school fee, per annum, is between US$6,429 and US$10,451 and the highest recorded school fee was US$54,264 (2006: 198) which is in excess of the British public school Eton.

It is significant that these schools prefer to recruit teachers for whom English is the mother tongue (Canterford 2009). It seems that for the parents of children in these schools, the significance of English is that it is the *lingua franca* of globalisation and therefore opens doors for access to elite English-speaking universities and to the global labour market for professional and executive jobs. In this sense it can also be seen as a mark of distinction (in Bourdieu's sense) that not only gives these international school students a cultural and credential advantage but also serves to exclude students who do not study or write and speak in English (Pak-Sang Lai and Byram 2006). Canterford (2009) has argued that there is a segmented labour market for teachers in which preferential recruitment takes place in favour of mother tongue English speakers.

These figures suggest that whatever the nature of the programmes that international schools run they are indeed largely, although certainly not exclusively, the preserve of the wealthiest strata on the globe. However, it is worth noting that for the May 2006 IB diploma examinations 65 per cent of the 53,540 candidates were from state institutions and in October 2006, 52 per cent of the 1,888 IB schools in 123 countries were state schools that received no tuition fees (Hill 2007: 32) (source: www.ibo.org/facts/schoolstats/progsbycountry. cfm). This suggests that North American state schools are using the IB qualification as a way of gaining advantage in the national positional competition for credentials. In effect, what we may be seeing is the adoption of global credentials, such as the IB Diploma, by state schools in order to counter the advantage that credentials like the IBD may have given private international schools. In the light of these data it is important to stress that our interest in this monograph is primarily with fee paying international schools that attract the privileged children of global professional workers and their national counterparts. However, the development of IB schools within national systems also raises questions about whether those attending these schools can gain an advantage within the national positional competition for credentials. In other words, it may be that IB credential holders may gain access to national professional middle-class jobs, if not those relating to the global economy.

The literature supports the theory of a positional advantage for international schooling graduates in order to access elite higher education. In her study into the needs of American graduates who spent a significant amount of their developmental years in international education, Useem (1993) found that four times as many international school graduates went on to achieve a bachelor's degree than the national average. With respect to state education adoption of the IB, Elizabeth Fox makes a telling point:

It was in North America, where the national consciousness had been ignited by government publications (*A nation at risk*) deploring the state of public education, that the IB began to be adopted as a viable programme for state schools in pursuit of excellence . . . By the mid 1980s public schools in Atlanta, Houston, Winnipeg, Chicago, Milwaukee, and Los Angeles, using the IB as a focal or magnet programme with an emphasis on academic standards and excellence, were successful in attracting system wide enrolments of able students, thus improving their image within the local community and reversing the trend of losing gifted students to the private sector.

(Fox 1998: 73–4).

Canterford's (2009) study reinforces the view of the exclusivity of international schools. In his study, 94 per cent of international schools stated that the USA or Britain featured as one of the top three destinations for higher education. When this data is combined with that of the cost of an international education, it is strongly indicative of an education for an elite.

This discussion underlines the point that those attending international schools can be understood as advantaged. This leads to a typology of three distinct types of international school: first, fee-paying schools teaching to an international curriculum and comprising a predominantly expatriate composition where students are not usually citizens of the country in which the school is situated. Second, fee-paying schools teaching to an international curriculum comprising a mix of international students and those who are national citizens; and last, state schools teaching to an international curriculum based upon the international baccalaureate but with students who are national citizens. This distinction is important in order to contextualise issues of culture and citizenship and how they connect to different sectors of the international schooling community. These issues are raised in the following discussion.

The privileged nature of international schools: class consciousness and character

One of the early attempts to come to terms with the privileged nature of many international schools and their implications for the culture and consciousness they may foster is that of Wilkinson (1998). We focus on his paper in this section because it provides a clear account of one of the issues that we need to consider, which are twofold. First, that of the relationship of highly mobile students to questions of citizenship, especially with respect to their host nations. Here there is a question of the tension between their mobility and privilege and how they might understand their rights and obligations. Second, can we understand the education that these mobile students receive as giving them not only a credential advantage but also an advantage as regards the type of character fostered by international schools?

In discussing the role and significance of international schooling for a contemporary global age, Wilkinson has observed that international schools *'have often been described as elitist and hence of little relevance in the widest global terms'* (1998: 227, emphasis in original). Wilkinson disputes this in pointing to the rapid growth in the emergence of international schools in recent years, suggesting that for a significant section of high stratum society international schooling is considered the educational system of choice. Certainly, the value of international schooling is recognised by key officials within the national system of higher education system in India. During her speech at the IB Heads conference in Jakarta (March 1996) Mrs A. S. Dessai, chairperson of the University Grants Commission, observed that as international students represented such a significant transnational elite it was necessary to inculcate in such students a sense of global responsibility: '[T]hey need to develop a knowledge base which gives them the potential to influence decisions to create a more equitable world' (Dessai in Hayden and Thompson 1998: 231). While in itself contradictory, implicit within this statement is the assumption that the international students of today represent a powerful and influential future cadre of global professionals and therefore it is essential to harness the potential for positive change by promoting a curriculum rooted in values consistent with an equitable and egalitarian future. Wilkinson shares this vision for international schooling and yet his discussion as to how to set about such a task highlights a key tension underpinning the notion of global responsibility: how to foster a global versus a national identity for international students.

For example, the relationship between international schools and the countries in which they are located has been of fundamental importance for the United World College (UWC) movement as well as for the international qualification on which they base their educational programme: the International Baccalaureate (IB). Both place a strong emphasis upon the national culture of the 'host' country in encouraging links with the wider community. Wilkinson cited two established UWCs: Li PO Chun in Hong Kong and the Mahindra college in India which recruit a *'significant number'* of students from the host country, not simply a token measure but recognised as 'fundamental to the concept of crossing frontiers and is the only answer to those who see international education as equivalent to the education of a multinational and first world-dominated elite' (Wilkinson 1998: 231).

Despite such attempts, Wilkinson acknowledges the difficulty facing less privileged 'local' students in meeting the expensive schooling fees incurred in pursuing this form of education. He believes a more effective way to establish links with the host country is by forging links with (state) schools through teacher exchange programmes with state schools. This, however, is not an easy task with respect to the difficulties associated with, for instance, unequal pay scales, terms and conditions. While raising some of the pragmatic issues associated with forging links between schools with a view to 'learn from' the culture of the host nation, Wilkinson fails to develop an answer to the fundamental question: how can the cultures of the host nation and the international schooling community be successfully integrated? It appears that Wilkinson is suggesting that simply by dint of greater access between the disparate social worlds of international school and local community these different cultures may magically come together with the outcome of fostering a new set of cultural values (within the international students at least), that are somehow more worthy than the sum of both parts:

> The internationally mobile families, whose children form the core of many international schools and who make up the majority of IB examination entries, increasingly share a set of values and attitudes quite different from those of their own or their host communities. In themselves these values including openness, self sufficiency and tolerance of difference, are important. They are however, only one subset of the values of a wider and much less privileged world. They can only be honed and shared through wider contact, through which they will form the mature beliefs of a new generation that is committed to changing the world, and changing it for the better.
>
> (Wilkinson 1998: 233)

In order to understand the problems associated with notions of global citizenship for the mobile international schooling community it is helpful to refer to the literature on third culture kids (TCKs) and transnational nomads who comprise the mobile clientele of international schools. Useem (1976) was the first to research the needs of American internationally mobile young adults and found there were commonalities in experiences of repatriation to their passport countries. In coining the term 'third culture kids' Useem found that:

> Although they have grown up in foreign countries they are not integral parts of those countries. When they come to their country of citizenship (some for the first time) they do not feel at home because they do not know the lingo or expectations of others – especially of those their own age. Where they do feel most themselves is in that interstitial culture, the third culture, which is created, shared and carried by persons who are relating societies, or sections thereof, to each other.
>
> (Useem 1976 in Langford 1998: 29)

In more recent times such issues pertaining to TCKs have been identified in a wider cohort of internationally mobile young people from other national-ities who, owing to their parents' occupation, have spent a significant amount of their developmental years living in one or more countries outside their passport country. This has given rise to the term 'global nomads' who are 'members of a world-wide community of persons who share a unique cultural heritage. While developing some sense of belonging to both their host culture(s) and passport culture(s) they do not have a sense of total ownership in any' (Schaetti 1993 in Langford 1998).

A number of studies into the experiences of TCKs and global nomads have identified a range of common characteristics pertaining to a notion of multi-culturalism. These include: the ability to speak a number of languages, cross-cultural awareness and three-dimensional world view (Langford 1997). Aspects of such broad types of world view include skills and aptitudes necessary to operate very successfully with others who are different in reference to: diplomacy, flexibility, patience and tolerance (Kilham 1990; Langford 1997). However, they also refer to the ability to be self-sufficient, including characteristics such as independence, maturity and the ability to cope in a crisis (Stuart 1992).

How then are we to understand the relationship between the characteristics of TCK students and the global labour market? In order to explore this it is illuminating to contextualise these characteristics of 'ideal type' TCKs/ Global Nomads against the attributes sought for key workers in high-end managerial, and research and design positions.

International school cultures and the demands of MNCs

Drawing upon interviews carried out by Brown *et al.* (2010) with HR personnel within a range of transnational corporations (TNCs) across diverse industries such as financial services, automotives and retail, a number of core behavioural competencies were consistently raised across these varied fields. These were firmly rooted in the importance of 'soft skills' such as: interpersonal and communication skills, team work, nuanced understanding of multiple cultures and a flexible adaptable outlook. Such requirements are neatly encapsulated in an interview with HR managers at an electrical TNC in Korea:

> To be a global manager [requires] to be a kind of a cultural translator. I think this really requires a lot of the softer skills that have not been a traditional focus of Korean management. And I think that is something that we have to become more sophisticated about you know being a little bit more nuanced in your interactions, just being more, being more aware and again being more flexible and not you know you hear the old adage you know treat others as you would like to be treated. It is treat others as they want to be treated and I think that just by learning more so it is not just going to a country and being the, you know the tourist, but really you know empathising.

In order to maintain a relevance to multiple cultures, it was apparent that the culture and identity of the TNC was of fundamental importance. This was reflected in attributes sought in staff such that while it was necessary for key employees to be adept in multiple cultures, it was of equal importance to maintain a commitment to the distinct culture of the corporation as explained in an interview with a global bank in Beijing:

> This kind of people is not only very capable for the softer skills for leadership, communication, interpersonal and something like that but also the people who knows very well our company and our culture because for [X bank] it has already 140 years history and why we can run so smoothly because we have the core culture inside.

In one sense we could see a straightforward correspondence between the student characteristics of TCK children and the way they are fostered within international schools and the 'third culture' of TNCs. For example, an HR executive for a leading electronics TNC commented: 'X is really a company with a very strong culture, globally. It doesn't mean you are US, or UK, or China, we have this consistent culture', while another electronics HR manager spoke of the common values that were necessary: 'You can't have a different set of er . . . er . . . value system or a code of conduct in India different than Europe, it, it's same across the globe.' A banking TNC HR manager spoke in similar terms: 'The organisation is attempting really to fuse together cultures . . . Er hopefully they'll absorb the best of each.'

What is interesting about these cases is that the TNCs all originally started in quite different nations and cultural settings but they appear to have moved to a common culture which seeks similar sets of personal characteristics in their elite recruits.

However, before being too carried away with the notion of correspondence it is important to add some qualifications. First, while TNCs may be able to articulate what they see as desirable qualities at a certain level of abstraction, whether they are able to identify potential recruits with any precision is another matter. Moreover, as Alvesson (2001) has noted, there is considerable ambiguity in both the qualities that are required for knowledge work and a considerable amount of impression management in judgements that are made about such workers. Furthermore, while at one level it is surprising that HR managers seek the same qualities and skills, despite different cultural locations, there may nevertheless be different cultural interpretations of what these qualities and skills mean in practice.

The rationale for positing the emergence of a transnational ruling class

This section introduces three different positions on the implications of a global economy upon forms of power and decision making. The first position to be discussed is neo-Marxist, which hypothesises the emergence of a transnational ruling class (Robinson 2004). According to this perspective, power is wielded through those who control the means of production. As production processes have become globalised, so ruling classes become divorced from nation states and instead can be seen to operate upon a global scale. The second position, a Weberian perspective, would not accept the concept of a unitary transnational class but instead sees issues of power in terms of elites that are related to different power bases (Parkin 1979). For example, there may be elites created through their access to the top jobs in the labour market or political or educational elites, all of which have different power logics and dynamics as well as differential rules by which individuals may enter these elites. Hence the Weberian perspective understands power as comprising different forms (political, social, economic) and as operating across different playing fields within the national and across the global. This raises problems in defining universal ruling parties that can be understood as a ruling global class. The third position is nationalist and sees globalisation in terms of an imperialist competition between nations. This position is opposed to seeing processes of globalisation as breaking down the power of nation states. On the contrary, this perspective sees key states as becoming stronger in terms of the power they may wield across a global platform. In particular this position argues that there are winners and losers in the stakes for global competitive advantage, typically the West becoming the losers and the East standing to gain. However, within these nation states there may well be either a ruling class in neo-Marxist terms or a combination of ruling elites in Weberian terms. In fact in China the notion of class, although changing, has to be understood differently to that in the West because of the dominant role of the People's Party (He Quinglian 2000).

In neo-Marxist theories, in order for a class to be formed it must have a common basis in the means of production: for the ruling class by either owning or organising production and for the working class by selling their labour to the owners and organisers of production. The rationale for arguing that we now have a global basis for production is that transnational corporations have indeed created a global form of production (Robinson 2004). For example, a leading German car manufacturer has a 24-hour design team that follows the sun with centres in Germany, India and the United States. The point about this team is that it works on the same problem round the clock, when the German part of this team closes down, the one in India opens and so on.

The idea of the formation of a transnational ruling class needs to be seen as in the process of developing. Here it is important to distinguish between a *class-in-itself* and a *class-for-itself*. The former refers to the objective conditions that make the formation of a class possible, such as the global production of goods and services. However, a *class-in-itself* may not see or act as a class with an awareness of its economic and political interests, an agenda to fulfil them and a rationale or ideology that it seeks to disseminate as a way of legitimising its interests. In contrast, a *class-for-itself* acts on all these fronts. Clearly, a global transnational *class-for-itself* would be greatly facilitated by the kinds of common experience that private international schools may provide as well as the elite universities its graduates might attend.

However, it is noticeable that the key talking shop for global capitalists – the annual meeting at Davos – includes not only the owners and organisers of global production but also politicians and key policy makers. This suggests that the classical Marxist account given by Robinson (2004) needs extending. Sklair (2001) has argued that a theory of a transnational ruling class would need to include TNC executives, politicians and high level national and multilateral agency bureaucrats who are active in formulating global economic rules, professionals who act as consultants and operate think tanks seeking to influence global policy and those involved in global trading, media and advertising. The extension of the transnational ruling class in this way implies that politicians and bureaucrats, for example, are active in the construction of the rules and processes of globalisation as well as the organisation of production. This is intuitively plausible in that if we take the World Trade Organisation (WTO), for example, it is clear that its bureaucrats have actively helped to establish the rules of the present form of economic globalisation.

It is significant that for Sklair (2001) the ideology that legitimises the transnational class is that of neo-liberalism: the ideology that privileges individual freedom within the market and elevates the market to the key organisational principle of society. In relation to globalisation, market freedom is applied to the breaking down of trade barriers to enable powerful transnational corporations (TNCs) to extend their markets. In this sense there appears to be a coherent logic behind the idea of a transnational ruling class: they have a common objective position in terms of global production, they have common interests and a common ideology.

It may be objected that they do not all hold the same interests in common. For example, manufacturing TNCs may have quite different agendas from financial TNCs. For example, it can be argued that the City of London as once the financial centre of the world drew off talent and resources from manufacturers in Britain. Equally, we now know that financial TNCs' pursuit of profit has had a direct impact on manufacturers since the financial crisis has reduced consumers' ability to buy their goods. The Marxist account has coped with this objection by identifying within the overall ruling class, class fractions such as those relating to manufacturing and finance. The general point, however, is that at a sufficiently high level of abstraction, they share common interests, both requiring open markets in pursuit of profit. The difficulty arises when the practices of one fraction, the financial, are so profligate that they plunge the other fractions into a crisis. The best that can be said is that if there is a transnational ruling class it is now in disarray and reliant on nation states for its survival, as indeed is the neo-liberal ideology that rationalised and legitimised their actions. These comments do not take into account the possibility, which we pursue below, that this crisis is not so much a crisis of a transnational or global ruling class but of a particular group of Western transnational TNC executives and policy makers; albeit one that has fundamental implications for society and for the limits of a finance-driven system of capitalist growth (Arrighi 2007).

So far we have concentrated on neo-Marxist accounts that have focused on production and trade but there is another aspect to this which relates more to a Weberian inspired account focusing on the emergence of global labour markets. Rather than entertaining the concept of a transnational or global ruling class it would focus more on the influence of global elites. The key theorist in this context is Robert Reich.

Reich's theory (1991) underlying his book *The Work of Nations* argues that global economic technologies and practices have created a global labour market producing an elite of symbolic analysts. In effect these are people who 'speak the language(s)' of IT and maths and who are needed to do business in the modern world. He identifies three types of symbolic analysts: those who innovate and problem solve in the production of goods and services; those that understand the market and how customers needs can be met through niche products; and those that link problem solvers and identifiers, who manage ideas and are 'strategic brokers'.

The key to understanding the situation of symbolic analysts in relation to international schools, Reich argues, is that symbolic analysts become detached from national education and welfare systems because they can afford portable forms of education, health and welfare in line with their privileged Bedouin existence across the globe. This has negative implications at a national level as it removes the middle class symbolic analyst voice from debates on national educational provision, as well as health and welfare.

While Reich's position can be understood as broadly Weberian in its emphasis on labour markets rather than production, nevertheless it is an important part of the jigsaw in understanding the impact of globalisation on opportunity, power and wealth. While his work makes no general claims as to ideologies that enable these symbolic analysts to cohere into a group or indeed class, it is safe to say that many may view national systems of education, health and welfare with either indifference or disdain and these views may be consistent with neo-liberal ideology.

Moreover, global systems of production will require global labour markets through which talented graduates can be recruited to oversee the systems and processes of global production. It follows, logically, that a global productive system requires a global labour market from which to recruit and promote individuals across the globe. A focus on global production systems may be primary in understanding global class formation but it tells us little about the individuals who fill the class positions created by such a system and with respect to education, this is crucial.

Reich's account of the symbolic analysts is important in that it enables us to understand how and why certain groups in society can ascend to the leading global decision-making positions and the routes by which they get there. We saw above that there appeared to be a correspondence between the characteristics and culture of third culture kids in international schools, the kinds of qualities and skills they may acquire in them and how these related to the demands of TNCs with respect to the recruitment of the most talented graduates (Lauder 2006). When the technical abilities that may be acquired at leading universities are added to these characteristics it is clear why this group may appear so advantaged.

National interests versus those of a transnational ruling class

To date we have considered the plausibility of the idea of a transnational ruling class. Underlying this idea or indeed hypothesis is the view that global productive systems are becoming more closely integrated on the basis of the shared interests of a transnational ruling class. However, there is an alternative account that sees the development of the global economy as similar to attempts to integrate global production and commerce before the First World War. Here, global economic development is seen to be driven by the interests of nation states rather than a global ruling class. At times these interests may coalesce in forms of cooperation, while at others, cooperation may break down through intense rivalry or competition. In this respect it could be argued that the period of globalisation which the West initiated in the early 1980s and which it has dominated until recently has now come to an end. That period could plausibly be seen as initiating the development of a transnational ruling class legitimised by neo-liberal ideology. However, the rise of China and India in particular raises questions about the transnational ruling class thesis.

There are two general points to be made about this observation. First, class formation would have to be seen as occurring primarily at the national level, although clearly outward-looking in relation to global economic development. Second, it would need to be recognised that class formation in China is very different from that in the West. This is because the People's Party remains central to economic decision making and opportunities for advancement and influence.

Broadly speaking, there are three issues that need to be considered in advancing the claim that it is national interest rather than the interests of a global transnational class that is driving change in the global economy.

The first of these relates to the domestic situation in a country such as China. Here China's state market economy (Arrighi 2007) needs to address the aspirations of its people if serious social unrest is not to threaten, something about which the authorities are extremely concerned. With a growth rate averaging over 9 per cent for the past decade, China has been able to reduce the incidence of poverty more quickly than any other country in history (Winters and Yusuf 2007). However, the current global recession may reverse some of these gains, as well as creating social unrest. The Chinese government is particularly concerned with unemployed graduates who they see as leading protests.

When contextualising the literature detailing the growth in East Asian economies such as China and India it is pertinent to consider the views of policy makers in such countries in order to explore how they conceive the global market economy. The following extracts underline the strategies key countries have taken with regard to processes of globalisation in order to generate what they see to be a competitive advantage above the West.

In talking about the growth in increased foreign direct investment in China, a leading policy maker spoke of the draw of the cost advantage of situating research and design work in China that has also led to an increase in skills and technology:

> They want to share the same advantage, for example, cheap labour, or market . . . The best way to prevent your know-how from being lost is to cooperate with your competitors, only in this way you can control your competitors internally . . . products made in China, which you find in western countries, have been upgraded, almost everything is made in China now.

A similar view was voiced by an Indian policy maker who spoke of the competitive edge that low cost has given to their core industries of manufacturing and IT:

> Ultimately what is going to happen is that more than one activity . . . go to places where they can be done best, and they can be done cheapest. I think that is the only way that businesses can survive . . . . It is really vital that companies must grow and increasingly you need to achieve those economies of scale, you need to achieve the skill, you need to access markets,

you need to diversify – you know, instead of one market. And this is where a very healthy trend actually is emerging. What we are finding – once again – it is a sign of growing confidence in us – if the company is competitive, the economy is competitive, they'll try to achieve economies of scale on all global platforms . . . . And you know – coming to the second issue, an interesting point you made, are companies becoming larger? You just saw the latest billionaires list, one tenth of the new entrants were Indian companies.

Another senior policy maker in India described how the government has encouraged firms to invest abroad in order to gain the skills and technology that can be repatriated back to India, as a process of learning:

> Today we say that to acquire a company outside, you can invest equal to a 100 per cent of your net worth of your company – if you are a 10 million dollar company, you can invest 10 million dollars outside. Now we are looking at it – paper with me right now on the table – saying how to further that, incentivise it, because people, our pharmaceutical companies want to buy up companies outside, partly because of the trademarks that they hold etc, but more because of the market access that it gives them. And a lot of our manufacturing companies, particularly in automobile forging units – are wanting to buy up group Thyssen, the German company. The premium company called . . . . Has made a gunning for that. But we are saying that it is because – as the costs of producing are becoming high overseas, the Indian investors see an opportunity of taking it over, initially produce there, Indian management style, . . . and maybe in the course of time relocate here.

Evidence such as this provides a new angle to consider the role of international schooling in generating a national competitive advantage. Where governments who are key players within a global economy welcome in transnational corporations they are clear that they do so only within the parameters enabled by national political power. It is clear from these accounts that should such arrangements not prove beneficial for the economy of such key players in the East, the global labour market might look somewhat different. From this perspective we could see economic globalisation, as it is now, as driven by national interest which can often coincide with those of other nations in the global economy. For example, the current recession has prompted calls of protectionism for workers in the United States, which in 2007 lost 5 million jobs overseas, mainly to China. And the United States has also sought to apply pressure to China to raise its currency because it has been seen as 'artificially' low in order to keep its exports cheap.

On this view of globalisation, the period that we have identified can be seen as one of transition from a neo-liberal phase through to one where TNCs have acted as a conduit in the rise of China and India (Brown *et al.* 2010), through to a new phase that some have suggested will be driven by China (Henderson 2008).

However, it remains an open question as to whether it is the TNCs who are the principal drivers of the global economy or whether it will be the newly rising economies of China and India. The fact is that the TNCs still retain significant power with respect to investment, jobs, and research and development. Indeed, it can be argued that by their strategies they have been able to cream off national resources and talent in pursuit of their own aims (Lauder *et al.* 2008). However, while many of the European TNCs appear to operate beyond national interests, the newly emerging TNCs of China and India seem far more closely allied to nationalist goals. It is precisely these issues that underlie the debate between Wood (2002) and Robinson (2007). In the light of the recent developments we have described it seems that a new position needs to be adopted that takes account of national interests while acknowledging the continuing power of the TNCs. Where the power lies in the global economy will determine whether we consider a transnational ruling class or national ruling classes or elites as the principle decision makers in its development.

However, the state at the national level needs to be factored into this equation since it could either promote the growth of international schools or indeed seek to find ways of preventing their citizens from participating in a form of education that will give an additional impetus to the life chances of those who are already privileged.

The role of the state and the development of international schools

International schools are variously treated in different countries. In many, they are part of a market system of education but not in all. The key point here concerns what Brown (2000) has called the democratic deficit. He notes that when a system of schooling such as that of international schools stands outside national systems citizens cannot participate in decisions as to how the rules of the competition for credentials should be constructed. In essence, international schools are reliant on the wealth and wishes of parents, rather than on the abilities and motivations of children. In turn, the question of whether children attending international schools gain an unfair advantage in the competition is not one that can be addressed through normal democratic channels. This has led to states taking different approaches to the problem these schools pose with respect to the democratic deficit. For example, Turkey does not support international schools for its nationals, although the IB has been adopted for some national schools. For schools offering the IB diploma there have been difficulties with its integration into a prescribed curriculum that focuses on the creation of secular Turkish citizens. All schools (state and private) are required by law to teach to the Turkish National Curriculum, which is not a natural fit with the IB diploma. In order to graduate from high school all Turkish students must comply with the national curriculum requirements upon which the high school diploma is solely based. Therefore, those students studying for the IB diploma have an additional workload. This high school diploma is essential for any Turkish student wishing to enter a Turkish university; indeed most Turkish universities do not even recognise the IB diploma (Halicioglu 2008). In effect the ministry of education in Turkey has created a barrier for its nationals being educated in international schools.

In contrast, South Korea has recently allowed the children of Korean nationals to attend ISs. However, these students are unlikely to have access to the main educational channels to economic and political power because these are related to the high schools and elite universities students attend. So far cultural practices and norms in South Korea have trumped the power of wealth to gain advantage. Some nations are undecided about whether they should open the market for ISs or whether they should retain control of their schools for purposes of a national citizenship education and indeed a nationally regulated competition for credentials.

One of the most interesting responses in this respect is that of the Netherlands (Prickarts 2009). Dutch pre-university students can take the IB Diploma Programme Pilot at government sponsored schools instead of following the Dutch pre-university programme. The question is why would the state provide funding in this way? The hypothesis that Prickarts entertains is that the state is caught between a concern with equity, which would indicate that international schools should not be supported, and the sense that Dutch nationals need to be promoted through the international school system so that they gain access to the key global decision-making processes.

What this example clearly points to is the tension that economic global-isation has created for the state centred on the democratic deficit. The Dutch case is an example of the trade-offs that Hobson and Ramesh (2002) refer to when states are confronted with the demands of economic globalisation.

However, the number of countries that restrict their nationals from access to ISs is diminishing and our account suggests that while the children of transnational families may relate to the trans-cultural values of transnational corporations and seek to travel where the work is, children of the national elite who attend international schools for the curriculum and skills they offer may well have fostered a strong sense of national identity and utilised the advantage offered from their schooling in order to maximise their competitive advantage within their own home nation.

Conclusion

This chapter has provided evidence that international schooling caters for children of elite professional families, both those who are internationally mobile and, increasingly, those with high aspirations for their children within the home nation. However, there are debates around how we may understand this advantage: in relation to fostering a set of formal qualifications (the IB), or in relation to the softer skills connected to trans-cultural understanding and know-how. Furthermore, we may question how a future cadre of international schooling graduates may come to relate to the world and their responsibilities towards it. Can we understand this in relation to neo-Marxist theories of a transnational ruling class founded upon principles of coordination of global production? Or can we see the role of the ISs as key to the positional competition within nations? How we understand the role of the nation depends on our view of globalisation: is it driven by neo-liberal mechanisms or by competition between states' imperialism? Perhaps the most convincing argument so far is the Reichian perspective that a transnational elite may emerge, divorced from state but formed upon the different lines of industry. However, we may understand some convergence between such elites in political terms in relation to key principles of trade and production and in relation to prevailing ideologies that may support their common interests. The key to such questions lies in how different types of international student, whether national or transnational, may construe issues of identity and citizenship, on local and global levels. While at this juncture we may only speculate as to the future of the global economy and what role international schools may have within it, the relationship of such schools to a global hierarchy of higher education institutions formed by a neo-liberal agenda, and to national and international elites is a question well worth pursuing.

The relationship between IS students and the top universities, which in turn feed the top TNCs enables some understanding of how this advantage operates. Yet in turn this leads us to a final question. In an increasingly unstable global economic climate can we really expect future IS graduates to forgo the advantages they had in the decisions they make for their children, in the pursuit of a more equitable future?

References

Alvesson, M. (2001) Knowledge work: ambiguity, image and identity, *Human Relations* 54(7): 863–86.

Arrighi, G. (2007) *Adam Smith in Beijing*, London: Verso.

Brown, P. (2000) The globalisation of positional competition, *Sociology* 34(4): 633–53.

Brown, P., Lauder, H. and Ashton, D. (2010) *The Global Auction: The Broken Promises of Education, Jobs and Rewards*, Oxford: Oxford University Press.

Brummitt, N. (2009) Facing up to global recession, *International School Magazine* 12(1): 13–14.

Callinicos, A. (2009) *Imperialism and the Global Political Economy*, Cambridge: Polity Press.

Canterford, G. (2003) Segmented labour markets in international schools, *Journal of Research in International Education* 2(1): 47–65.

Canterford, G. (2009) *Segmented Labour Markets in International Schools*, Bath: University of Bath, Ed. D.

Fox, E. (1998) The Emergence of the International Baccalaureate as an impetus for curriculum reform. In M. Hayden and J. Thompson (eds) *International Education: Principles and Practice*, London: Kogan Page, pp. 65–76.

Gellner, E. (1983) *Nations and Nationalism*, Oxford: Blackwell.

Halicioglu, M. (2008) The IB Diploma programme in national schools: the case of Turkey, *Journal of Research in International Education* 7: 164.

Hayden, M. and Thompson, J. (eds) (1998) *International Education: Principles and Practice*, London: Kogan Page.

Hayden, M. C. and Thompson, J. J. (2000) International education: flying flags or raising standards, *International School Journal* XIX(2): 48–56.

Henderson, J. (2008) China and global development: towards a global-Asian era? *Contemporary Politics* 14(4): 375–92.

He Quinglian (2000) China's listing social structure, *New Left Review* 5: 69–99.

Hill, I. (2007) International education as developed by the International Baccalaureate Organization. In M. Hayden, J. Levy and J. Thompson (eds) *The SAGE Handbook of Research in International Education*, London: Sage, pp. 25–37.

Hobson, J. and Ramesh, M. (2002) Globalisation makes of states what states make of it: between agency and structure in the state/globalisation debate, *New Political Economy* 7(1): 5–22.

Kilham, N. (1990) World-wise kids, *The Washington Post*, 15 February, p. B5.

Langford, M. E. (1997) Internationally mobile pupils in transition: the role of the international school. MA dissertation, University of Bath.

Langford, M. E. (1998) Global nomads, third culture kids and international schools. In M. Hayden and J. Thompson (eds) *International Education: Principles and Practice*, London: Kogan Page, pp. 28–43.

Lauder, H. (2006) International schools, education and globalisation: towards a research agenda. In M. Hayden, J. Levy and J. Thompson (eds) *The SAGE Handbook of Research in International Education*, London: Sage, pp. 441–9.

Lauder, H., Brown, P. and Ashton, D. (2008) Globalisation, skill formation and the varieties of capitalism approach, *New Political Economy* 13(1): 19–35.

MacDonald, J. (2006) The international school industry, *Journal of Research in International Education* 5(2): 191–213.

Pak-Sang Lai and Byram, M. (2006) The politics of bilingualism: a reproduction analysis of the policy of mother tongue education in Hong Kong after 1997. In H. Lauder, P. Brown, J. Dillabough and A. H. Halsey (eds) *Education, Globalization and Social Change*, Oxford: Oxford University Press, pp. 490–504.

Parkin, F. (1979) *Marxism and Class Theory: A Bourgeois Critique*, London: Tavistock.

Prickarts, B. (2009) *The Future of the Dutch International School*, Education Department, University of Bath.

Reich, R. (1991) *The Work of Nations*, New York: Simon and Schuster.

Robinson, W. (2004) *A Theory of Global Capitalism*, Baltimore: Johns Hopkins University Press.

Robinson, W. (2007) The pitfalls of realist analysis of global capitalism, *Historical Materialism* 15: 71–93.

Sklair, L. (2001) *The Transnationalist Capitalist Class*, Oxford: Blackwell.

Stuart, K. D. (1992) Teens play a role on moves overseas, *Personnel Journal* 71: 72–8.

Sylvester, R. (2007) Historical resources for research in international education (1851–1956). In M. Hayden, J. Levy and J. Thompson (eds) *The SAGE Handbook of Research in International Education*, London: Sage, pp. 11–24.

Useem, R. H. (1976) Third culture kids, *Today's Education* 65(3): 103–5.

Useem, R. H. (1993) TCKs four times more likely to earn bachelor's degree, *Newslinks* XII(5): 27, available online: www.tckworld.com/useem/art2.html.

Wilkinson, D. (1998) International Education: a question of access. In M. Hayden and J. Thompson (eds) *International Education: Principles and Practice*, London: Kogan Page, pp. 227–34.

Winters, L. and Yusuf, S. (2007) *Dancing with Giants: China, India and the Global Economy*, Washington: Institute for Policy Studies, the World Bank.

Wood, E. M. (2002) Global capital, national states. In M. Rupert and H. Smith (eds) *Historical Materialism and Globalisation*, London: Routledge.

4 International schools and micropolitics

Fear, vulnerability and identity in fragmented space

Richard Caffyn

Introduction

Micropolitics has begun to develop considerably as an area of focus in educational management. It is usually associated with closed doors and the secret underworld of school organisation (Ball 1987; Hoyle 1989). However, to fully understand how micropolitics works, it is very useful to consider the sociological and emotional side of schools as organisations. It is also important to understand that organisational politics affect all aspects of schools, including the curriculum, learning and pedagogy. This concept suggests that an organisation is a maze of interconnected relationships (Watson 2002) and that each affects the other in some way.

Ball regards schools as, above all, complex organisations where struggles are the norm for scarce resources, control and power: 'The structure of social relations in the school is the outcome of ongoing tensions and rivalries, conflicts and realignment which are played out in and through both formal and informal types of context' (Ball 1987: 213). The hidden power balances within the school are a critical aspect of micropolitics. Blase and Anderson (1995) have investigated the importance of leadership and staff relationships with principals, focusing on the principal as the main agent of micropolitics. They see the importance of principal type and categorise principals as well as the staff reactions when faced with different principals (Blase and Anderson 1995; Anderson 1991; Blase 1991). Their work centres on the political perspectives of individuals within schools. They argue that these political viewpoints are the result of values, beliefs, impressions and experience: 'both patterns of micropolitical action seem to emanate from tensions surrounding core values and school contextual values' (Blase and Anderson 1995: 65). In defining micropolitics, Hoyle argues that 'Micropolitics can be said to consist of the strategies by which individuals and groups in organisational contexts seek to use their resources of authority and influence to further their interests' (1989: 66).

Hoyle put forward the idea that there are tactics used by those in organisations to achieve what they want, such as bargaining, manipulating, controlling and displacing. Baldridge (1989) also suggests that subcultures and subgroups articulate interest in different ways, using politics and often conflict to engage with other groups. These views are in contrast to the tidy arguments often put forward in various management models such as bureaucracy and collegiality.

Management of such diverse and complex institutions as schools, especially international schools, cannot be categorised so easily. Etic management and managerialist structures can fail because of distance from professional and local school conditions (Wright 2001; Thrupp and Willmott 2003; Hey and Bradford 2004). Locality and global trends are often particular concerns of international schools. In discussing the contemporary view of micropolitics, it is important to acknowledge the increasing complexity of definitions of the term and the variety of perspectives from which researchers and authors look at school management.

Hargreaves looks at the link between power and institutional micropolitics. He regards change in education as ultimately a political act. 'They are attempts to redistribute power and opportunity within the wider culture' (1998: 282). It is interesting to point out that many commentators view power as a contentious issue (Bates 1989; McNay 1994; Gewirtz *et al.* 1995; Brundrett 1998; Findlay and Newton 1998; Zaretsky 2004). Often this materialises as management having power over staff and the unequal power distribution within school organisation (Webb *et al.* 2004; Herr 2005). Lenski suggests that 'Institutional power takes many forms, but it always involves the possession of certain enforceable rights which increase one's capacity to carry out one's own will even in the face of opposition' (1986: 250).

But what is power in education and in schools? Is it the ability to change, to control, to not be questioned? Control is not necessarily power. Power is more focused on being in a position to bring about these things: it is about positioning (Troman 2000; Wrigley 2003; Vidovich 2004).

In Weberian terms, power is in the bureaucracy, the hierarchy; this is power as authority (Lukes 1974). With the development of society and the increase in collegial organisations, the continued need for this kind of structure is highly contentious. Other forms of management and organisational structure such as collegiality and ambiguity reveal the complexity of power in schools. There are a variety of stakeholders all vying for the vacuum of power that the managerial charade of bureaucracy has left behind. Bush (1995) argues that power in schools is both official, in the forms of positional power, and informal. This demonstrates the problematic nature of power as contested between groups, especially legitimate power and informal power. Conflict can emerge through these contested zones. The problem here, according to Bush, is the structural ambiguity of the educational institution; a loose coupling where the balance between classroom and department autonomy can clash with administrative control. 'The partial autonomy of teachers and their authority of expertise, together with the sectional interests of different subunits, leads to this structural looseness and the prevalence of micropolitics . . .' (Bush, 1995: 86).

One of the problems of micropolitics is that it can be seen as viewing all problems and decision making as inherently conflict-based and problematic (Wallace 2000, 2001). It can be used as the main explanatory theory of school organisation, creating polarities of reaction and view. Research into international schools has generally concentrated on defining what such schools are (Hayden and Thompson (1995, 1996, 2000a, 2000b) and what international means (Hayden *et al.* 2000). There has been some discussion of problematising issues of diversity in international schools (Allan 2002; Pearce 2003; Cambridge 2003; Cambridge and Thompson 2004). Heyward discusses the problems of the post-welfare world in the context of international education. In his study into an international school in Indonesia, he looks at the nature of the international school culture and suggests that what is needed is cultural literacy and understanding. Yet he goes on to suggest a real concern with the contemporary picture of these schools, a world where there are 'complex cultural flows and growing global cultural interdependence' (2000: 31).

In international school research, it is the deeper social interrelationships that are usually lacking sufficient investigation. For example, Ellwood (1996) sees the promotion of values as part of the relationships and contexts of the people involved in international schools. She suggests this is a complex procedure in such a multicultural and diverse institution as an international school. Diversity of experience, background and values are important in investigating international school and these are often overlooked in research. Emotions and the psychodynamics of schools (Dunning *et al.* 2005; James *et al.* 2006) are also areas relatively new to international school research, yet critical because of the emotional focus that these schools can generate.

The two most significant problems with literature on micropolitics within schools are access to data and the focus on the negative aspects of politics. Of all the authors, only a few such as Blase and Anderson (1995) see positive politics coming from these forces. Few have sympathy or try to analyse the factors that directly impact on management as part of a larger global education problem.

The other issue is access, where politics, conflict and power in organisations are difficult and often problematic areas to research. In school research into politics, the emphasis is on the manifestations of micropolitics and the dynamics of leadership. In particular, headship is under-represented in data (Ball 1987; Muijs and Harris 2003), or seen as overly dominant (Tourish and Pinnington 2002), or the focus is on a teacher–victim perspective (Ball 1990b; Doyle 1998; Blase and Blase 2003, 2004).

Organisational micropolitics

School politics is usually focused towards the outward manifestations of conflict. Significant theories that were developed during the 1980s and 1990s concentrated on the use of metaphors to describe the manifestations of political activity (Ball 1987; Blase 1989; Hoyle 1989; Hargreaves 1994, 1997).

This is useful to consider when looking at international schools but then to develop towards understanding micropolitics as a psychodynamic phenomenon (James *et al.* 2006).

Ball (1987) introduces the concept of departments contesting for power and control of scarce resources in the form of baronial politics. Ball sees schools as neither static nor predictable. He suggests that the realities of the messiness and conflict-laden underworld of school realpolitik are masked by the school's image, a constant source of concern in a complex era of market economies, rivalry and survival. 'The specific distribution of the strong baronies and weak baronies will differ between institutions and will change over time; it is the outcome of on-going conflicts and rivalries' (ibid: 222).

Relationships are important between individuals in an organisation, especially towards those who have real or perceived influence or power. Ball goes on to discuss the idea of creating influence, stressing the politics of the organisation and the use of it towards individual objectives. This is an important point, one that Ball expands externally from the school by looking at clientele power and positioning for economic advantage (Ball 2003). The issue of gaining power can also be seen from a clientele perspective where social power and cultural capital are unequally distributed and access to it important for economic and social positioning (Fowler 1997; Ecclestone and Field 2003).

Ball goes on to discuss meetings and committees as forums for politics and rivalries. He regards them as the communication mediums through which some of the politics of the organisation are visible. These formal systems also reveal the fact that much political interplay goes on informally. This is not just through departmental politics but subcultures and subgroups (Ball 1987; Bell 2003; Busher 2006). International schools can be affected by baronial politics, in that they are often isolated and open to problems of scarce resources, economic constraints and contested influence. They could well be places for powerful individuals to rise unchecked, for rivalries between departments and the rawness of conflict between personalities.

Hoyle (1989) argues that the realities of organisations are as places of bargaining and manipulation. He discusses at length basic micropolitical strategies used particularly by management in controlling outcomes, arguing that it is the inequality of the institution's players that encourages the micropolitical. The inequality of power access in schools is an important theme. In schools, groups have different possibilities for power and control, reflecting Foucault's view of diffused power (Foucault 1986, 1994, 2004). However, micropolitics implies a more restrictive, repressive, dominant view of power contrary to Foucault (Ball 1990a).

Contrived collegiality suggests that collaboration is something that is controlled and implemented, rather than being flexible and emergent. Hargreaves points out that organisations need 'to facilitate collaboration and collegiality, not to control it' (1994: 199). Ultimately he sees the control of teachers and their time 'In contrived collegiality, collaboration among teachers was compulsory, not voluntary; bounded and fixed in time and space; imple- mentation- rather than development-orientated; and meant to be predictable rather than unpredictable in its outcome' (1994: 208).

Hargreaves' work (1995, 1997, 2001; Hargreaves and Goodson 1996) on internal school fragmentation and the effects of post-welfare society on schools has relevance for the discourse of international schools. Troman (2000) argues that isolation is a major bi-product of contrived collegiality, and this pers- pective has resonance to international schools that are often isolated socially, mentally and physically from their immediate location, from homelands and from other international groups.

Balkanisation looks at school cultures, and the fragmentation and splitting of schools through subgroups, departments and alliances (Hargreaves 1994, 1995; Nias 1999; Johnson 2003; Flores 2004). Hargreaves (1994: 214–15) suggests that there are four main factors in balkanisation:

- Low permeability
- High permanence
- Personal identification
- Political complexion.

This approach is tied with Ball's concept of baronial politics and the importance of considering departmental groups when investigating politics within an organisation. Retallick and Butt discuss the isolation in the development of fragmented groups.

> In contrast, teachers' work dissatisfaction derives, to a major extent, from negative intercollegial relations . . . . school staffs are more likely to be characterised by dysfunctional status differentiation due to seniority, gender, subject or professional cliques; and by balkanisation, where power is abused and not shared.
>
> (Retallick and Butt 2004: 99)

Although not discussing international schools, several authors suggest that there are strong differences between teachers, implying that leadership is crucial in developing collaborative systems (Flores 2004; Roberts 2005). However, attributing such power and influence to leadership over complex situations can be too straightforward a solution and does not address the impact and power of internal and external factors on schools. Balkanisation is certainly useful in understanding international schools with their diverse groups, structures and locations.

The politics of leadership, styles of management and hierarchical structures have powerful effects on staff and schools (Blase 1989; Blase and Anderson 1995; Blase and Blase 1995, 2002). It is this aspect of control in schools and the pressures on management to organise and discipline staff that are particularly interesting when investigating international school organisation.

Although Blase and others are writing in the context of US educational systems (Blase and Blase 2004), their view of schools as controlled, as places of power imbalance, can be transferred to the discussion on international schools. Different views on leadership, diverse experiences of management and attitudes towards hierarchy are often contentious fields and open to opinion, experience, background and emotion.

Rizvi (1986) regards conflict in schools as inevitable because of the complexity of social relationships. He suggests that each school is unique and has its own history and features (1989). Schools as unpredictable and complex are themes of micropolitical literature (Hargreaves and Goodson 1996; Oldroyd and Hall 1997; Achinstein 2002; Beach and Carlson 2004; Oplatka 2004). Hierarchical control can be the problem as this creates contested space that results in resistance and conflict (Foucault 1977; Walton 1997; Whitty 1997; MacDonald 2004).

In international schools, the many perspectives and views of stakeholders, the isolation of schools, the managerial etic constructs on existing school cultures can all enable political conflict. Leadership is a complex exercise and skill (Wallace and Huckman 1996; Whitehead 1998; Reid *et al.* 2004), especially in international environments. There is little literature critically addressing the complexities of international school leadership, especially the issues of politics, cultural friction and power (Littleford 1999; Zsebik 2000; Blandford 2001; Blandford and Shaw 2001). Several authors discuss the manifestations of conflict in international schools but it is often seen as issues of cross-cultural dialogue rather than the impact of more wide-ranging sociological factors (Shaw 2001).

Bargaining over access to resources and the scarcity of resources is often a cause of micropolitical behaviour especially between departments or individuals (Ball 1987; Gewirtz 2000; Sachs 2001; Case and Selvester 2002). Ashforth and Saks suggest that organisational politics has much to do with control and access: 'Control has been cast as bargaining power, referent power, formal authority, informal leadership, job autonomy, knowledge/skill/ability utilisation, participation, access to resources, and so on' (2000: 313).

This suggests a wider understanding of what micropolitics is and the levels at which it affects an organisation. However, to focus just on management relations and resources is too narrow a view of micropolitics. Micropolitics and studies into schools should focus on the intricate complexities of organisational life and culture (Hoyle 1989; Hammick 1996; Davies 1994; Young and Brooks 2004).

Evans (1998) investigates what influences teachers' attitudes towards their jobs. In particular she focuses on morale, satisfaction and motivation, using case studies and in-depth interviews with a small number of teachers to collect her data and investigate their responses. One of the most useful conclusions that Evans highlights here is the idea of different schools having different climates; where teachers can find themselves in the wrong working environment. As Evans points out, leadership is vital in determining teacher morale, satisfaction and motivation. What is useful to conclude here is the importance of individual perceptions, perspectives, values and needs.

Blase (1989, 1991) suggests that schools are places where leadership theory is limited and does not really investigate the realities of school life.

> Schools are complex, unpredictable social organisations that are extremely vulnerable to a host of powerful external and internal forces. They exist in a vortex of government mandates, social and economic pressures, and conflicting ideologies associated with school administrators, teachers, students, and parents.
>
> (Blase 1991: 1)

Hoyle sees the importance of the mix of interests that are part of micropolitics and that 'individual interests cannot be isolated from other interests' (1999: 215). Each individual comes to the organisation with a different agenda. There are overlaps of interest, for example departmental, cultural, experiential and other categories. However, how individuals perceive a school is extended in an international school, where diversity of staff experiences and perceptions can be the cause of further conflict and struggle for control (Pearce 2003; Robertson 2003).

Clientele power and positioning is an important aspect of schools driven by marketplace ideology and a factor that is creating tension in schools (Bidwell *et al.* 1997; Tomlinson 2001; Bubb *et al.* 2005; De Regt and Weenink 2005; Green and Vryonides 2005). Zaretsky (2004) suggests that parents can create tension and emotions in schools, something that can directly impact on the way the school is run.

Part of this is concerned with middle class strategies for social and economic reproduction (Ball 2003). This can become a tension in international schools where parents have considerable cultural capital and positional power (Phillips 2002; Zilber 2005). Often international schools will attempt to placate parental concerns and views by accountability or controlling staff (Robertson 2003). However, these techniques are usually about disciplining and policing (Clegg 1998; Gewirtz 2000; Perryman 2006). Sklair's work (1997, 2001) on transnational capitalist class is relevant here when looking at applying clientele power to international organisations. Sklair argues that the power these groups have directly affects the policy and management decision making in schools. It is this aspect of globalisation and post-welfare society that creates such imbalances of power, and as Cambridge (2003; Cambridge and Thompson 2004) suggests, can be seen in the way international schools are managed and promoted.

Teachers can become controlled by powerful elites for economic objectives (Power and Whitty 1999; Cairns *et al.* 2003; Green and Vryonides 2005; Hatcher 2005). This becomes a form of biopower to discipline a subservient workforce (Danaher *et al.* 2000). As Poulantzas says, 'power relations do not constitute a simple expressive totality, any more than structures or practices do; but they are complex and dislocated relations, determined in the last instance by economic power' (1986: 152).

How then do international schools bring a multidimensional, quasi-national and transient/permanent staff together as one? This is the essential paradox of such a school. Can it do this effectively and, if it tries, what is the cost? It can be argued that, ultimately, international schools are not collaborative organisations. They are artificial structures placed in complex environments with a diverse populace. They cannot create consensus because they are too diverse. The idea of creating a school culture and meaning is at odds with a profession that thrives on diversity. Therefore it must be a structure that is imposed, no matter how beneficently, and this gives rise to the strong possibility of power struggles, conflict and political manoeuvring. All stakeholders have different reasons to be in the school, different ideologies, goals and power (Foucault 1977; Hargreaves 2000; Sklair 2001; Ball 2003). Short-term goals, managerial firefighting and the models of balkanisation and baronial politics can become the modus operandi of transient leadership and management.

Rizvi's later work has looked at the effects of globalisation and the increase in power and influence of transnational corporations and global elites (Rizvi and Lingard 2000). Much of this argument is similar to that of other literature looking at globalisation, internationalism and economic power in contemporary society (Hargreaves 1997; Braslavsky 2003; Brown and Lauder 2004). As Rizvi and Lingard (2000) suggest, greater differences are occurring between groups with regard to economic and social power. This issue can and should be looked at when considering how and what micropolitics occurs in international schools. Is it because of social fragmentation caused by greater social inequality, especially between clientele and school staff, and consequently greater power imbalance?

History is an often-neglected medium of investigation when it comes to researching schools. Even with such a deep discussion of any particular institution, the historical perspective can be superficially utilised. An institution is not static; it has developed and changed over the years since its foundation. Its history makes it unique, shapes its cultures and is, in turn, affected by the people associated with it (Caffyn 2008; Foucault 1984, 1986). Politics are intertwined with the institution's history and its location. They are part of it and have been formed by it. Organisations have history, traditions and environments (Handy and Aitken 1986). It is important to look at the history of schools as social structures, seeing them less as fixed and more as fluid and changing. The effects of history and incidents and individuals within that history have long-term significance (O' Farrell 1999; Lave 2003; Morris 2000; Rizvi 1989).

Power

Power is an important aspect of micropolitics. It can be seen as fluid, accessible, sometimes about synergy though invariably about conflict (Lenski 1986;

Poulantzas 1986; Morley 2000). It is not just about authority and influence, but also about position and resistance. Foucault (2004) and Bourdieu (2004) are particularly useful in understanding power as a critical aspect of organisations. There is a behavioural and sociological element and this can be applied to looking at international school power.

> Although Foucault did not regard individuals as mere pawns of power, he did not believe that they were aware of the broader consequences of their actions . . . . In other words, the tactics involved in the operation of power may involve the conscious subject but the overall strategy of a particular field of power-knowledge relations is ultimately non-subjective.
>
> (Jones 1990: 93)

Power and who has it within a school are not easy areas to investigate. The obvious power structure in a school is intermixed with informal power, manipulative power, personality cults and alliances. There is a whole spectrum of possible scenarios, events and episodes that yield a multidimensional and complex picture to any analysis of power within an organisational structure. In discussing the politics of control over the definition of the school, Anderson sees a complex, ineffective organisation where individuals vie for ascendancy.

> That schools are loosely coupled, bureaucratic and coercive forms of control, are seldom effective, that the relationship between principals and teachers is an essentially political one, and that the control versus autonomy battle is fought out in subtle and not-so-subtle ways daily among principals, teachers, parents, and students in schools.
>
> (Anderson 1991: 120)

Busher (2006) argues that power is not only the assertion of values and choice, but the challenge and prevention of choice to others. He stresses the importance of authority and influence, where all have access to power but that there is no equality in that access.

It is this view of schools that forms an important aspect of the micropolitical argument. Schools are political places but the power issue is not clearly defined or obvious. The school is a place of alliances, battles, manipulation, leaders, followers, conflict and cooperation. It is critical to see micropolitics as a discourse of power reflecting organisations as places of social interplay, fear and vulnerability (Watson 2002; Fineman 2003, 2005). Usually a school's power is seen in its hierarchy. Yet this view pays no regard to the subtlety of power and the complexity of such organisations as having diffused and contested power (Foucault 1977; Hoy 1986; Sachs 2001; Ball 2004).

Ball (1987, 1990b) sees the importance of who has a claim to power rather than the formal structures of power; the invisible and hidden rather than the ritual. This is Foucault's concept of organisational discipline and punishment, rather than ritualised demonstrations of power (Foucault 1977).

It is on occasions deliberately displayed in public events; rituals are employed to confirm order and celebrate and reinforce institution verities. Process and interaction are less obvious and visible, normally available only in private and backstage settings where agreements may be tested and altered, verities challenged.

(Ball 1987: 215)

The consequences of this are that disciplinary practices are created to keep dominant groups in control through the normalisation and regulation of employees. This becomes biopower: techniques of power for subjugation and control (Danaher *et al.* 2000; Herr 2005). This links with Foucault's work on subjugation and disciplinary practices, and is something that is part of the discourse of globalisation (Bottery 2006; Wrigley 2003; Ball 2003). As a theoretical concept it can be applied to international schools as isolated places of elite transnational classes.

Power in schools invariably offers an extremely complex and chaotic scenario. Schools are never totally alike and although one can try to apply theory to explain such phenomena, it is more a case of investigating each school, its players, its history and its environment (Howes and Kaplan 2004; Busher 2006). As Rizvi points out, 'Each situation has to be examined in the content of its own unique historical and social features' (1989: 227).

Economic power and the issue of positioning is an area that Ball (2003) looks at in detail. He regards schools as being increasingly used as arenas for class struggle and self-interest. In many ways schools have always been polit-ical arenas for economic positioning. Perhaps with greater individualism and the break-up of social welfare systems, the reality of their existence is more exposed. In international schools, this self-interest is a very powerful force where clientele power can manipulate and control school agendas (Caffyn 2007). It is the class structure of capitalist elites and the normalisation of teachers as 'power over' that is of important concern to international schools. The ideology of internationalism can easily be compromised by transnational capitalist agendas and self-interest (Cambridge and Thompson 2004).

With the increase in globalisation and transnational elites, this kind of power will become more crucial. Within an international school the various players' views on who should have power and how it should be used are wide and varied, often dependent on cultural and historical conditions. Each school will also have differing systems of power flow. For Foucault, power is closely associated with knowledge where power relations are linked to control over discourse (Foucault 1977, 2004; Atkinson 2000; Quicke 2000).

The psychodynamic micropolitical perspective

Schools are places of emotion (Watson 2002; Woods and Carlyle 2002); though there is little investigation of emotions in schools (Day and Leitch 2001). Educational institutions are regarded by a number of authorities as places of anxiety, especially in working relationships (Beatty 1999; James 1999; James *et al.* 2006). Rajan (2000) goes on to suggest that leadership in organisations should be concerned with understanding emotions and that critical to leadership is the concept of having emotional intelligence. There is often little in management and leadership manuals or texts that gives advice on how to deal with emotions.

Lave (2003) demonstrates the emotions revolving around the local international school that were a product of history, location, power, control and fear. Vulnerability and insecurity were integral with the transient and permanent groups that fought for control over the focal points of the community such as the school. Often, there can be powerful emotional ties within groups in international schools (Pearce 2003).

As Hargreaves (2001) discusses, the emotional geographies of school staff, such as personal, cultural, professional, moral, physical and political, directly affect relationships with colleagues. The masking of emotions in schools will often give a false reality, suggesting that schools are places of order, control and without emotional activity. Day and Leitch (2001) argue that emotional power and history impact on the teachers' workplace, and that personal situations and issues are critical in understanding how people behave. Clientele, as well as school staff, have emotional capital inherited in a school, particularly middle classes (Ball 2003). This could also be applied to the transnational classes who are usually associated with international schools.

Zembylas (2003) addresses the complexities of teacher identity, suggesting that there is an emotional aspect to school culture and power relations. He argues that both emotion and politics are part of the identity of each teacher. This is very useful, in that here is an attempt to demonstrate that the psychodynamic and the political exist together. Dunning *et al.* (2005) see that, through the practice of splitting and projecting, individuals are using emotions to create political reactions. Conscious and unconscious feelings and fears can therefore become manifest as views, reactions and ideology. Individual or group opinions and actions can be the result of strong emotions that are consequently interpreted and made sense of.

As James *et al.* (2006) discuss, the realist and psychodynamic perspectives on micropolitics do not easily fit together. The former focuses on self interest and scarce resources (Hoyle 1989), whereas the latter looks at emotion originating from fear and identity. Yet these two apparently divergent views can be drawn together as they both suggest the importance of the self and the group. In each perspective there is a stress on conflict, power and the need for agency. As an heuristic device, combining these perspectives helps understand the importance of people and determination in organisations. It draws on organisational politics, but places the concepts of human agency and emotion as critical aspects of any organisation. 'The emotional experience, mental forces and the defences against emotional experience are fundamental to organising in schools and are highly influential in organisational micro-politics in educational institutions' (James *et al.* 2006: 48).

Understanding international schools as micropolitical places

This section centres on addressing why international schools might be susceptible to political interplay. It will discuss issues of location, history, control, isolation and fragmentation (Caffyn 2010a) as critical in understanding the politics particular to international schools. From this discussion will come a way forward for applying a theoretical approach to international school micropolitics and a deeper understanding of these kinds of schools.

In looking at international schools, Haywood (2002) stresses the factor of headship as the most important in achieving school success. He argues that the main management function is to have a vision and to involve all stakeholders within it. Leadership is a complex exercise, and it is useful to consider the dynamics of power within international schools and the access to power that certain groups have, both departments and subcultures.

Powerful clientele and leadership can have strong power bases often owing to the isolation of the schools from mediating and controlling regulatory systems. Robertson (2003) looks at the creation of hegemonic consensus through legitimising the interests of powerful groups through various mediums. He goes on to suggest that globalisation and market trends as well as clientele interests could affect teacher accountability in international schools. Neo-liberal principles and the powerful capitalist global elites have considerable power to determine the direction of international organisations (Sklair 2001). Etic systems of management and control of human resources can have profound and devastating effects on local norms, where global systems of dominance, normalisation and acculturation can result in resistance, fragmentation and tension (Ferner and Quintanilla 1998).

Much international school research fails to begin to look at the complex problems of social-cultural perspectives on power and the conflict caused through differing goals and visions within such schools (Hayden and Thompson 1996; Blandford and Shaw 2001; Hardman 2001; Haywood 2002). Hayden and Thompson (2000b) suggest that diversity is deeper than the obvious cultural differences and argue that the market-driven nature of many international schools is important to understand. Often leadership is naively associated with managing the culture of international schools and therefore fails to comprehend the complexity of culture and the limitations of the leadership model (Littleford 1999). Schools are seen as open to manipulation and control, a hegemonic and monocultural model divorced from the reality of schools as complex and highly diverse political places (Hoyle 1986; Ball 1987; Hargreaves 1994). Schools are commonly regarded as places of coercive assignment and the categorisation of people and norms (Meighan 1993; St. Pierre 2000; Ball 2000; McInerney 2003).

Zsebik (2000) argues that there is almost an unwillingness to acknowledge educational politics or conflicts of interest in international education. He suggests that there is possibly a 'culture of silence' that ties in with the idea of dominant groups and survival in power-orientated organisations (Zsebik 2000: 64). International schools work very much in isolation and this factor may be one of the causes why discussion of who has power is rarely initiated. There is no system to protect those who do not have power from the vagaries, micropolitical manoeuvring and power plays of those who have it.

The effects of globalisation can be that it creates greater protectionism and possibilities for increased managerialism in organisations (Bottery 2006). Are international schools heading towards a pseudo-internationalism where the use of 'international' within education is controlled politically for economic advantage and market-orientated, managerialist goals by leadership and powerful transnational groups (Gold 2001; Wright 2001)?

Through its huge variety of staff and because of its isolation, the international school has the potential for enormous conflict as well as synergy. In trying to shape a school's direction or primary task (James *et al.* 2006), a manager has a highly problematic exercise. International schools usually have a mixture of permanent or transient staff and parents, differing goals, and diverse views on and experiences of education. Is it possible to create a neat model that serves to encapsulate a corporate culture? Maybe international schools are more about collaboration through conflict and synergy, and high levels of stress and troubleshooting are the norm. To survive as an organisation, schools (Roberts 2005) and possibly more so an international school, may resort to more Machiavellian tactics, but at what cost to its long-term development?

This can also impact on the way curriculum is used. Does it become a system to give access to global markets and social capital? Curriculum in international schools can become a part of organisational politics, where values-led programmes are marginalised or used as tokenistic for a more pragmatic and economic reality. Phillips (2002) and Cambridge and Thompson (2004) suggest that this is part of the discourse of globalisation, at odds with the internationalist ideologies of many international schools.

The conflict that can emerge over curriculum is largely a product of the tension between expressive order values and testing. Part of this is also to do with ideological statements such as international mindedness and global citizenship. The pressure here is the use of education for capital and control (Ball 2003; Bourdieu 2004) and increasing hegemonic social practice (Matthews and Sidhu 2005). The political impact of global capitalist elites (Sklair 2001) can mean that the curriculum becomes a tool for economic reproduction rather than the construction of any real democratic, ideological or global change.

In critiquing Foucault's model of organisational power, Quicke (2000) argues that it is vital to know the realities of power and understand the conflictual and diverse nature of a school. Each school and its cultures are a unique maze of power relationships, environmental pressure, personal histories and significant events. When assessing the concerns of an international school, these factors can take on a much stronger significance. Fragmentation, personality, national culture, isolation and market pressure add to this. Within this are formal and

informal group structures; formal groups based on departments and divisions, informal groups based on variables such as culture, socialisation,
nationality, interest, family structure and job-position (Caffyn 2007). Groups
are diverse and have different historic backgrounds, experiences and objectives,
which can create tensions (Hargreaves 1997; Busher and Harris 1999; Wildy
and Louden 2000; Persson *et al.* 2004). Such tensions are also evident between
groups in international schools (Hayden and Thompson 1995; Richards 1998;
Lave 2003).

Towards a developed theory of international school micropolitics

What has come out of the discussion so far is the need to develop an approach
to school and organisational politics (Hoyle 1986; Blase 1989) that takes into
account not only issues of power and conflict, but emotions. It is this latter
lens that is discussed by James *et al.* (2006), where fear, identity, vulnerability
and boundary control are critical in understanding school psychodynamics
(Gabriel 1999; Watson 2002). This has emerged throughout the discussion
on organisational micropolitics and international schools as places of political
interplay.

Individuals within and outside a school bring in powerful emotions, often
developed from experience, background, perceptions and views, that impact
heavily on the way the school works. This draws on earlier micropolitical theory
and the concept of organisational politics with psychodynamics in organisations. In an international school there is a strong possibility for conflict
and politics to occur due to extreme opposites of orientation such as long-
term (permanent) and short-term staff (transient). International schools are
located in very different arenas to many other schools, notably because of
their 'international' dimension, being isolated within host countries (Allen
2002). Clashes of interest, experience, background and identity can unfold in
differing ways inside the school. International schools are under immense
pressures as focal points of expatriate, international and local communities.
The creation of identity, especially by displaced individuals and groups,
often impacts on the psychodynamics of a school. This can develop into
subcultures, fragmented groups, isolated individuals and short-term solutions
to complex organisational problems. Micropolitics in international schools
needs to be looked at from a synthesis of early organisational theory (Ball 1987)
and understanding organisations as places of vulnerability, fear and identity
(James *et al.* 2006). One aspect of this is the concept of splitting and projecting,
especially where there is organisational stress. What happens is that emotions,
particularly feelings of good and bad, are projected onto people, events or
decisions, and then these feelings are split as a form of making sense and
of 'social defence' (Dunning *et al.* 2005). This perspective is important in the
attempt to synthesise psychodynamic and organisational micropolitics. Such
a view is:

grounded in psychoanalytical concepts, which sees organisational politics as arising from individual and collective, conscious and unconscious fears about identity, worth and vulnerability. These anxieties can be at the heart of very powerful emotions such as anger and euphoria and can be the basis of more commonplace feelings such as annoyance and happiness. By way of contrast, a realist micropolitical perspective sees political behaviour as a complex net of individual explanations and agendas, initiated and constructed by the mobilisation of self-interest.

(Dunning *et al.* 2005: 245)

This tension between these two perspectives need not be antagonistic. Like all organisations and group structures, schools are places of social interplay, determined by both political and emotional factors. An international school is a place of powerful emotions, notably fear and vulnerability. Therefore, it can be suggested that politics in such schools is not just about organisational political manipulation and control, but reactions to complex and unstable locations.

Schools have multiple boundaries, both internal and external, which are negotiated continuously. As Hernes argues, organisational boundaries are not static but constantly evolving. He suggests that boundaries can be subdivided into mental, social and physical: 'Organisational boundaries influence the ways and the extent to which an organisation may act outwards to exert influence on other organisations' (2004: 27).

What is significant with this interpretation of boundaries for international schools is that it places them firmly in intricate and dynamic relationships with other organisations, groups and cultures around them, including expatriate and local organisations. The emotional and social aspects of the international school, and its actors and groups, can become highly politically active. This is particularly so when groups and individuals are isolated and fragmented, and where the school becomes a surrogate family focus. Hope discusses risk-taking behaviour around traversing boundaries in internet use. He suggests that boundaries are risky places, often giving an 'illusion of control' (2007: 90). Taking this concept further, the emotional and social boundaries in and around international schools are complex and risky.

Psychologically, individuals and groups removed or marginalised, looking for identity, vulnerable and diverse in structure, can use these boundaries for many different reasons. Strong needs and fears can enable these to become political, where groups and individuals interact for control, identity and survival.

Although I wish to bring a fusion between the two perspectives of micropolitics, organisational and psychodynamic, it is useful to look closely at how international schools can become susceptible to strong emotions. The factors of fragmentation and isolation (Caffyn 2007) are significant in causing emotion and enabling the school to become a focal point of identity, conflict, power and therefore political activity.

International schools and their communities can become isolated from their immediate locality (Caffyn 2010a, 2010b) and from their homelands. This can, in turn, intensify relationships due to limited social possibilities and both psychological and linguistic isolation. As Morgan (1997) argues, this kind of environment produces a psychic prison, which increases distance, frustration and emotional tension (James *et al.* 2006; Gabriel 1999). There are different levels of interaction, diverse groups and subcultures, made up of permanence or transience. Lave (2003) stresses the power distance and politics caused by these emotional plays between permanent and transient groups in an international expatriate community. The boundaries of these groups can isolate them from outside and fragment them from within.

Fragmentation takes place both inside and outside an international school, where diverse individuals with different backgrounds, nationalities, experiences and profiles are forced together. The need to create identity and the considerable vulnerability of being in a new location can impact in deepening group boundaries (Gold 2001). Hargreaves (1997) argues that greater internationalism can mask deeper tribalism, and this can be evidenced in international schools where curricula can further divide. The phenomena of emphasising differences, exotica (Cambridge 2000), orientalism (Cambridge 2006) and colonialist agendas (Pennycook 1994, 1998) can mask emotional complexities and divisions. In two case study schools, I concluded that fragmentation was a critical factor in creating micropolitics; fragmentation between structural departments and formal divisions in each school, and between informal groups, subcultures and individuals (Caffyn 2010a). This latter aspect was both organisational and psychodynamic in construction, thus emphasising the importance of understanding international school micropolitics as a dynamic interplay between the emotion and the political.

Conclusion

The chapter attempts to put forward the importance of extending research into the social-political structure of international schools and especially subcultures, enclaves (Lave, 2003) and the transient transnational classes (Sklair 1997, 2001). It also poses questions that could serve as developing the growing research field into the sociology, culture and politics of international schools. What is critical to conclude about developing a theory of micropolitics that can be usefully used in international school research is the need to consider the psychodynamics and emotions that individuals and groups bring to schools. These experiences, views, prejudices and fears serve to create an emotional melting pot, out of which emerges some semblance of identity and reality. The politics, so often caused in schools, and particularly in international schools, are affected by these fears and vulnerabilities. This does not mean that all political behaviour is emotional, but suggests that the added vulnerability of isolation and distance in international school settings fuels political interplay as a medium for emotional outlet.

What is problematic about international schools is that they cannot be categorised easily or, until now, with any real robust typological framework (Hayden 2006). These schools inhabit very diverse places and structures, with differing and often complex staff structures, pupil make-up, parental backgrounds, management systems and historical trajectories. They are also emotional places and therefore any theory of understanding the international school needs to address the social reality of such locations. By using organisational theory with psychodynamics, a more realistic and relevant paradigm can be constructed.

Further research needs to be done into the locations of international schools and how these impact on their infrastructure. There also needs to be investigation of the different groups and how these affect the school itself, the learning and its management. Micropolitical research into international schools should address the different aspects of a school and school life, aiming to gain a closer and more realistic understanding of the myriad of tensions, emotions and political intrigues that are part of organisational life. All areas of a school, such as curriculum, pedagogy, assessment and learning, are interlinked to how individuals and groups work together. By understanding both the complexities and interrelationships within a school, a way of dealing with their problems and challenges can be addressed.

References

Achinstein B. (2002) Conflict amid community: the micropolitics of teacher collaboration, *Teachers College Record* 104(3): 421–55.

Allan, M. (2002) Cultural borderlands: cultural dissonance in the international school, *International Schools Journal* XXI(2): 42–53.

Allen, K. (2002) Atolls, seas of culture and global nets. In M. C. Hayden, J. J. Thompson and G. Walker (eds) *International Education in Practice*, London: Kogan Paul, pp. 129–44.

Anderson, G. L. (1991) Cognitive politics of principals and teacher: ideological control in an elementary school. In J. Blase (ed.) *The Politics of Life in Schools*, London: Sage, pp. 120–38.

Ashforth, B. E. and Saks, A. M. (2000) Personal control in organisations: a longitudinal investigation with newcomers, *Human Relations* 53(3): 311–39.

Atkinson, E. (2000) The promise of uncertainty: education, postmodernism and the politics of possibility, *International Studies in Sociology of Education*, 10(1): 81–99.

Baldridge, J. V. (1989) Building the political model. In T. Bush (ed.) *Managing Education: Theory and Practice*, Milton Keynes: Open University Press, pp 57–65.

Ball, S. J. (1987) *The Micropolitics of the School*, London: Routledge.

Ball, S. J. (1990a) Introducing Monsieur Foucault. In S. J. Ball (ed.) *Foucault and Education: Disciplines and Knowledge*, London: Routledge, pp. 1–7.

Ball, S. J. (1990b) Management as moral technology: a Luddite analysis. In S. J. Ball (ed.) *Foucault and Education: Disciplines and Knowledge*, London: Routledge, pp. 153–66.

Ball, S. J. (2000) Educational studies, policy entrepreneurship and social theory. In S. J. Ball (ed.) *Sociology of Education, Volume III: Institutions and Processes*, London: RoutledgeFalmer, pp. 1524–53.

Ball, S. J. (2003) *Class Strategies and the Education Market: The Middle Classes and Social Advantage*, London: RoutledgeFalmer.

Ball, S. J. (2004) Performativities and fabrications in the education economy: towards the performative society. In S. J. Ball (ed.) *The RoutledgeFalmer Reader in Sociology of Education*, London: RoutledgeFalmer, pp. 143–55.

Bates, R. (1989) Leadership and the rationalisation of society. In J. Smyth (ed.) *Critical Perspectives on Educational Leadership*, Lewes: Falmer Press, pp. 131–56.

Beach, D. and Carlson, M. (2004) Adult education goes to market: an ethnographic case study of the restructuring and reculturing of adult education, *European Educational Research Journal*, 3(3): 673–90.

Beatty, B. R. (1999) Teachers and their leaders: the emotionality of teachers' relationships with administrators, Paper presented to the *International Study Association on Teachers and Teaching Conference*, Dublin, June.

Bell, D. (2003) Mythscapes: memory, mythology, and national identity, *British Journal of Sociology* 54(1): 63–81.

Bidwell, C. E., Frank, K. A. and Quiroz, P. A. (1997) Teacher types, workplace controls, and the organisation of schools, *Sociology of Education* 70 (October): 285–307.

Blandford, S. (2001) Middle management in international schools. In S. Blandford and M. Shaw (eds) *Managing International Schools*, London: RoutledgeFalmer, pp. 136–52.

Blandford, S. and Shaw, M. (2001) The nature of international leadership. In S. Blandford and M. Shaw (eds) *Managing International Schools*, London: RoutledgeFalmer, pp. 9–28.

Blase, J. (1989) Teachers political orientation vis-à-vis the principal: the micropolitics of the school. In J. Hannaway and R. Crowson (eds) *The Politics of Reforming School Administration*, Lewes: Falmer Press, pp. 113–26.

Blase, J. (1991) The micro-political perspective. In J. Blase (ed.) *The Politics of Life in Schools*, London: Sage, pp. 1–18.

Blase, J. and Anderson, G. (1995) *The Micropolitics of Educational Leadership*, London: Cassell.

Blase, J. and Blase, J. (1995) The micropolitics of successful supervisor-teacher interaction in instructional conferences. In D. Corson (ed.) *Discourse and Power in Educational Organisations*, Cresskill: Hampton Press, pp. 55–70.

Blase, J. and Blase, J. (2002) The dark side of leadership: teacher perspectives of principal mistreatment, *Educational Administration Quarterly* 38(5): 671–727.

Blase, J. and Blase, J. (2003) The phenomenology of principal mistreatment: teachers' perspectives, *Journal of Educational Administration* 41(4): 367–422.

Blase, J. and Blase, J. (2004) The dark side of school leadership: implications for administrator preparation, *Leadership and Policy in Schools* 3(4): 245–73

Bottery, M. (2006) Educational leaders in a globalising world: a new set of priorities? *School Leadership and Management* 26(1): 5–22.

Bourdieu, P. (2004) The forms of capital. In S. J. Ball (ed.) *The RoutledgeFalmer Reader in Sociology of Education*, London: RoutledgeFalmer, pp. 15–29.

Braslavsky, C. (2003) Teacher education for living together in the 21st century, *Journal of Research in International Education* 2(2): 167–83.

Brown, P. and Lauder, H. (2004) Education, globalisation and economic development. In S. J. Ball (ed.) *The RoutledgeFalmer Reader in Sociology of Education*, London, RoutledgeFalmer, pp. 47–71.

Brundrett, M. (1998) What lies behind collegiality, legitimation or control? an analysis of the purported benefits of collegial management in education, *Educational Management and Administration* 26(3): 305–16.

Bubb, S., Earley, P. and Totterdell, M. (2005) Accountability and responsibility: 'rogue' school leaders and the induction of new teachers in England, *Oxford Review of Education* 31(2): 255–72.

Bush, T. (1995) *Theories of Educational Management*, London: PCP.

Busher, H. (2006) *Understanding Educational Leadership: People, Power and Culture*, Maidenhead: Open University Press.

Busher, H. and Harris, A. (1999) Leadership of school subject areas: tensions and dimensions of managing in the middle, *School Leadership and Management* 19(3): 305–17.

Caffyn, R. (2007) Fragmentation in international schools: a micropolitical discourse of management, culture and postmodern society. In M. C. Hayden, J. J. Thompson and J. Levy (eds) *The SAGE Handbook of Research in International Education*, London: Sage, pp. 339–50.

Caffyn, R. (2008) Understanding the historical context: history as an investigative lens in studying the micropolitics of international schools, *International Schools Journal* XXVII(2): 29–36.

Caffyn, R. (2010a) 'We are in Transylvania, and Transylvania is not England': Location as a significant factor in international school micropolitics, *Educational Management, Administration and Leadership* 38(3): 321–40.

Caffyn, R. (2010b) *Micropolitics of International Schools*, Saarbrucken, VDM (pending).

Cairns, G., McInnes, P. and Roberts, P. (2003) Organisational space/time: from imperfect panoptical to heterotopian understanding, *Ephemera* 3(2): 126–39.

Cambridge, J. (2000) International schools, globalisation and the seven cultures of capitalism. In M. C. Hayden and J. J. Thompson (eds) *International Schools and International Education*, London: Kogan Page, pp. 179–90.

Cambridge, J. (2003) Identifying the globalist and internationalist missions of international schools, *International Schools Journal* XXII(2): 54–8.

Cambridge, J. (2006) Realism and antirealism in international education research. In M. C. Hayden, J. J. Thompson and J. Levy (eds) *The SAGE Handbook of Research in International Education*, London: Sage, pp. 412–25.

Cambridge, J. and Thompson, J.J. (2004) Internationalism and globalization as contexts for international education, *Compare* 34(2): 161–75.

Case, P. and Selvester, K. (2002) Watch your back: reflections on trust and mistrust in management education, *Management Learning* 33(2): 231–47.

Clegg, S. (1998) Foucault, power and organisations. In A. McKinlay and K. Starkey (eds) *Foucault, Management and Organisational Theory*, London: Sage, pp. 29–48.

Corson, D. (1995) Discursive power in educational organisations: an introduction. In D. Corson (ed.) *Discourse and Power in Educational Organisations*, Cresskill: Hampton Press, pp. 3–15.

Danaher, G., Schirato, T. and Webb, J. (2000) *Understanding Foucault*, London: Sage.

Davies, L. (1994) *Beyond Authoritarian School Management: The Challenge for Transparency*, Ticknall: Education Now Books.

Day, C. and Leitch, R. (2001) Teachers' and teacher educators' lives: the role of emotion, *Teaching and Teacher Education* 17: 403–15.

Deem, R. and Brehony, K. J. (2005) Management as ideology: the case of 'new managerialism' in higher education, *Oxford Review of Education* 31(2): 217–35.

De Regt, A. and Weenink, D. (2005) When negotiation fails: private education as a disciplinary strategy, *Journal of Education Policy*, 20(1): 59–80.

Doyle, J. (1998) Power and contentment, *Politics* 18(1): 49–56.

Dunning, G., James, C. and Jones, N. (2005) Splitting and projection at work in schools, *Journal of Educational Administration* 43(3): 244–59.

Ecclestone, K. and Field, J. (2003) Promoting social capital in a risk society: a new approach to emancipatory learning or a new moral authoritarianism? *British Journal of Sociology of Education* 24(3): 267–83.

Ellwood, C. (1996) The matter of values, *International Schools Journal* XVI(1): 39–45.

Evans, L. (1998) *Teacher Morale, Job Satisfaction and Motivation*, London: PCP.

Ferner, A. and Quintanilla, J. (1998) Multinationals, national business systems and HRM: the enduring influence of national identity or a process of 'Anglo-Saxonization', *The International Journal of Human Resource Management* 9(4): 710–31.

Findlay, P. and Newton, T. (1998) Re-framing Foucault: the case of performance appraisal. In A. McKinlay and K. Starkey (eds) *Foucault, Management and Organisational Theory*, London: Sage, pp. 211–29.

Fineman, S. (2003) *Understanding Emotion at Work*, London: Sage.

Fineman, S. (2005) Appreciating emotion at work: paradigm tensions, *International Journal of Work Organisation and Emotion* 1(1): 4–19.

Flores, M. A. (2004) The impact of school culture and leadership on new teachers' learning in the workplace, *International Journal of Leadership in Education* 7(4): 297–318.

Foucault, M. (1977) *Discipline and Punish: the Birth of the Prison*, London: Allen Lane.

Foucault, M. (1984) Des espaces autres, architecture, *Mouvement et Continuité*, October: 1–10.

Foucault, M. (1986) Disciplinary power and subjection. In S. Lukes (ed.) *Power*, New York: New York University Press, pp. 229–42.

Foucault, M. (1994) Truth and power. In J. D. Faubion (ed.) *Michel Foucault: Power*, London: Penguin, pp. 111–33.

Foucault, M. (2004) Power/knowledge: selected interviews and other writings 1972–1977, online at: www.thefoucauldian.co.uk/bodypower.htm.

Fowler, B. (1997) *Pierre Bourdieu and Cultural Theory: Critical Investigations*, London: Sage.

Gabriel, Y. (1999) *Organisations in Depth*, London: Sage.

Gewirtz, S. (2000) Bringing the Politics back in: A critical analysis of quality discourses in education, *British Journal of Educational Studies* 48(4): 352–370

Gewirtz, S., Ball, S. J. and Bowe, R. (1995) *Markets, Choice and Equity in Education*, Buckingham: Open University Press.

Gold, S. J. (2001) Gender, class and network: social structure and migration patterns among transnational Israelis, *Global Networks* 1(1): 57–78.

Green, A. and Vryonides, M. (2005) Ideological tensions in the educational choice practices of modern Greek Cypriot parents: the role of social capital, *British Journal of Sociology of Education* 26(3): 327–42.

Hammick, M. (1996) Validation of professional degrees: the micropolitical climate and ethical dilemmas, *Quality Assurance in Education* 4(1): 26–31.

Handy, C. and Aitken, R. (1986) *Understanding Schools of Organisations*, London: Penguin.

Hardman, J. (2001) Improving recruitment and retention of quality overseas teachers. In S. Blandford and M. Shaw (eds) *Managing International Schools*, London: RoutledgeFalmer, pp. 123–35.

Hargreaves, A. (1994) *Changing Times, Changing Teachers*, Toronto: OISE Press.

Hargreaves, A. (1995) Renewal in the age of paradox, *Educational Leadership* 52(7): 1–5, online at: www.ascd.org/readingroom/edlead/9504/hargreaves.html.

Hargreaves, A. (1997) Reconstructing restructuring: postmodernity and the prospects for educational change. In A. H. Halsey, H. Lauder, P. Brown and A. Stuart Wells (eds) *Education: Culture, Economy and Society*, Oxford: Oxford University Press, pp. 338–53.

Hargreaves, A. (1998) Pushing the boundaries of educational change. In A. Hargreaves *et al.* (eds) *International Handbook of Educational Change*, London: Kluwer, pp. 281–94.

Hargreaves, A. (2000) Four ages of professionalism and professional learning, *Teachers and Teaching: History and Practice* 6(2): 151–82.

Hargreaves, A. (2001) The emotional geographies of teachers' relations with colleagues, *International Journal of Educational Research* 35: 503–27.

Hargreaves, A. and Goodson, I. (1996) Teachers' professional lives: aspirations and actualities. In I. Goodson and A. Hargreaves (eds) *Teachers' Professional Lives*, London: Falmer Press, pp. 1–27.

Hatcher, R. (2005) The distribution of leadership and power in schools, *British Journal of Sociology of Education* 26(2): 253–67.

Hayden, M. C. (2006) *Introduction to International Education: International Schools and their Communities*, London: Sage.

Hayden, M. C. and Thompson, J. (1995) International schools and international education: a relationship reviewed, *Oxford Review of Education* 21(3): 327–45.

Hayden, M. C. and Thompson, J. (1996) Potential difference: the driving force for international education, *International Schools Journal* XVI(1): 46–57.

Hayden, M. C. and Thompson, J. (2000a) International education: flying flags or raising standards? *International Schools Journal* XIX(2): 48–56.

Hayden, M. C. and Thompson, J. (2000b) Quality in diversity. In M. C. Hayden and J. Thompson (eds) *International Schools and International Education*, London: Kogan Page, pp. 1–11.

Hayden, M. C., Rancic, B. A. and Thompson, J. J. (2000) Being international: student and teacher perceptions from international schools, *Oxford Review of Education* 26(1): 107–23.

Haywood, T. (2002) An international dimension to management and leadership skills for international education. In M. C. Hayden, J. J. Thompson and G. Walker (eds) *International Education in Practice*, London: Kogan Paul, pp. 170–84.

Hernes, T. (2004) Studying composite boundaries: a framework of analysis, *Human Relations* 57(1): 9–29.

Herr, K. (2005) Administrators mandating mediation: tools of institutional violence cloaked in the discourse of reconciliation, *International Journal of Leadership in Education* 8(1): 21–33.

Hey, V. and Bradford, S. (2004) The return of the repressed? The gender politics of emergent forms of professionalism in education, *Journal of Education Policy* 19(6): 691–713.

Heyward, M. (2000) Intercultural Literacy and the International School, *International Schools Journal* XIX(2): 29–36.

Hope, A. (2007) Risk taking, boundary performance and intentional school internet 'misuse', *Discourse* 28(1): 87–99.

Howes, A. and Kaplan, I. (2004) A school responding to its cultural setting, *Improving Schools* 7(1): 35–48.

Hoy, D. C. (1986) Power, repression, progress: Foucault, Lukes, and the Frankfurt School. In D. C. Hoy (ed.) *Foucault: A Critical Reader*, Oxford: Blackwell, pp. 1–27.

Hoyle, E. (1986) *The Politics of School Management*, London: Hodder and Stoughton.

Hoyle, E. (1989) The micropolitics of schools. In T. Bush (ed.) *Managing Education: Theory and Practice*, Milton Keynes: Open University Press, pp. 66–80.

Hoyle, E. (1999) The two faces of micropolitics, *School Leadership and Management* 19(2): 213–22.

James, C. R. (1999) Institutional transformation and educational management. In T. Bush, L. Bell, R. Bolam, R. Glatter and P. Ribbins (eds) *Educational Management: Redefining Theory, Policy and Practice*, London, PCP, pp. 142–54.

James, C. R., Connolly, M., Dunning, G. and Elliott, T. (2006) *How Very Effective Primary Schools Work*, London: PCP.

Johnson, B. L. (2003) Those nagging headaches: perennial issues and tensions in the politics of education field, *Educational Administration Quarterly* 39(1): 41–67.

Jones, R. (1990) Educational practices and scientific knowledge: A genealogical interpretation of the emergence of physiology in post-revolutionary France. In S. J. Ball (ed.) *Foucault and Education: Disciplines and Knowledge*, London: Routledge, pp. 78–104.

Lave, J. (2003) Producing the future: getting to be British, *Antipode* 35(3): 492–511.

Lenski, G. (1986) Power and privilege. In S. Lukes (ed.) *Power*, New York: New York University Press, pp. 243–52.

Littleford, J. (1999) Leadership of schools and longevity of school heads, *International Schools Journal* XIX(1): 23–34.

Lukes, S. (1974) *Power: A Radical View*, London: Macmillan.

MacDonald, A. (2004) Collegiate or compliant? Primary teachers in post-McCrone Scotland, *British Educational Research Journal* 30(3): 413–33.

McInerney, P. (2003) Moving into dangerous territory? Educational leadership in a devolving education system, *International Journal of Leadership in Education* 6(1): 57–72.

McNay, L. (1994) *Foucault: A Critical Introduction*, Cambridge: Polity Press.

Matthews, J. and Sidhu, R. (2005) Desperately seeking the global subject: international education, citizenship and cosmopolitanism, *Globalisation, Societies and Education* 3(1): 49–66.

Meighan, R. (1993) *The Theory and Practice of Regressive Education*, Nottingham: Educational Heretics Press.

Morgan, G. (1997) *Images of Organisation*, London: Sage.

Morley, L. (2000) The micropolitics of gender in the learning society, *Higher Education in Europe* 25(2): 229–35.

Morris, A. (2000) Charismatic leadership and its after-effects in a Catholic school, *Educational Management Administration and Leadership* 24(4): 405–18.

Muijs, D. and Harris, A. (2003) Teacher leadership – improvement through empowerment? An overview of the literature, *Educational Management Administration and Leadership* 31(4): 437–48.

Nias, J. (1999) Primary teaching as a culture of care. In J. Prosser (ed.) *School Culture*, London: PCP, pp. 66–81.

O'Farrell, C. (1999) Postmodernism for the uninitiated. In D. Meamore, B. Burnett and P. O'Brien (eds) *Understanding Education: Contexts and Agendas for the New Millennium*, Sydney: Prentice Hall, pp. 11–17.

Oldroyd, D. and Hall, V. (1997) Identifying needs and priorities in professional development. In L. Kydd, M. Crawford and C. Riches (eds) *Professional Development for Educational Management*, Buckingham: Open University Press, pp. 130–47.

Oplatka, I. (2004) The characteristics of the school organisation and the constraints on market ideology in education: an institutional view, *Journal of Education Policy* 19(2): 143–61.

Pearce, R. (2003) Cultural values for international schools, *International Schools Journal* XXII(2): 59–65.

Pennycook, A. (1994) *The Cultural Politics of Education as an International Language*, Harlow: Pearson Education.

Pennycook, A. (1998) *English and the Discourses of Colonialism*, London: Routledge.

Perryman, J. (2006) Panoptic performativity and school inspection regimes: disciplinary mechanisms and life under special measures, *Journal of Education Policy* 21(2): 147–61.

Persson, A., Andersson, G. and Nilsson Linström, M. (2004) Successful Swedish head-masters in tension fields and alliances, *International Journal of Leadership in Education* 8(1): 53–72.

Phillips, J. (2002) The third way: lessons from international education, *Journal of Research in International Education* 1(2): 159–81.

Poulantzas, N. (1986) Class power. In S. Lukes (ed.) *Power*, New York: New York University Press, pp. 144–55.

Power, S. and Whitty, G. (1999) Market forces and school cultures. In J. Prosser (ed.) *School Culture*, London: PCP, pp. 15–29.

Quicke, J. (2000) A new professionalism for a contemporary culture of organisational learning in contemporary society, *Educational Management Administration and Leadership* 28(3): 299–315.

Rajan, A. (2000) Leadership in the knowledge age, *Royal Society of Arts Journal* 153 (4593).

Reid, I., Brain, K. and Comerford Boyes, L. (2004) Teachers or learning leaders? Where have all the teachers gone? Gone to be leaders, everyone, *Educational Studies* 30(3): 251–64.

Retallick, J. and Butt, R. (2004) Professional well-being and learning: a study of teacher–peer workplace relationships, *Journal of Educational Enquiry* 5(1): 85–99.

Richards, N. (1998) The Emperor's new clothes? The issue of staffing in international schools. In M. C. Hayden and J. Thompson (eds) *International Education: Principles and Practice*, London: Kegan Paul, pp. 173–83.

Rizvi, F. (1986) *Administrative Leadership and the Democratic Community as a Social Ideal*, Burwood: Deakin University Press.

Rizvi, F. (1989) In defense of organisational democracy. In J. Smyth (ed.) *Critical Perspectives on Educational Leadership*, London: Falmer Press, pp. 205–34.

Rizvi, F. and Lingard, B. (2000) Globalisation and education: complexities and contingencies, *Educational Theory* 50(4): 419–26.

Roberts, A. (2005) Transposing a culture: reflections on the leadership of a closing school, *Improving Schools* 8(3): 237–53.

Robertson, J. E. (2003) Teachers' perceptions of accountability at an international school, *Journal of Research in International Education* 2(3): 277–300.

Sachs, J. (2001) Teacher professional identity: competing discourses, competing resources, *Journal of Education Policy* 16(2): 149–61.

Shaw, M. (2001) Managing mixed-cultural teams in international schools. In S. Blandford and M. Shaw (eds) *Managing International Schools*, London: RoutledgeFalmer, pp. 153–72.

Sklair, L. (1997) Social movements for global capitalism: the transnational capitalist class in action, *Review of International Political Economy* 4(3): 514–38.

Sklair, L. (2001) *The Transnational Capitalist Classes*, Oxford: Blackwell.

St. Pierre, E. A. (2000) Poststructural feminism in education: an overview, *Qualitative Studies in Education* 13(5): 477–515.

Thrupp, M. and Willmott, R. (2003) *Education Management in Managerialist Times: Beyond the Textual Apologists*, Maidenhead: Open University Press.

Tomlinson, S. (2001) *Education in a Post-Welfare Society*, Buckingham: Open University Press.

Tourish, D. and Pinnington, A. (2002) Transformational leadership, corporate cultism and the spirituality paradigm: an unholy trinity in the workplace? *Human Relations* 55(2): 147–72.

Troman, G. (2000) Teacher stress in the low-trust society, *British Journal of Sociology of Education* 21(3): 331–53.

Vidovich, L. (2004) Towards internationalising the curriculum in a context of globalisation: comparing policy processes in two settings, *Compare* 34(4): 443–61.

Wallace, M. (2000) Integrating cultural and political perspectives: the case of school restructuring in England, *Educational Administration Quarterly* 36(4): 608–32.

Wallace, M. (2001) Sharing leadership of schools through teamwork: a justifiable risk? *Educational Management Administration and Leadership* 29(2): 153–67.

Wallace, M. and Huckman, L. (1996) Senior management teams in large primary schools: a headteacher's solution to the complexities of post-reform management? *School Organisation* 16(3): 309–23.

Walton, R. E. (1997) Managing conflict in organizations. In M. Crawford, L. Kydd and C. Riches (eds) *Leadership and Teams in Educational Management*, Buckingham: Open University Press, pp. 110–15.

Watson, T. J. (2002) *Organising and Managing Work: Organisational, Managerial and Strategic Behaviour in Theory and Practice*, Harlow: Pearson.

Webb, L., McCaughtry, N. and MacDonald, D. (2004) Surveillance as a technique of power in physical education, *Sport, Education and Society* 9(2): 207–22.

Whitehead, S. (1998) Disrupted selves: resistance and identity work in the managerial arena, *Gender and Education* 10(2): 199–215.

Whitty, G. (1997) Marketization, the state, and the re-formation of the teaching profession. In A. H. Halsey *et al.* (eds) *Education: Culture, Economy and Society*, Oxford: Oxford University Press, pp. 299–310.

Wildy, H. and Louden, W. (2000) School restructuring and the dilemmas of principal's work, *Educational Management Administration and Leadership* 28(2): 173–84.

Woods, P. and Carlyle, D. (2002) Teacher identities under stress: the emotions of separation and renewal, *International Studies in Sociology of Education* 12(2): 169–89.

Wright, N. (2001) Leadership, 'bastard leadership' and managerialism: confronting twin paradoxes in the Blair Education Project, *Educational Management Administration and Leadership* 29(3): 275–90.

Wrigley, T. (2003) Is 'school effectiveness' anti-democratic? *British Journal of Educational Studies* 51(2): 89–112.

Young, B. and Brooks, M. (2004) Part-time politics: the micropolitical world of part-time teaching, *Educational Management Administration and Leadership* 32(2): 129–48.

Zaretsky, L. (2004) Advocacy and administration: from conflict to collaboration, *Journal of Educational Administration* 42(2): 270–86.

Zembylas, M. (2003) Interrogating 'teacher identity', emotion, resistance, and self-formation, *Educational Theory* 53(1): 107–27.

Zilber, E. (2005) International school educators and their children, *Journal of Research in International Education* 4(1): 5–22.

Zsebik, P. (2000) The politics of international education. In M. C. Hayden and J. Thompson (eds) *International Schools and International Education*, London: Kogan Page, pp. 62–9.

5 Teachers for the international school of the future

Mary Hayden and Jeff Thompson

International school teachers today

The international school context today is characterised by rapid change, and a lack of shared terminology or agreement about when or where such schools originated. It would be safe to claim, however, that international schools had their recent origins principally in the need for globally mobile professional parents to arrange education for their children while located away from the home context, and that the majority of such schools have been and continue to be English medium. It is not surprising, therefore, that the majority of teachers attracted to, and sought by, such schools have been native English speakers educated themselves in an English-medium environment (Hayden and Thompson 2008). In the absence of a shared accepted definition of the concept of an international school it is impossible to be precise about the exact number of such teachers. The conclusion reached by Canterford (2003), however, based on an analysis of international school details held by International Schools Services (ISS 2010) in 1997–8, that the teaching staff of such schools are dominated by Americans and British, seems plausible. Equally plausible is the anecdotal evidence suggesting that increasing numbers of native English speakers from New Zealand, Australia, Ireland, Canada and South Africa are now joining the teaching staff of such schools. The balance of nationalities among international school teachers varies in different parts of the world and may relate not only to their native language, or how far they wish to travel from 'home', but also the extent to which taking a teaching post outside one's home country appears attractive. Joslin points out that 'Unlike international companies where personnel are posted from headquarters in the home country to other locations, and are given pre-departure cross-cultural training and orientation programmes, teachers choose to apply for a post overseas' (2002: 34). Whether teachers choose to move from their home context may be influenced by the extent of the risk such a choice will represent. Sutcliffe, observing in 1991 that most teachers in international schools at that time were British or American, linked this point to the fact that teachers in the UK and USA are not civil servants. For those in countries where teachers are classified as civil servants, he argued, reluctance to move outside the 'home' education system may be linked to 'the lack of freedom to move and to respond to openings as they occur, the national career and pension structures, and the general bureaucracy' (1991: 175).

Individual reasons for moving to an international school teaching post undoubtedly vary. Certainly it appears that among the teaching staff of international schools are many teachers who have chosen to combine their relatively portable career with a desire to travel the world, often with an expectation of returning to the home country in due course. Also to be found are those who began their international school teaching career with such intentions, but then decided to stay in the international school sector by taking a number of postings in different locations. And then there are those who, effectively, put down roots in one new location – perhaps because they marry a local resident, or feel that no other school or location could compare with the one they have found. Such differences are influenced, of course, by myriad factors in any individual situation, including employment law and tax law. The nature of the school's contracts can also be influential, given that teaching contracts in the international school sector typically last for maybe 2 or 3 years: though potentially renewable, many move on after a first contract. These and other factors can all affect an individual and the length of his/her term of employment at a particular international school. And no school, of course, is above the law of the country in which it is located. So in a country where homosexuality is illegal, for instance, a school cannot appoint to its staff an openly homosexual teacher; where cohabiting of non-married couples is illegal, an international school cannot arrange, or be seen to condone, accommodation shared by a single teacher with someone of the opposite sex. Teaching in an international school can thus raise many new challenges for teachers who move for the first time from schools in their home context.

There are, then, large numbers of globally mobile teachers staffing international schools worldwide, many of them native English speakers, some staying only a few years before returning home, while others effectively make a career of international school teaching. It would be misleading, though, to suggest that all teachers in international schools are from such backgrounds. Indeed the majority of international schools will have on their staff at least a small number of host country teachers, often employed to teach the local language and culture. It is frequently the case, too, that an international school will have at least one senior manager/administrator from the host country, who understands the legal, tax and other systems of that country and acts as a cultural interpreter between the school and the country in which it is located. To view the teaching population of most international schools as made up of expatriates and local teachers, however, would be to over-simplify what is in many cases a complex situation. Hardman, in analysing a range of issues relating to teachers in international schools, argued that it is possible to categorise 'overseas' teachers in international schools 'according to what motivates them and what they offer the school' (2001: 131). Hardman's categorisation suggests that overseas teachers applying for posts in international schools can generally be considered to fall into one of the following groups:

- childless career professionals
- 'mavericks' ('free and independent spirits')
- career professionals with family.

and among the more senior teachers (older, with no dependent children):

- senior career professionals
- senior mavericks
- senior Penelopes ('faithful to the country they had adopted'; based on Ulysses' wife in Homer's Odyssey, who for 20 years waited faithfully for her husband to return from the Trojan war).

Garton (2000), however, is among those who point out that the overseas teachers described by Hardman are only one 'type' among several to be encountered in this context, highlighting what he describes as the 'widespread practice of having a teaching staff that can be grouped into three distinct categories':

- host-country nationals
- 'local hire' expatriates
- 'overseas hire' expatriates.

As also noted by Cambridge (2002), the category to which an individual teacher belongs relates not only to his/her nationality and/or geographical origins but also to the contract of employment. Where such groupings exist (and they tend to be found largely in international schools in developing countries), those teachers appointed on an 'overseas hire' contract will generally have the most advantageous pay and conditions: quite possibly enjoying a higher salary, and better benefits (such as paid flights at the end of the school year, private health care, reduced or waived fees for their own children) than those in either of the other two categories. The availability of 'local hire' expatriates for recruitment meanwhile, as Garton points out, 'is almost always dependent on the fact that they have spouses or partners who work for embassies, aid agencies or multinational companies in that particular country, or who are . . . residents of the country in question' (2000: 88). Sometimes described as the 'trailing spouse', such teachers can be difficult to distinguish in many respects from the overseas-hire teacher, but tend to be 'recruited at considerably less cost, as it is perceived that they do not require housing, flights or most of the other fringe benefits regarded as axiomatic for overseas-hire recruits' (2000: 88). 'Host country nationals', meanwhile, may be paid lower salaries again and be entitled to few if any benefits – though often (again, in developing countries) they are still paid a higher salary than they would earn in the local state system.

It would be misleading to suggest that such typologies are to be found in every international school. Where they *are* found, they tend to be defended on the basis of market forces, given that an experienced overseas teacher may only take up the post if the salary offered is competitive internationally, but to pay such salaries to all teaching staff would render the school financially non-viable. Such distinctions can appear unpalatable, and can also cause difficulties for the schools in which they apply. As Hardman points out, they can lead to

> hidden resentment towards overseas teachers by local members of staff, most commonly the result of differential pay scales and special benefits paid to teachers ... doing equal jobs ... (resulting in) friction, and sometimes overt conflict, creating a negative impact on the working environment.
>
> (Hardman 2001: 128)

Teachers for future international schools: some key issues

Future international schools

In October 2009 Brummitt estimated there were then in existence 5,374 English-medium international schools catering for 2.3 million students. His future projections suggested that by the year 2015 8,000 such schools will exist, while 11,000 international schools catering for 4.9 million students would be in place by 2020.

In attempting to gaze into the crystal ball of future international school developments, however, it is worth considering a little more closely the nature of the growth within the sector to date, as it is arguably within one part of the sector that the greater growth has been observed. Until relatively recently growth had been within what might be described as the 'traditional' international schools established, often by parents, in response to a local need to cater for globally mobile expatriate children. Anecdotal evidence, however, would seem to suggest that – while the numbers of such 'traditional' international schools continue to grow – the greater growth can be observed within the more 'modern' type of international school. These schools may cater for expatriates, but be established on a for profit, proprietary basis by an individual owner or commercial organisation. Instead of being a parent-led individual institution responding to specific local needs, such a school may be part of a group of schools located either regionally or worldwide. Undoubtedly the growth in this 'modern' type of international school arises in response to a market made up principally not of expatriates, but of host country affluent families who either lack confidence in their own country's education system

(Cambridge 2000: 181) or seek a competitive edge for their child over his/her peers (Lowe 2000: 24–5). Attending an English-medium school and following a non-national curriculum (which may be an international curriculum such as the International Baccalaureate (IB, 2010a), the International GCSE (IGCSE: CIE 2010 and Edexcel 2010) or International Primary Curriculum (IPC 2010), or a curriculum imported from a national context such as the English A level) can be perceived as providing status, as well as access to highly regarded universities internationally.

The growing demands of what has been described as the 'transnational capitalist class' (Sklair 2001: 8) should be viewed against a backdrop of changes such as those described by Friedman (2005) as arising from the world's third era of globalisation, where the dynamic force is no longer countries or companies globalising, but the 'new found power of *individuals* to collaborate and compete globally' (2005: 10). At the same time, the international school sector seems certain to be affected by the 'demographic explosion' anticipated in the early twenty-first century by Rischard, for instance, who predicts a global population of around 8 billion by 2020–5, growing from 5 billion in 1990 and 6 billion in 2002; 95 per cent of the 2 billion by which the earth's population is predicted to increase between 2002 and 2025 will, says Rischard, be living in developing countries and most will flock to the cities, leading to the existence of around 60 cities worldwide with more than 5 million inhabitants – almost twice as many as in 1990 (2002: 6).

So what are the implications for international schools in such a changing global environment? Rischard's predicted large expansion in the global population and increased city sizes may have little impact on international schools if those increased numbers arise among the poorest sections of the population in the developing world. Where the increasing numbers are, however, among the relatively affluent and aspirational middle classes who wish for their children that competitive edge provided by English-medium education and a non-national curriculum, then the increase in demand for international schools is potentially enormous. An important limiting factor, it would seem, is national governments' stance on attendance at international schools by their citizens: whether like Singapore, for instance, where host country nationals are forbidden by law from attending international schools (Allen 2000: 130–1), or like Thailand, whose recent deregulation has allowed Thai nationals to attend international schools, seeing a steady growth in their numbers as a result (MacDonald 2006). A change of policy in just one country such as China, which normally forbids host country nationals from attending mainland Chinese international schools, could lead to a rapid rise in numbers of such schools in a short space of time, with an emphasis on provision for socio-economically advantaged Chinese citizens. Clearly the backwash effect of such provision on the national education system of countries whose middle classes effectively remove their children from that system is potentially marked, and is no doubt a factor in the decisions of some countries to restrict international school access to expatriates.

Undoubtedly the place of English as the (currently) unchallenged global language is an element in any consideration of the future of international schools, with research into reasons for parental choice of international schools suggesting an English-medium education as the highest priority for native and non-native English speakers alike (Deveney 2000; MacKenzie *et al.* 2003; Potter and Hayden 2004). Predictions are that the pre-eminence of English as the global *lingua franca* will ultimately decrease, with an estimated half the population of the world (about 3.5 billion) speaking or learning English by 2015 before numbers drop so that, by around 2050, other languages will be more widely spoken internationally (Gray 2006). There is evidence, nevertheless, to suggest that at least in the relatively short term the bilingualism (mother tongue plus English) that is currently the norm for educated elites worldwide will become the norm for many more (Thomas 2006), thus contributing to the growth in demand for English-medium international schools. The impact on teacher recruitment of the growing numbers of such schools is likely to be significant.

Issues of pedagogy

Demand for English-medium education by non-native as well as native speakers of English impacts upon the nature of the education provided within the schools in question. It is clearly the case that international school classrooms are composed increasingly of multilingual and multicultural student populations that were less prevalent in many earlier international schools, where native English-speaking globally mobile expatriate families accounted for a higher proportion of the mobile student population than is now the case. The growth in cultural and linguistic diversity of many international schools seems set to continue. Other changes will also directly affect both international and national schools in the coming years. Steadily growing understanding, for instance, of how the brain functions is likely to impact upon education systems globally as an increased awareness develops of how learning actually takes place in young people. Of no less potential impact upon the way in which students are educated are the sophisticated forms of information and communications technology becoming increasingly available. Not only can such technology be effectively used in the classroom, as is already the case in large numbers of schools worldwide; the technology could, it is argued by some, lead to the traditional form of school becoming largely redundant. When teachers can communicate with students electronically, what need is there for students to gather together in one building, day after day, for face-to-face interaction with a teacher? Cannot young people work individually from home, supported electronically by a teacher who sets work, responds to queries, provides formative feedback and generally supports the student in developing his/her learning? Such an approach was adopted recently by at least one international school during temporary closure due to concerns about the H1N1 virus. These issues, again, do not relate to international schools only, but what is distinctive about the international school network is that many of its number cater for the globally mobile expatriate child away from his/her home context. If learning can be supported electronically and remotely within a local area, could it not also be supported on a similar basis from the other side of the world? A child who moves countries following his/her parents' career could thus continue to be educated not by attending a local international school in the new location, but through electronic links with a school (or teachers, with or without a school building) based in his/her home country. The questions raised by such an approach to education, including who would supervise such home-based, computer-assisted learning (stay-at-home parent?, 'helper'?, private tutor?), are many and varied in relation to the economic and social implications of such a change in the traditional nature of the school-based learning/teaching relationship.

Issues of teaching method and style may also arise in respect of the increasing diversity of contexts from which international schools will recruit future teachers, which could have important implications for pedagogy and for teachers' initial and continuing professional development. The institutional model proposed by Thompson (1998) for the learning environment appropriate for the promotion of international-mindedness includes the centrality of an experiential learning approach to the development of the values associated with an international education as promoted in many international schools. Indeed, the prevailing style of learning/teaching to be found in international schools worldwide is undoubtedly what might be described as a Western liberal, student-centred, constructivist approach which, while familiar to many of those recruited to teach in international schools, will pose challenges for those trained in a context where a more teacher-centred, didactic style is the norm. Such teachers are likely to need to make adjustments to their previous practice, and to require professional development support as they do so. Differences in pedagogic approach may also prove to be a source of conflict within schools between overseas and host country teachers, where adaptation to new ways of teaching is either resisted or ineffective. Flexibility and adaptability in pedagogy seem likely to be at a premium rather than adherence to any specific style of teaching, not least as a response to the range of ways in which young people learn.

One additional point of relevance here relates to the increasing interest within national education systems in the international dimension of education. The USA, the UK and Australia are just three examples among many of countries becoming increasingly aware of the importance of young people developing broader perspectives than those traditionally delimited by national boundaries. For pragmatic reasons, such national systems are increasingly recognising that those young people who lack an appreciation of other countries and cultures, or an understanding of how the world works, are likely to be left behind in a globalised marketplace (Hastings 2003: 3). For reasons that are ideological in part, as well as pragmatic, national education systems are acknowledging the importance of young people understanding that the major problems facing our planet need to be addressed from an international perspective, as well as the importance of young people growing up to feel responsibility for addressing such problems. As national education systems increasingly internationalise the educational experience of their students, a question could arise about the likely future differences between the education offered by international schools and that offered by their national counterparts. Whereas in the past many international schools were quite different from national schools in respect of their multicultural student populations and the international focus of their curriculum, with the growing international focus in many national schools worldwide, and the increasingly multicultural nature of student populations, it is arguably the case that such differences are gradually being eroded. Will this change in the nature of national educational systems impact upon international schools and, if so, how might that impact be manifested?

Sources of future international school teachers

As the number of international schools worldwide increases, one might wonder where the teachers will be found to staff them. While, as already noted, the 'traditional' form of international school has tended to be staffed largely by expatriates (with some, but not many, host country teachers), some of the newer international schools, catering principally for a host country student population, may have a higher proportion of host country teachers making up the teaching staff. The growing number of international schools in India, for instance, are likely to recruit many Indian teachers who, while they may need to develop expertise in different pedagogies than those in which they were initially trained, will already not only be expert in the prevailing pedagogy but also be fluent English speakers. International schools located where English is not widely spoken, on the other hand, will need to recruit more teachers from outside the country.

It is clear that Heads and senior managers of international schools are finding it increasingly difficult to recruit expatriate teachers to fill all the posts available (Wigford 2007). So who are the teachers who make up the international school labour market? And how do Heads go about recruiting them to international school posts? In his predictions of future growth for international schools, Brummitt (2009) suggested that from a point in October 2009 where 221,000 teachers were employed by international schools, by 2015 the number likely to be needed will be in the region of 320,000 and, by 2020, could be as many as 450,000: in other words, the number of teaching staff needed by international schools in 2020 could be approximately double what it was in 2009. Little research has been conducted into international schoolteacher recruitment (Millican 2000); in one of the few studies undertaken to date, Canterford (2003) explored the nature of the international school-teacher labour market and, in particular, the nationalities of teachers working within the sector. Canterford acknowledged the limitations on his analysis, given the imprecise and incomplete nature of the data available: the only database accessible that included data on teacher nationalities was that provided by International Schools Services (ISS), based on data supplied by member schools, with teacher nationalities broken down only into the four categories of US, UK, host country and 'other'. Accepting these limitations, Canterford's analysis is nevertheless interesting in showing that of the 500 schools and 27,432 teachers included in his study, over 52 per cent of teachers were either British or American, with some variation across different regions of the world. More interesting in considering issues for future international school teachers are the points Canterford goes on to make in exploring why international schools apparently favour US and UK teachers, and operate within what are described as segmented labour markets (Doeringer and Piore 1985; Dibb and Simkin 1996). With respect to the so-called customer discrimination aspect of segmentation theory, where in the international school context the customer is the parent, Canterford suggests that there is often parental pressure placed upon schools to recruit not only native English speakers but also teachers who are 'Western' trained. Indeed research by Walsh (1999) suggests that parents of international school students (whether local nationals or expatriate) would only accept non-native English speaking, non-Western trained, teachers for their child if they were to teach only 'local' subjects such as 'local' languages. Garton (2000), meanwhile, an experienced international school Head, also makes the case that international school parents often '"prefer" their child to be taught by a native English-speaking, "Western trained" overseas-hire expatriate, for reasons that may be founded rather more on prejudice than on a well-informed evaluation' (2000: 87). Garton's latter point is reinforced by the work of a number of critics of the assumption that non-native speakers are less effective as language teachers than native speakers, summarised by Grimshaw (2007), who argues that non-native speakers 'often have more understanding of the language-learning needs and strategies of their students than do "native speakers"' (2007: 373), which enables them to act as 'imitable models of the successful language learner of English' (Medgyes 1992: 39).

There are complex issues at work here, but the nature of the international school teaching population is clearly an issue that will be crucial as the sector develops in the future: which sources will provide the teachers of the future? Will they continue to be largely recruited from native English-speaking 'Western' countries? Will the discrimination described by Canterford continue to operate? No less important a question in the context of education worldwide relates to the impact on national systems of increasing numbers of teachers being recruited for the international school market, for the most part from English-speaking countries. The removal of large numbers of teachers from the teaching force of the country that trained them, at a time when those countries may themselves be facing teacher shortages, raises social and ethical issues about the relationship between the international and national school sectors that will become more marked as the international school sector increases in size.

Central to the question of the recruitment of international school teachers is the means by which they are recruited, and recent years have seen many changes in this regard. International schools recruiting today, for instance, are less likely to rely on glossy promotional brochures to attract potential teachers than on comprehensive and well maintained websites. Some factors may be much as they were previously: newspapers are still used to advertise posts, raising questions of where to advertise since the location will undoubtedly influence the nature of the pool of applicants from whom the appointment will be made. The use of technology is likely to improve the quality and efficiency of recruitment in the sense that, currently, overseas-hire international school teachers often accept a new post without ever visiting the school or, even, meeting face to face those with whom they will work most closely. The use of facilities such as Skype seems likely to lead to both interviewer and interviewee being better informed than they might otherwise have been and/or to schools reducing costs incurred through recruiters flying around the world for face-to-face interviews, as well as reducing for Heads the large amount of time spent in recruiting annually, compared with those with similar responsibilities in national contexts, as a result of the relatively high turnover of teachers on short-term contracts (Odland and Ruzicka 2009).

This last point raises the question of the future of agencies and recruitment fairs, which have to date been a central part of recruitment strategy for many international schools. Agencies including Gabbitas, International Schools Services (ISS), the Council of International Schools (CIS), Teachers International Consultancy (TIC) and Search Associates can help with advertising and shortlisting (Garton 2000: 90). Some agencies run recruitment fairs, where large numbers of recruiters and job-seekers come together in a large centrally placed hotel for several days of interviews culminating, it is hoped, in recruiters having filled all their vacant posts for the next school year and job-seekers having accepted a job offer. Though many successful appointments have undoubtedly been made at such fairs, their popularity may be waning (Wigford 2007). With increasingly sophisticated telecommunications systems likely to become available, it will not be surprising if the perceived need for international travel and face-to-face meetings in the recruitment process diminishes with time.

Skills and attributes for future international school teachers

It has already been noted that increasing understanding of the processes of learning arising from the rapidly developing field of brain research, as well as developments in technology, will impact upon the skills required of future classroom teachers in both international and national schools. The training provided for the new teacher of the future, and/or the ongoing professional development available to the already qualified teacher of the future, will need to take into account these new developments and suggest possible new pedagogical approaches.

What sort of prior preparation, then, will be needed for those about to embark upon teaching in an international school? Currently it is generally assumed that if someone has been trained to teach in a national context, has a certain amount of experience (perhaps two or three years) and has a reasonably adaptable personality, they will be able to teach successfully in an international school. Teachers new to the international school sector for the most part learn the skills required in that context 'on the job'. In an international school similar to that they have left behind (such as a British-experienced teacher moving into a British-type international school with mostly British students and teachers, and following the English national curriculum) this may not raise many challenges. For teachers moving to a very different context, however, the burden of providing support can fall on their new colleagues, may lead to learning by 'trial and error', and may be demotivating as they feel 'unexpectedly "de-skilled" in a new school because an unfamiliar set of pupils react to them differently' (Stirzaker 2004: 32). Almost certainly the need for some form of preparation for teachers embarking on international school teaching will lead to the development of courses and qualifications (Snowball 2007), raising questions about how specific such preparation should be (can the same course prepare teachers to teach in an international school in Japan and an international school in Mumbai?), who should offer it, and how it should cater both for those who are very experienced in their own national context, and for others with little prior teaching experience of any sort.

One skill likely to be needed by the future international schoolteacher relates to the growing number of international school students who are not native speakers of English. Clearly there will continue to be specialist teachers whose main responsibility is the provision of support for such students as they develop fluency in the English language. Arguably, however, it will become increasingly important for all teachers, and not only language specialists, to have some ability to support the needs of such students in the non-specialist language learning context. Programmes such as ESL in the Mainstream (2010) might thus gain increasing prominence.

Equally important to the future international schoolteacher will be the trait of intercultural awareness and sensitivity. In many international schools, teachers may be working with students from forty or more national/cultural backgrounds. While it would be unreasonable to expect any one teacher to be familiar with cultural practices of all the different backgrounds of students in an international school setting, an open-mindedness and willingness to give the benefit of the doubt to those whose practices are different from one's own, and to learn about the practices of those other cultural backgrounds, are likely to be attributes sought in recruitment and encouraged through professional development opportunities. Similarly, and particularly in the type of international school where many students move school on a regular basis, the future international schoolteacher will need to have an understanding of how to support those experiencing transition. The needs of such students are becoming ever more well documented, and ways in which international schools can support them (and, indeed, their less mobile peers who regularly experience the upheaval of friends moving on) are increasingly well understood (see, for instance, Langford 1998; McKillop-Ostrom 2000; Dixon and Hayden 2008). Indeed, anecdotal evidence suggests that growing numbers of international school teachers were themselves globally nomadic children and have lived those experiences first hand. Those who have not may need to develop sensitivity to and understanding of the experiences of those they teach.

It has long been possible to observe in international schools what have been described as the pragmatic and ideological dimensions (see, for instance, Hayden 2006), where the pragmatic dimension relates to the preparation of young people for an increasingly globalised world where knowledge and understanding of international geography, history and politics, linguistic skills and intercultural literacy (Heyward 2002) will be advantageous. The ideological dimension, meanwhile, relates to the preparation of young people to be global peace-makers who will promote respect and understanding across cultural and linguistic borders, help to break down the barriers that arise through prejudice and ignorance, and feel responsibility for finding solutions to those global problems that transcend national borders. As the twenty-first century progresses, there is likely to be growing pressure on young people not only to cope pragmatically in a world increasingly influenced by the growing forces of globalisation, but also to develop those attributes that will enable them to help to create a better world. If these are the skills needed by the young people of tomorrow, they are also the skills that will be needed by the international school teachers of tomorrow – who will not only require the technical skills to teach languages, politics, geography and history in a multicultural environment, but will also need to model the values that international schools aim to imbue in their students.

Support for future international school teachers

If these, then, are the skills and attributes anticipated in the future international schoolteacher, what forms of support will they need in that future? Some may be relatively self-evident: teachers are likely to need help, for instance, in understanding how they can best support their students with respect to English language learning (in English-medium international schools) and global mobility. They will also need support in developing intercultural sensitivity and awareness, as well as the traits associated with the ideological dimension of the mission of many international schools. Future international school teachers seem likely also to need some preparation for teaching in such a context, in relation not only to the content of new programmes but also to the Western liberal, child-centred approach to pedagogy found in many international schools. If the backgrounds from which international school teachers are recruited become more varied than they have been to date, there is likely to be increasing need for professional development for those teachers whose previous experience has been acquired in a different pedagogic context.

Much of the support needed by the future international schoolteacher is likely to be similar in principle, if not in detail, to that needed by teachers in schools anywhere. Those moving to a new school will need some form of induction or orientation, though this will need to take account of the diversity among new teaching recruits who may be much more varied in terms of previous experience than would be expected in a national context (see Stirzaker 2004). They will also require some ongoing form of what might be described as appraisal in identifying their strengths and areas for improvement (see, for instance, Matthews 2006). Where the curriculum they are working with is provided by an external organisation such as the International Baccalaureate, Cambridge International Examinations or the International Primary Curriculum, they will also require support in understanding the curriculum requirements and how best to support their students in meeting them – which may be provided by more experienced colleagues within the same school, as well as through courses and workshops provided by those organisations. As the number of such international programmes increases (as seems likely), the provision of such support will become increasingly important.

For both pragmatic and professional reasons, it is likely that many future international school teachers will continue to aspire to the achievement of academic qualifications such as Masters and Doctoral degrees. As the number of such teachers increases, more universities worldwide are likely to see the value of catering for such a market, and as technology becomes more sophisticated it will become decreasingly necessary for teachers to travel to a particular location in order to engage in such courses. The motivation for some international school teachers, at least, in gaining such qualifications will undoubtedly be the acquisition of a competitive edge over others with promotion ambitions but no such qualification. Indeed it could be argued that the increasing number of international school teachers now holding or working towards Doctorates arises from the fact that, as holding a Master's degree becomes increasingly the norm in the international school sector, the Doctorate now provides the competitive edge that at one time was provided by the Master's degree. It is interesting to speculate as to what might ultimately take the place of the Doctorate, as that qualification become more widely held by staff in international schools worldwide. Will a new post-doctorate qualification emerge? Or will an expansion be seen in programmes recently introduced that recognise particular forms of experience, such as the International Teacher Certificate (ITC 2010) developed as a means of recognising international school teaching experience, or the International Baccalaureate Teacher Award designed to recognise those who have experience of teaching one or more of the three IB programmes (IB 2010b)? Such means of recognising particular forms of relevant experience seem certain to grow in number. In a related area, the encouragement for practice-based research provided to date through schemes such as the Jeff Thompson Research Fellowships, recently introduced by the International Baccalaureate (IB 2010c), seem likely to increase. It will be interesting to observe in coming years the extent to which such recognition will come to form part of the selection process for the international schoolteacher of the future.

Career progression possibilities

Issues raised have so far focused largely on the classroom teacher, rather than on those leaders or managers (Heads, Principals, Directors, for instance) often referred to in international schools as administrators. Many international school administrators have made a career in this context, beginning as young classroom teachers and working their way up, often through a number of different international schools in various parts of the world. Conversely, there are international schools which, in seeking a new senior administrator, look for experience not so much from the international school sector as from a national system: for an international school with a national allegiance, for instance, 'recent and relevant' experience of that national context may be considered more desirable than experience elsewhere. Those who assume, however, that such a transfer will be no different from moving between schools within a national context could be in for a surprise as the new cultures encountered (not only with respect to students, parents and teachers from different cultural, national and linguistic backgrounds, but also to the culture of the school itself and its local environment) lead to different kinds of challenges than have previously been encountered. Dimmock and Walker make the points that leadership 'is a culturally and contextually bounded process inextricably intertwined with its larger environment (organisational, local community and larger environment)' and that cultural influence on leadership is multidimensional, 'often difficult to discern, subtle and easy to overlook – to the point that it is underplayed by many, and even dismissed by some' (2005: 3–4). In the context of international schools in particular, Shaw (2001) discusses some of the challenges raised by managing mixed-culture teams, highlighting the increased likelihood of dissonance in international schools compared with national schools, when expectations may fail to be met through misunderstanding rather than by intention.

Lack of space prevents the discussion here of many interesting and detailed issues, some of which are considered at more length in Hayden and Thompson (2008). Two issues which often surface are administrator turnover and long-term planning. The former cannot be considered without reference to the wide variety of governance models found in international schools, including the single owner with no recognisable Board as such, the not uncommon heavily parent-influenced Board, the self-perpetuating and elected Board models, and the somewhat confusingly inconsistent terminology referring *inter alia* to Board members, governors, directors and trustees. More detailed discussion of some Board-related issues can be found in Hayden (2006), but undoubtedly one issue that often causes tension between Board and Head in international schools is that of the boundary between their respective responsibilities for policy development and implementation. Reference in such situations to micro-management is not uncommon, with schools experiencing difficulties 'when a Board attempts to step into an operational or management role. Such micro-management, however well-meaning, almost inevitably leads to role confusion and potential conflict' (Powell 2001: 13). Though little research exists, evidence suggests that there may be a link between Board/Head tensions and the relatively high turnover of Heads in international schools compared with most national systems (Hawley 1994 and 1995).

In a context where turnover of Heads is often high, the notion of what might be described as long-term planning, strategic planning or development planning can be problematic (Leggate and Thompson 1997). While more difficult to organise and to implement than in more stable contexts, it is arguably at least as important as, if not more important than, it would be in such contexts. As Nelson, an experienced international school Head, points out: 'Certainly, strategic planning is demanding of time, but so too is the alternative – not planning! Being in a constantly reactive mode is time-consuming, wasteful of resources and ultimately debilitating to students, staff and parents alike' (2000: 171). Undoubtedly one of the ironies of administrative/leadership roles in the international school context is that in the very situation where relative instability increases the need for long-term planning, it is that lack of administrative stability that can militate against such plans being devised.

Summary

This chapter has raised issues, and asked questions, about teachers in international schools and has suggested what may be important issues for such teachers in the future. One challenge to anyone working in this area is the dearth of research that could at least begin to answer some of the many questions being asked. Although the research base is gradually growing, principally through practitioners engaging in postgraduate research degrees and disseminating the outcomes of their studies, there is still a clear need for more research and, ideally, more large-scale funded research projects focusing on issues arising from international schools and their student/teacher populations. There is also a need for better records with respect to the nature of the teaching populations in international schools: as Canterford's research highlighted (2003), those databases that do currently exist are not comprehensive and do not allow for sufficiently meaningful analysis of the data that could contribute to a better understanding of the context.

The forces of globalisation are certain to continue to impinge upon, and contribute to, the growing numbers of international schools worldwide, generating many important issues that would benefit from further research. Such research could not only be illuminating for the international school sector itself, but might also inform practice in national education systems. That this growing field be not only better documented but also more extensively researched would seem to be essential for those adults and young people whose lives will be influenced by the international schools of the future.

References

Allen, K. (2000) The international school and its community: think globally, interact locally. In M. C. Hayden and J. J. Thompson (eds) (2000) *International Schools and International Education: Improving Teaching, Management and Quality*, London: Kogan Page, pp. 124–39.

Brummitt, N. (2009) Presentation to IPSEF Conference, London: 22 October 2009.

Cambridge, J. (2000) International schools, globalization and the seven cultures of capitalism. In M. C. Hayden and J. J. Thompson (eds) *International Schools and International Education: Improving Teaching, Management and Quality*, London: Kogan Page, pp. 179–90.

Cambridge, J. (2002) Recruitment and deployment of staff: a dimension of international school organization. In M. C. Hayden, J. J. Thompson and G. R. Walker (eds) *International Education in Practice: Dimensions for National and International Schools*, London: Kogan Page, pp. 158–69.

Cambridge International Examinations (CIE) (2010) available at: www.cie.org.uk/qualifications/academic/middlesec/igcse/subjects (accessed 6 January 2010).

Canterford, G. (2003) Segmented labour markets in international schools, *Journal of Research in International Education* 2(1): 47–65.

Deveney, M. (2000) An investigation into the influences on parental choice of an international school in Thailand. Unpublished dissertation for MA in Education (International Education), University of Bath.

Dibb, S. and Simkin, L. (1996) *The Market Segmentation Workbook: Target Marketing for Marketing Managers*, London: Routledge.

Dimmock, C. and Walker, A. (2005) *Educational Leadership: Culture and Diversity*, London: Sage Publications.

Dixon, P. G. S. and Hayden, M. C. (2008) 'On the move': primary age children in transition, *Cambridge Journal of Education* 38(4): 483–96.

Doeringer, P. B. and Piore, M. J. (1985) *Internal Labour Markets and Manpower Analysis*, London: Sharpe.

Edexcel (2010) available at: www.edexcel.com/quals/igcse/Pages/default.aspx (accessed 6 January 2010).

ESL in the Mainstream (2010) available at: www.decs.sa.gov.au/curric/default.asp?id= 17258&navgrp=615 (accessed 6 January 2010).

Friedman, T. (2005) *The World is Flat: a Brief History of the Globalized World in the 21st Century*, New York and London: Allen Lane (Penguin).

Garton, B. (2000) Recruitment of teachers for international education. In M. C. Hayden and J. J. Thompson (eds) (2000) *International Schools and International Education: Improving Teaching, Management and Quality*, London: Kogan Page, pp. 85–95.

Gray, K. (2006) The globalisation of English. Public lecture given at the University of Bath, 8 February 2006.

Grimshaw, T. (2007) Critical perspectives on language in international education. In M. C. Hayden, J. Levy and J. J. Thompson (eds) *The SAGE Handbook of Research in International Education*, London: Sage, pp. 365–78.

Hardman, J. (2001) Improving recruitment and retention of quality overseas teachers. In S. Blandford and M. Shaw (eds) *Managing International Schools*, London: Routledge Falmer, pp. 123–35.

Hastings, S. (2003) Fun and games, *TES Go Global Supplement*, 7 November 2003.

Hawley, D. B. (1994) How long do international school heads survive? A research analysis (Part I) *International Schools Journal* XIV(1): 8–21.

Hawley, D. B. (1995) How long do international school heads survive? A research analysis (Part II) *International Schools Journal* XIV(2): 23–36.

Hayden, M. C. (2006) *Introduction to International Education: International Schools and their Communities*, London: Sage.

Hayden, M. C. and Thompson, J. J. (eds) (1998) *International Education: Principles and Practice*, London: Kogan Page.

Hayden, M. C. and Thompson, J. J. (2008) *International Schools: Growth and Influence*, in UNESCO International Institute for Educational Planning (IIEP) Fundamentals of Educational Planning series, Paris: UNESCO, available at: www.iiep.unesco.org/information-services/publications/abstracts/2008/fundamentals_92.html.

Heyward, M. (2002) From international to intercultural: redefining the international school for a globalised world, *Journal of Research in International Education* 1(1): 9–32.

International Baccalaureate Organization (2010a) available at: www.ibo.org (accessed 6 January 2010).

International Baccalaureate Organization (2010b) available at: www.ibo.org/programmes/pd/award/ (accessed 6 January 2010).

International Baccalaureate Organization (2010c) available at: www.ibo.org/announcements/jeffthompson_research.cfm (accessed 6 January 2010).

International Primary Curriculum (2010) available at: www.internationalprimary curriculum.com (accessed 6 January 2010).

International Schools Services (ISS) (2010) available at: www.iss.edu (accessed 6 January 2010).

International Teacher Certificate (ITC) (2010) available at: www.internationalteacher certificate.com/ (accessed 6 January 2010).

Joslin, P. (2002) Teacher relocation: reflections in the context of international schools, *Journal of Research in International Education* 1(1): 33–62.

Langford, M. (1998) Global nomads: third culture kids and international schools. In M. C. Hayden and J. J. Thompson (eds) *International Education: Principles and Practice* London: Kogan Page, pp. 28–43.

Leggate, P. M. C. and Thompson, J. J. (1997) The management of development planning in international schools, *International Journal of Educational Management* 11(6): 268–73.

Lowe, J. (2000) Assessment and educational quality: implications for international schools. In M. C. Hayden and J. J. Thompson (eds) *International Schools and International Education: Improving Teaching, Management and Quality*, London: Kogan Page, pp. 15–28.

MacDonald, J. (2006) The international school industry: examining international schools through an economic lens, *Journal of Research in International Education* 5(2): 191–213.

MacKenzie, P., Hayden, M. C. and Thompson, J. J. (2003) Parental priorities in the selection of international schools, *Oxford Review of Education* 29(3): 299–314.

McKillop-Ostrom, A. (2000) Student mobility and the international curriculum. In M. C. Hayden and J. J. Thompson (eds) *International Schools and International Education: Improving Teaching, Management and Quality*, Kogan Page: London, pp. 73–84.

Matthews, M. (2006) *Appraisal for Teachers and Heads in International Schools*, Great Glemham: John Catt Educational.

Medgyes, P. (1992) Native or non-native: who's worth more? *ELT Journal* 46(4): 340–9.

Millican, E. A. (2000) Managing the Recruitment of Teaching Staff in International Schools. Unpublished MA in Education dissertation: University of Bath.

Nelson, N. (2000) Strategic planning for international schools: a roadmap to excellence. In M. C. Hayden and J. J. Thompson (eds) *International Schools and International Education: Improving Teaching, Management and Quality*, London: Kogan Page, pp. 169–78.

Odland, G. and Ruzicka, M. (2009) An investigation into teacher turnover in international schools, *Journal of Research in International Education* 8(1): 5–29.

Potter, D. and Hayden, M. C. (2004) Parental choice in the Buenos Aires bilingual school market, *Journal of Research in International Education* 3(1): 87–111.

Powell, W. (2001) Roles and responsibilities: what does a school board do? In W. Powell, N. Bowley and G. Schoppert (eds) *School Board Governance Training: A Sourcebook of Case Studies*, Great Glemham: John Catt Educational, pp. 13–21.

Rischard, J. F. (2002) *High Noon: 20 Global Problems, 20 Years to Solve Them*, New York: Basic Books.

Shaw, M. (2001) Managing mixed-culture teams in international schools. In S. Blandford and M. Shaw (eds) *Managing International Schools*, London: Routledge Falmer, pp. 153–72.

Sklair, L. (2001) *The Transnational Capitalist Class*, Oxford: Blackwell.

Snowball, L. (2007) Becoming more internationally-minded: international teacher certification and professional development. In M. C. Hayden, J. Levy and J. J. Thompson (eds) *The SAGE Handbook of Research in International Education*, London: Sage.

Stirzaker, R. (2004) Staff induction: issues surrounding induction into international schools, *Journal of Research in International Education* 3(1): 31–49.

Sutcliffe, D. (1991) The United World Colleges. In P. L. Jonietz and D. Harris (eds) *World Yearbook of Education 1991: International Schools and International Education*, London: Kogan Page, pp. 25–37.

Thomas, H. (2006) Personal Communication.

Thompson, J. J. (1998) Towards a model for international education. In M. C. Hayden and J. J. Thompson (eds) *International Education: Principles and Practice*, London: Kogan Page.

Walsh, P. (1999) International teacher recruitment: an empirical investigation. Unpublished MA in Education dissertation, University of Bath.

Wigford, A. (2007) Building capacity for international teacher recruitment, *Intercom* (newsletter of the Centre for the study of Education in an International Context, University of Bath) 24: 2–3, available at: www.bath.ac.uk/ceic/documents/24total.pdf.

6 Teaching and learning in international schools

A consideration of the stakeholders and their expectations

Helen Fail

The international school context

Before it is possible to discuss aspects of teaching and learning in international schools, it is important to come to a shared understanding of the context.

There have been a number of different typologies over the years that have attempted to facilitate an understanding of the very different international schools around the world (Leach 1969; Terwilliger 1972; Ponisch 1987; Matthews 1988; Hill 2002, 2006a). These have used various criteria in order to categorise the different types of school ranging from their curriculum (national or international), their purpose and reason for being (ideological or market-driven), their student population (multinational or predominantly one nationality), their faculty (multinational or not), their history (national schools overseas). Although these may be useful, as Pearce points out 'defining international schools is difficult, contentious and probably pointless . . . They cannot always be classified by the names they adopt and are best treated as a broad continuum' (Pearce 1994: 8). Hayden (2006) comes to a similar conclusion in advising that they are seen as a 'spectrum' 'with the ideological at one end and the market-driven at the other' (Hayden 2006: 16). For the purpose of this discussion, a broad understanding is adopted that includes quite a varied type of school ranging from the most ideological at one end (such as the United World Colleges (Peterson 1987)) to the for-profit schools at the market-driven end of the spectrum that often offer a national curriculum and are usually English-speaking medium. Jonietz (Jonietz and Harris 1991) rather naively claimed that international schools were alike in their 'international goals, and their multicultural, multinational and multilingual populations'. I would like to suggest that they may be alike in their multicultural, multilingual and multinational populations but these schools do not necessarily share international goals, unless they are towards the ideological end of the spectrum. They do often share multilingual and multicultural student populations (although there can be no assumptions about the predominant percentage from any one nationality) and this alone will have an impact on the teaching and learning that goes on within them. Another factor that is often taken for granted is that they are usually English medium. Although there are bilingual international schools in a number of countries (and of course the multilingual European schools) the majority of international schools are English medium and this has an impact on the faculty recruited and the nature of the teaching and learning that takes place (Hayden 2006).

Culture: essentialist and non-essentialist views

Another term that needs to be discussed is the notion of culture. In order to examine the cultural influences on teaching and learning, it is necessary to adopt a shared meaning for the term culture. There seem to be two opposing tendencies. One is the essentialist view that can lead to stereotyping (Holliday 1999; Hinton 2000). The essentialist view suggests that each culture has an observable, identifiable list of behaviours and customs that characterise the culture (Hofstede 1997; Smith *et al.* 2006). Where does this list of characteristics come from? One possible source is cross-cultural research (Hofstede 1997, 2001; Smith *et al.* 2006) although different cultures tend to categorise other cultures with stereotyped views (Hinton 2000). These are what Brislin (2000) calls 'shortcuts to thinking' or what Moscovici (1981) would call social representations. The obvious danger with this view is the temptation to assume that each individual from a particular culture must exhibit all of the culture's characteristics. Hofstede (1997) does warn that this is an 'ecological fallacy' and it should not be assumed that individuals from a culture will exhibit all the characteristics assigned to that culture.

The non-essentialist approach suggests that cultural influence is one of many factors affecting cross-cultural interactions. The teacher should therefore not rely totally on cultural influence in explaining interactions. With this approach, culture can be used along with other considerations in analysing particular interactions. This does make an analysis of what goes on in the classroom in the international school much more complex. With this approach, cultural influence can be considered and analysed and seen as part of the influence on the context. The approach advocated by Holliday (1999) (an interpretive, ethnographic analysis of a specific classroom culture), is proposed as the most effective and rewarding way of looking at the international school classroom. It is still necessary to have an understanding of the essentialist view that provides a framework and reference for analysis and may account for actions and reactions to cross-cultural interactions.

Hofstede's (1997, 2001) seminal work on cultural differences (an essentialist approach) may be helpful in categorising and understanding cultural differences, but his work enables the student to fall prey to stereotyping people and situations in an effort to clarify understanding. At the other end of the spectrum, recent work by Van Oord (2005, 2008) in the international school context, suggests that all encounters should be seen as 'intergroup' interactions rather than interactions based on cultural differences.

How are we to proceed in order to consider teaching and learning in international schools? I think it is important to acknowledge that people do share different values, world views, behaviours and traditions according to their background. Although these attitudes and behaviours may result from their social class, socio-economic status, level of education, life experience, family life, religious background, it is important to remember that the context of all these experiences is also their nationality/cultural background. The country in which they were born and the nationality and language of their parents have an impact on all of those previously cited aspects: social class, education, socio-economic status, religion and family life (Inglis 2005). It would be foolish therefore to say that the national and geographical context has no impact on a person. The teacher should therefore not dismiss the categories that the essentialist offers as irrelevant, nor should s/he assume that all interactions can be explained simply with reference to cultural differences.

So what are some different definitions of culture and how are we to understand their influence?

Definitions such as culture is 'a body of learned behaviour, a collection of beliefs, habits and traditions, shared by a group of people and successively learned by people who enter society' (Mead 1951) and 'The members of a culture system share a set of ideas and values. These are transmitted from one generation to another by symbols. Culture is produced by the past actions of a group and its members' (Krober and Kluckhohn 1952) now seem rather dated. Although they contain the critical notion that culture is *learned*, they do suggest that society is somewhat static. Certainly, they highlight the notion of ideas and values, which is another problem. Empirical research is based on observable behaviour and customs. This is where the notion of culture as an onion ring (Hofstede 2001) or an iceberg (Kohls and Knight 1994; Fennes and Hapgood 1997) is helpful. In both these analogies, surface culture is seen in terms of visible and observable behaviours and characteristics (essentialist) that are underpinned by invisible beliefs and values. So let us agree that culture is learned. It is not inherited. This is true for all the different cultural contexts that we are a part of and in which we function effectively. We behave in different ways in different contexts and this is true regardless of the geographical country in which we are located. How we behave in school, in our families, with our peers, in formal and informal situations, if we should travel overseas varies according to the context. We have a repertoire of behaviours, language and attitudes that we employ in different situations. One of these contexts of course is the international school classroom. In fact the following definitions highlight that our shared behaviour is with particular groups (rather than society as a whole); 'Culture has been defined in a number of ways, but most simply, as the learned and shared behaviour of a community of interacting human beings' (Useem *et al.* 1963) and 'the collective programming of the mind which distinguishes the members of one group or category of people from another' (Hofstede 1997).

The essentialist view of culture does reduce all interactions to cultural interactions (Holliday 1999; Van Oord 2005). The non-essentialist view takes a more interpretive approach and draws on cultural analysis to understand interactions but does not necessarily reduce all interactions to their cultural underpinning. The following discussion on teaching and learning in international schools adopts an interpretive approach but does draw on essentialist views of culture in order to analyse the problematic nature of teaching and learning in international schools (Samovar *et al.* 2007).

Although stereotyping is frequently regarded in a detrimental way (Hinton 2000) it must be acknowledged that stereotypes are actually shared social representations within groups. The danger for the international schoolteacher in using authors such as Hofstede (1997, 2001) in order to enhance an understanding of other cultures is that s/he may be tempted to stereotype the behaviour of students and parents. One must therefore guard against seeking to understand and simplify cross-cultural teaching by using theoretical models that may reinforce stereotypes. Allan (2003) has undertaken some valuable research in the context of intercultural interactions in the international school classroom that highlights the complexity of the issues. He demonstrates how cultural dissonance leads to intercultural learning. It is important to realise that both the teacher and the student need to learn from these encounters. It is not merely a question of the student learning the new school culture. The teacher needs to be open to new perspectives as well. The notion of culture in this context will draw on both essentialist and non-essentialist paradigms, and encourages the reader to take a broader perspective to embrace the complexity of the interactions taking place in international schools.

So let us move on to the stakeholders in an international school and consider their expectations about the outcomes of the teaching–learning experience in the international school and how cultural influences might impact those encounters.

Teachers

Most teachers in international schools have been trained in English-speaking milieus in the Western world. There are often locally hired teachers in international schools who may be languages-other-than-English teachers (L.O.T.E.) but the majority of international schools are English-medium schools and being a native-English speaker is seen as an advantage. What goes hand in hand with being a native-English speaking teacher is the probability that one has been trained to teach in an English-speaking country. It is therefore important to consider the history of pedagogy in these countries and the consequent impact on the students. 'Our ideas, *our values*, our acts, even our emotions, are, like our nervous system itself, *cultural products*' (Geertz 1993: 50, emphasis added).

If teachers do not acknowledge the source of their ideas and values (Walker 2004), then they are in danger of not realising that the judgements that they make of their students are in fact a product of their own cultural background. Teachers' behaviour, attitudes and expectations of their students are usually rooted in their view of teaching and learning which is related to the culture in which they were trained to teach. Indeed, an article that assesses the global awareness of 700 college students in the United States concludes that civilization is becoming more international. In the context of the article, 'international' seems to be synonymous with American, and indicates how ethnocentric much research is (Clarke 2004). Much teacher behaviour is rooted in beliefs about behaviourism (Skinner 1969), cognitivism (Sternberg 1999) and social constructivism (Vygotsky 1986). Teachers hold beliefs about reward or punishment, the construction of meaning, motivation, original thought, independent learning, all of which are based in the history and development of theories about teaching and learning (Jordan *et al.* 2008). Are these ideas cultural? Piaget and Vygotsky were not native English speakers so there has been cross-cultural dissemination in educational theories. Philosophy, psychology and sociology have all played a part in how teachers view their role, their students and the way in which they teach. It would be naive to assume that all teachers share a similar view simply by virtue of having an English-speaking background. There are differences of views and opinion within individual countries and across generations. Recent research on the brain is starting to impact teaching and learning, and views about intelligence have divided educators over the years (Jordan *et al.* 2008). It is important to realise that cultural influence (such as Hofstede's (1997) power distance and individualism) is yet another ingredient in the complicated recipe. International school conferences for teachers' professional development (such as the annual ECIS conference) frequently host speakers whose purpose is to bring findings from the latest research about learning styles, brain-based learning, second-language learning, in order to influence teachers' practice and what goes on in the classroom. The teacher is a lifelong learner and professional constantly improving his/her practice based on the latest research.

Articles in the *Journal of Research in International Education* highlight issues in teaching and learning relevant to this debate. One focuses on Chinese teachers' expectations of their students in terms of rote learning (Tao *et al.* 2006) and another on the teaching of science to Islamic students where the theory of evolution cuts across their religious beliefs (Robottom and Norhaidah 2008). Both of these articles highlight the influence of cultural backgrounds that both teachers and students bring in terms of their expectations of how and what students learn. Deveney (2007) looks at teacher preparedness for teaching Thai students. Thai students' behaviour is assumed to be predictable and based on national and cultural characteristics. The teachers involved in her research felt that they were not necessarily helping their students achieve their full potential as a result of not having a full knowledge of their behaviour. Other researchers who have looked at teacher preparedness for teaching internationally also focus on learning as much as possible about other cultures in order to teach more sensitively (Duckworth *et al.* 2005; Snowball 2007). Samovar *et al.* (2007) write from the premise that multicultural students have different characteristics based on their cultural background and the teacher needs to have an awareness of and understanding of these differences. Although

Holliday (1999) argues against this expectation of how Japanese students will behave by virtue of being Japanese, it would be foolish to avoid learning as much as possible about different cultures by denying that there are cultural differences.

So what do international schoolteachers bring to the table in terms of their expectations? What sort of learners are they hoping to produce? This is where Van Oord (2005) raises a particularly relevant issue for the international schoolteacher. What he draws attention to (citing the work of Balagangadhara 1994) is the fact that each group (culture) not only selects the content of what should be learned (the curriculum) but how it should be learned (meta-learning). This has enormous implications for the teaching–learning debate in international schools. It suggests that one needs to pay attention not merely to the curriculum (i.e. is it international enough in terms of its content) but how it is taught and how the students learn. This raises another significant question in international education. Are the teachers responsible for how their students learn to learn or do the students bring their own background in how they learn with them? A view based on Bloom's taxonomy of learning is that certain skills are superior to others (Bloom and Krathwohl 1956). This is seen in the testing and assessment system. Skills such as evaluation and synthesis are rated more highly than description that may merely demonstrate memorisation and is low down on Bloom's taxonomy. How are students tested in international schools? Brown (2002) raises the issue of national and cultural assessment and the implications for international schools. Students are invariably marked on tests and examinations that have been taken as individuals and which favour original thought and interpretation (Brown 2002). These skills are not necessarily valued across all cultures (Hofstede 1997).

Although the temptation is to use essentialist cultural differences in order to make a point (Hall 1976; Hofstede 1997; Trompenaars and Hampden-Turner 1997; Smith *et al.* 2006; Samovar *et al.* 2007) it is helpful to use the iceberg (Kohls and Knight 1994; Fennes and Hapgood 1997) or the onion ring (Hofstede 2001) to show that values and attitudes influence behaviour. We may not want to describe behaviour and reduce culture to a visible and superficial list of characteristics but we are in a sense all culture-bound to the extent that the way we think and teach and our expectations of our students are actually a product of our own training and learned beliefs about teaching and how students learn. We may argue that we only want students to achieve their full potential. But what does that potential look like? Do we want them to fit back into their own home culture or become freethinking individuals who are anxious to do well and pursue their own goals? Teachers need to be aware that the sort of behaviour that they want students to produce (questioning, independent thought, verbally confident in front of others) may actually be at odds with the way they have been encouraged to learn in other classrooms (Samovar *et al.* 2007). Needless to say, these issues are not confined to international schools but to schools in many countries around the world with a multicultural student body. Are we imposing our values as educators on our students? We only have to think in terms of teaching about sex or same sex relationships to see how such views are largely linked to a particular country/culture's laws and may be completely at odds with the religious beliefs of students and their families. This brings us to the issue of the teaching of values in international schools (Bartlett 1992; Kotrc 1994; Walker 2004).

The teaching of values

The issue of shared values in international education has been a subject of debate (Mattern 1990; Ellwood and Davis 1991; Kotrc 1994) and Bartlett (1992) has argued that international schools afraid of addressing the values debate have sometimes created a *'values-vacuum'* in international schools. Schools in any culture pass on the values of that culture, whether consciously or unconsciously, and in so doing prepare students to live in it (Brislin 2000; Lee 2001). International schools have debated or avoided the issue of what values they pass on since values are often culture based (Mattern 1990; Ellwood and Davis 1991; Bartlett 1992; Geertz 1993; Kotrc 1994), and they do not want to be seen to be passing on culturally specific values. Kotrc (1994) investigated whether there were shared values in international schools and concluded that there is value relativism in international schools: 'No value is superior to the other, therefore needs to be equally accepted, and a sort of moral "anything goes" is the consequence' (Kotrc 1994: 72).

Whether the teaching of values is deliberate or not, they are a shared part of any community, and surely international schools should be paying attention to what values are being passed on to their students and how those values are preparing them for the future (Blackburn 1989). Work by Schwartz (1997) has sought to establish whether there are universal values across cultures so these are not issues confined to the international school arena. The work of Inglehart (2006) relating to world values adopts an essentialist approach in categorising different cultures. This is certainly a challenging area for the international schoolteacher to consider and one where there are no easy answers. Some would consider that international schools are bastions of cultural imperialism. It is important that teachers consider not just the content of what they are teaching, nor the way in which they teach it, but how they influence their students in more subtle ways through their attitudes and expectations. Where do those attitudes and expectations come from? Teachers do need to become more self-aware and analyse their own behaviour. It is not simply a matter of becoming culturally sensitive towards their students.

It would be foolish to assume that all teachers in international schools share similar views about teaching and learning. Schools that have staff from mainly one country may establish a more coherent policy and practice but there have been several misunderstandings between staff from different English-speaking nationalities (Fail 2000). When it comes to assessment and grading, one only has to put British and American teachers together and ask them to agree to realise that there are very different views on what and how students should be graded. Some research has been done on preferred teaching and student interaction styles in the international school arena (Van Oord and den Brok 2004). Although there were similar results between the students and teachers, it became apparent that actually teachers judged their own teaching style differently from the students (Van Oord and den Brok 2004).

There have been studies looking at teacher preparedness for teaching in international school contexts (Deveney 2007; Duckworth *et al.* 2005) and advice prepared for teachers entering the international school arena (Langford *et al.* 2002), but these tend to focus on the surface/essentialist level of how to behave and what to expect. In reality all the stakeholders involved in the teaching/learning nexus of international schools are going to be changed by the experience.

Cultural differences

In order to come to a decision about the validity of the research and theoretical claims about the impact of cultural difference, it is necessary to identify them. Hofstede's (1997, 2001) five dimensions could be said to influence the teaching and learning in international schools. It must be remembered that his findings were based on adults working for IBM around the world (the majority of whom were men), but his work has been so influential that it is important to consider the claims.

Power distance

The major way that this could impact on the teaching and learning in international schools is through the relationship between the teacher and the student and their expectations of one another. Where there is a higher power-distance the role of the teacher in relationship to the student is more distant and more powerful. This is most likely to have an impact on the teacher–student relationship and their treatment and attitude towards each other.

Individualism–collectivism

According to this continuum, the way that the classroom and learning are organised for students to work independently or collaboratively would indicate the cultural background of the teacher/students. This is also said to influence attitudes towards and the practice of plagiarism. In collectivist cultures, it is claimed that people care more about the group than about their individual success. This might affect speaking out as an individual in class. Most teachers in international schools come from individualist cultures.

Uncertainty avoidance

This is said to influence the extent to which students can work independently and confidently with ambiguity. Cultures with high uncertainty avoidance prefer much more highly defined assignments and tasks and do not like too much freedom when working.

Masculinity–femininity

This dimension is said to reflect achievement versus the emphasis on relationships and interpersonal communication in the classroom. It also has an impact on gender relationships and expectations within the classroom.

Confucius dynamism

This dimension is said to affect long- and short-term orientation and the issue of saving face. Certainly in the context of behaviour management and homework it is important to consider how issues are dealt with in order to avoid embarrassing anyone (Hofstede 1997, 2001).

There are a number of other theorists whose work has implications when teaching and learning cross-culturally. A relevant consideration related to face-saving is Spencer-Oatey's (2000) work on politeness theory. Hall's work on matters of time (monochromic versus polychronic) can impact the classroom and work deadlines and the issue of high and low context cultures can also have implications for the classroom and how much information is given/needed by the teacher/student (Hall 1976, 1981, 1984). Much of Trompenaars' and Hampden-Turner's (1997) work has similar dimensions to that of Hofstede (1997). Consideration of whether students are intrinsically or extrinsically motivated is relevant for teachers (Samovar *et al.* 2007) when considering motivating students to learn. Teachers often rely on their own beliefs and previous professional experience about how students are motivated and past practice may not always be relevant in the international school. Nisbett (2005) argues that how people interpret the world and what they see can be attributed to Aristotle or Confucius. He sees a binary divide in terms of perception, between analytical and holistic ways of seeing.

This is not a comprehensive list but it does raise awareness of the many and subtle ways in which teachers can reflect on their own cultural assumptions and what they might bring to the classroom. Smith *et al.* (2006) present a summary of most cross-cultural research in the area of social psychology that is of relevance to the international school classroom. Certainly, the detail they present shows how complex conducting cross-cultural research is. Looking to the future, both Munro (2007) and Tsolidis (2002) anticipate the impact of globalisation and its impact on cultural fluidity where it will be increasingly difficult to categorise and analyse intercultural encounters. Also, it is important to realise that personality differences can play a part. In any culture there are students with high uncertainty avoidance when it comes to work assignments. There are introverts and extraverts in any culture. Everything therefore must not be attributed to culture or there will be fundamental attribution error (Ross 1977).

Another area related to the impact of culture, is of course the nature of 'culture shock' (Ward *et al.* 2001). This is relevant to both the teacher and the student. How new a person is to a culture and how comfortable in the new setting will inevitably impact on his or her perceptions and actions in the situation. Culture shock has been well documented, with its various stages (Pollock and Van Reken 2001; Ward *et al.* 2001). Heyward (2002) assesses the implications of culture shock with specific reference to the international school context. There is other literature on cross-cultural transition focused on the international school context (Langford *et al.* 2002; Ezra 2003; Mclachlan 2007). These all indicate that the psychological effects of being in a new setting (whether school or country) will affect the behaviour, attitudes and sense of well-being of the person involved.

One area that is beyond the remit of this chapter is of course the issue of second-language learning and the fact that many students in international schools are learning English as an additional language. This, in itself, has huge implications in terms of how teachers treat such students. Are they judged according to a deficit model (Sears 1998; Murphy 2003)? What of contrastive-rhetoric and the Sapir–Whorf theory that the students' view of the world and thinking are shaped by their first language (Sapir 1958)? This is yet another dimension that brings its own influence to the teaching and learning that takes place in international schools and needs further consideration (Murphy 1990, 2003; Baker 2006; Carder 2007).

There are various researchers and practitioners in the international school arena who are highlighting the particular challenge of language learning in the international school (Sears 1998; Kusuma-Powell 2004; Carder 2007) as well as the important work in the United States by Thomas and Collier (2002) which has drawn attention to policy and successful practice in the teaching and learning of bilingual learners.

Students

Naturally, children are also key stakeholders involved in the learning at international schools. It is here that the problem of the essentialist/non-essentialist approach rears its head again. One way of describing the children who attend international schools is as third culture kids or global nomads (McCaig 1996; Langford 1998; Pollock and Van Reken 2001). A third culture kid (TCK) is

> an individual, who, having spent a significant part of the developmental years in a culture other than the parents' passport culture, develops a sense

of relationship to all of the cultures while not having full ownership in any. Elements from each culture are incorporated into the life experience, but the sense of belonging is in relationship to others of similar experience.

(Pollock and Van Reken 2001)

Pollock and Van Reken (2001) develop a comprehensive profile describing and illustrating their different characteristics. Although this form of categorisation could be argued as essentialist, as it seeks to establish a list of characteristics of these children, it is also extremely helpful in recognising how these children are different from their peers who may have never lived abroad. One of the key characteristics of these children is their adaptability. They behave one way at home and another way at school. They speak one language at home and another at school. This interpretive way of looking at how we all behave and adapt to many different social settings is perhaps just more accentuated in their cases. What are some of the other benefits that may be a product of their opportunity to live outside their home country and attend an international school? They are seen to have a more international world view, often speak more than one language, have cross-cultural skills, and are more confident (Langford 1998; Gerner *et al.* 1992; Pollock and Van Reken 2001). It is what Balagangadhara (1994) would describe as having different meta-learning skills at their disposal. They have been exposed to more than one way of doing something and have learned more than one way of doing something, be it speaking or learning, and as a result they have a wider choice in selecting a skill or type of behaviour for a particular occasion. It should be pointed out that whereas 'cosmopolitanism' is seen as a term to describe people who successfully integrate and conduct themselves in different languages and different cultures (Gunesch 2004) it is often assumed that the TCK does the same. What is not really addressed in the literature is the process of 'becoming' a TCK. The phase of not having the language at one's disposal, being new and different, not having the relevant cross-cultural skills, is often overlooked. Pearce (1998) has looked at the various 'validators' in the lives of these children and how important they are in the adjustment process. He sees the 'validators' as being critical to the identity development of these individual international schoolchildren. To be fair, the literature does document the 'challenges' of such a childhood; the complex issue of cultural identity and belonging (Pearce 1998; Pollock and Van Reken 2001; Fail 2002, Fail *et al.* 2004, 2007) and dealing with frequent and massive change. Although my own research has focused on the long-term outcomes of such a childhood (Fail 1995, 1996, 2002, 2007; Fail *et al.* 2004) it is helpful to realise that as children develop through their school careers, they are 'becoming' and therefore do not necessarily have all the 'benefits' at their disposal. Bennett (1993) does look at the response of students towards the experience of being marginal in repeatedly new environments. Although she concludes that they may either use their marginality in a positive way (constructively) or in a negative way (encapsulated) (Bennett 1993), it is important to consider what goes on in the international school context that might generate a positive rather than a negative outcome. Hence, the literature does deal with the impact of repeated transitions in the lives of these young people and their ability to cope with frequent change. International schools are usually environments with high turnover of both staff and students. This, by itself, presents its own challenges and impact that have been documented in the literature (Langford 1998; Pollock and Van Reken 2001; Ezra 2003; Mclachlan 2007).

So what can we conclude about the students? They are learning how to learn. Their teachers may have different expectations and behaviours from the teachers at their previous school (wherever it was) and they adapt and learn how to behave in this new situation. They are learning how to learn in this new situation, they are adapting to the new 'culture', which is the international school (Van Oord 2005). One interesting phenomenon documented and researched by Deveney (2005, 2007) is what happens when students do not leave their home country but whose parents send them to an international school. In her situation, the majority of the students were from Thailand. They are described as being passive learners who do not speak/engage in class. Here again Hofstede's (2001) categorisation of high power distance/collectivist countries with high uncertainty avoidance, tempts the reader and researcher to assume that all the students behave in the same way because they are Thai. However, what this situation does draw attention to, is that when there is a large group of students from the host culture and the teacher is from another country, both groups have to adjust and adapt to each other. The teacher needs to try different strategies to engage the students and facilitate learning. The students gradually learn what makes the teacher happy. It is important for the growth of the student and the teacher not to reduce people to a stereotype (Hinton 2000). It is imperative though, to recognise differences and accommodate them.

Parents

It is relevant to consider parents as stakeholders even though they are not directly involved in the teaching and learning in school. They still have expectations in terms of what goes on in international schools linked to their reasons for choosing the school in the first place. Why have they enrolled their children in these schools and what outcomes are they expecting?

This certainly is an under-researched area and what has been done suggests that the parents fall into certain categories. Hayden (2006) draws attention to the fact that some parents deliberately choose the school and some parents have no choice if they want an English-speaking education for their children. It must be remembered that international schools are mainly private schools and therefore they are attracting customers (the parents) from a certain socio-economic group (Mejia, 2002). Although in certain countries there may be associated assumptions about class and status, this is not always the case in international schools. When families are relocated overseas, there may be subsidy and sponsorship of school fees not available in the home country. One exception, of course, is the United World Colleges. Their students are usually on bursaries based on academic ability and nationality. As there are not usually schools available from the national country, parents are frequently buying into an English language education (MacKenzie *et al.* 2001, 2003; Potter and Hayden 2004). For families who relocate internationally regularly, continuity of language and curriculum are an advantage. It would not be beneficial to send children to the local school if it involved changing languages and education systems every two or three years. Surveys done on parents at international schools suggest that fluency in English is seen as the driving factor. This may be for future economic or career advantage (Ezra 2007). Whether parents choose British/American schools may depend on their own background and whether they foresee higher education spent in one of those countries. Certainly fluency in English is seen as a major factor (MacKenzie *et al.* 2001, 2003; Potter and Hayden 2004; Hayden 2006) in research that has been done into why parents send their children to particular schools. What many parents may not realise is that their children are not just learning a language but are being affected by a world view and particular values (Pasternak 1998; Stobie 2007). These may often affect their children in ways that they had not anticipated. This may not be obvious until the family returns to the home country. This area has been particularly investigated in relation to Japanese students returning to Japan (Goodman 1990; Willis *et al.* 1994; Fry 2007). If teachers are teaching their students to question everything they read or hear, then there may be very real problems for parents who take their children home to countries where this is not part of their learning culture. Perhaps the problem is more challenging for students at the higher education level who have been schooled in one tradition (Balagangadhara 1994) and then travel overseas for postgraduate study. Here the notion of critical reading and writing can be at odds with the notion of increasing knowledge.

Curriculum

Although we have looked at various 'ingredients' – the type of international school, a way of looking at the 'culture' of the school, and the various stakeholders involved in the school (teachers, students and parents) and their expectations – there is one final key ingredient. A not-yet-mentioned critical component is the curriculum offered by the school. This can be both the explicit and the hidden curriculum (Thompson 1998). In the same way that there are many types of international schools, there are also a variety of curricula. Some schools offer their national curriculum (indeed 'British' international schools are obliged to offer their national curriculum and also provide a British ethos). American schools also offer similar curricula to the United States including of course American history and their Advanced Placement tests. Although both the US and the UK do offer 'international' examinations or international equivalents, they are necessarily preparing students for higher education in their own national system.

Over the years, the high mobility of children moving from school to school led to the conclusion that an international curriculum would be of great advantage to students for a variety of reasons. One would have the ability to relocate and pick up the same curriculum in another country and another major rationale was the need to develop an international qualification that would act as a university entrance qualification for a variety of countries (Fox 1998; Hill 2002, 2006a, 2006b; Walker 2004). Alongside the practical and utilitarian issues was the ideological vision of creating world-citizens who would work towards world peace (Hill 2002). A key issue in developing an international curriculum, of course, was what to include in it. Indeed one of the *International Schools Journal* (ISJ) compendia on international schools (Murphy 2004) focuses on the problematic nature of which history to teach (Ainger 2004). In the same way that an essentialist view of culture reduces culture to readily identifiable and observable characteristics, it is tempting to do the same with an international curriculum. The history of the International Baccalaureate Organisation can be traced, with its dual aims of practicality and ideology (Drennen 2002). Historically, the IBO wanted its curriculum to be of practical use to students and to influence their values and goals. It is explicit in expressing its ideological goal to create world citizens who care not only about their own country but also about others from around the world (Hill 2002; Hayden 2006). There are various criticisms aimed at it. It is claimed that it presents a Westernised humanistic view of the world (Paris 2003), but it is at least attempting through its theory of knowledge course, to introduce students to other ways of seeing the world. Bearing in mind that it is impossible for any curriculum to be value-free (Stobie 2007) one returns to the problematic nature of whose values are being transmitted either overtly or implicitly via the International Baccalaureate diploma? Munro (2007) would question how international the learning outcomes are because of the cultural background of the students. Thus at every stage (teacher/learner/context/curriculum) there is a complex and problematic interface.

The temptation is to simplify and explain differing world views and ways of learning by categorising in neat boxes, for example 'This student has behaved in this way because he is from a collectivist country'. Although such ideas may be helpful in analysing different cultural views of learning, it is important not to have a reductionist view that simplifies and may make erroneous judgements. The challenge of the third culture kid is that he or she no longer can be said to represent the 'home culture' but is a person who can make choices about which skills to draw on in a variety of contexts. The international schoolteacher needs an enlarged frame of reference that embraces and recognises many different viewpoints as valid.

Conclusions

So what can we conclude? Nothing is straightforward! There are different ingredients in the cake. Although the basic ingredients for the recipe might be the same (teachers, students, curriculum), the amount and the type and source of the ingredients will lead to a very different outcome in each situation. In international schools, teachers and students are learning from each other. Good teachers are on a particularly steep learning curve if they are sensitive to their context, their students and if they desire to become better teachers. We are all lifelong learners. We do not want the simplistic answers that reduce our students to representatives of a nation. We want to learn from each other. We want to find out whether there are better ways of doing things. Is our view of how students learn applicable in every situation? If teachers have a student-centred approach and want to adjust their teaching to the individuals in the class (going back to Rousseau 1762), this is particularly relevant for the international school context. It is important not to make assumptions. It is important not to teach the same thing in the same way. The more research carried out in the international school context, the more teachers realise that the situation is complex and there is no easy formula. How can one measure the outcomes of an international school? What do the mission statements reveal? What do the grades and results say about the teaching and learning that has been going on in the school? Are the students measured by their linguistic ability, their long-term success? One thing for sure, is that it is hard to measure what is going on in the schools. Various accreditation teams may assess by describing the statistics and recording a narrative from the school, but an international school is an incredibly diverse place. Do not be tempted to stereotype. Embrace the complexity and enjoy the challenge of teaching and learning in international schools.

References

Ainger, H. (2004) (originally published in 1992) Thinking about multicultural history: an anthropological perspective. In E. Murphy (ed.) *The International Schools Journal Compendium. Vol. 3: The International School Classroom: Adapting Lessons for a Culturally Diverse Student Body*, Saxmundham: John Catt Educational, pp. 88–94.

Allan, M. (2003) Frontier crossings: cultural dissonance, intercultural learning and the multicultural personality, *Journal of Research in International Education* 2(1): 83–110.

Baker, C. (2006) *Foundations of Bilingual Education and Bilingualism* (4th edn), Clevedon: Multilingual Matters.

Balagangadhara, S. N. (1994) *The Heathen in His Blindness: Asia, the West and the Dynamic of Religion*, Leiden: E. J. Brill.

Bartlett, K. (1992) Defining international education: a proposal for the future, *International Schools Journal* Spring 23: 45–52.

Bennett, J. M. (1993) Cultural marginality: identity issues in intercultural training. In R. M. Paige (ed.) *Education for the Intercultural Experience*, Yarmouth, ME: Intercultural Press, pp. 109–35.

Blackburn, R. (1989) An interview with Robert Blackburn, Deputy Director of IBO London, 25 Sept 1989. In P. L. Jonietz and D. Harris (1991) (eds) *International Schools and International Education: World Yearbook of Education*, London: Kogan Page, pp. 217–23.

Bloom, B. and Krathwohl, D. (1956) *Taxonomy of Educational Objectives: The Classification of Educational Goals, by a Committee of College and University Examiners. Handbooks 1 to 3: The Cognitive, Affective and Psychomotor Domain,* New York: Longmans Green.

Brislin, R. (2000) *Understanding Culture's Influence on Behaviour* (2nd edn), TX, USA: Harcourt Inc.

Brown, R. (2002) Cultural dimensions of national and international educational assessment. In M. Hayden, J. Thompson and G. Walker (eds) *International Education in Practice: Dimensions for Schools and International Schools*, London: Kogan Page, pp. 66–79.

Carder, M. (2007) *Bilingualism in International Schools: A Model for enriching Language Education*, Clevedon: Multilingual Matters.

Clarke, V. (2004) Students' global awareness and attitudes to internationalism in a world of cultural convergence, *Journal of Research in International Education* 3(1): 51–70.

Deveney, B. (2005) An investigation into aspects of Thai culture and its impact on Thai students in an international school in Thailand, *Journal of Research in International Education* 4(2): 153–71.

Deveney, B. (2007) How well-prepared do international school teachers believe themselves to be for teaching in culturally diverse classrooms? *Journal of Research in International Education* 6(3): 309–32.

Drennen, H. (2002) Criteria for curriculum continuity in international education. In M. Hayden, J. Thompson and G. Walker (eds) *International Education in Practice: Dimensions for National and International Schools*, London: Kogan Page, pp. 55–65.

Duckworth, R. L., Levy, L. W. and Levy, J. (2005) Present and future teachers of the world's children: how internationally-minded are they? *Journal of Research in International Education* 4(3): 279–311.

Ellwood, C. and Davis, M. (1991) An international curriculum for the middle school years, *International Schools Journal* Spring 27: 47–55.

Ezra, R. (2003) Culture, language and personality in the context of the internationally mobile child, *Journal of Research in International Education* 2(2): 123–49.

Ezra, R. (2007) Caught between cultures: a study of factors influencing Israeli parents' decisions to enrol their children at an international school, *Journal of Research in International Education* 6(3): 259–86.

Fail, H. (1995) Some of the outcomes of international schooling. MA dissertation, Oxford Brookes University.

Fail, H. (1996) Whatever becomes of international school students? *International Schools Journal* XV(2): 31–6.

Fail, H. (2000) The spectre of prejudice, *IS International School – ECIS Magazine* 2(3): 9.

Fail, H. (2002) The life histories of a group of former international school students. Ph.D. Thesis, University of Bath.

Fail, H. (2007) The potential of the past in practice: life histories of former international school students. In M. Hayden, J. Thompson, and J. Levy (eds) *Handbook of Research in International Education*, London: Sage, pp. 103–12.

Fail, H., Thompson, J. and Walker, G. (2004) Belonging, identity and third culture kids: life histories of former international school students, *Journal of Research in International Education* 3(3): 319–38.

Fennes, H. and Hapgood, K. (1997) *Intercultural Learning in the Classroom*, London: Cassell.

Fox, E. (1998) The emergence of the International Baccalaureate as an impetus for curriculum reform. In M. Hayden and J. Thompson (eds) *International Education: Principles and Practice*, London: Kogan Page, pp. 65–76.

Fry, R. (2007) Perspective shifts and a theoretical model relating to kaigaishijo and kikukushijo, or third culture kids in a Japanese context, *Journal of Research in International Education* 6(2): 131–50.

Geertz, C. (1993) *The Interpretation of Culture*, London: Fontana Press.

Gerner, M., Perry, F., Moselle, M. A. and Archibold, M. (1992) Characteristics of Internationally Mobile Adolescents, *Journal of School Psychology* 30: 197–214.

Goodman, R. (1990) *Japan's 'International Youth': The Emergence of a New Class of School-children*, Oxford: Clarendon Press.

Gunesch, K. (2004) Education for cosmopolitanism: cosmopolitanism as a personal cultural identity model for and within international education, *Journal of Research in International Education* 3(3): 251–75.

Hall, E. T. (1976) *Beyond Culture*, New York: Anchor Press.

Hall, E. T. (1981) *The Silent Language* (2nd edn), New York: Anchor, Doubleday.

Hall, E. T. (1984) *The Dance of Life: The Other Dimension of Time*, New York: Anchor, Doubleday.

Hayden, M. (2006) *Introduction to International Education*, London: Paul Chapman.

Heyward, M. (2002) From international to intercultural: redefining the international school for a globalized world, *Journal of Research in International Education* 1(1): 9–32.

Hill, I. (2002) The history of international education: an International Baccalaureate perspective. In M. Hayden, J. Thompson and G. Walker (eds) *International Education in Practice: Dimensions for Schools and International Schools*, London: Kogan Page, pp. 18–29.

Hill, I. (2006a) Student types, school types and their combined influence on the development of intercultural understanding, *Journal of Research in International Education* 5(1): 5–33.

Hill, I (2006b) Do International Baccalaureate programs internationalise or globalise? *International Education Journal* 7(1): 98–108.

Hinton, P. R. (2000) *Stereotypes, Cognition and Culture*, East Hove: Psychology Press.

Hofstede, G. (1997) *Cultures and Organizations: Software of the Mind*, London: McGraw.

Hofstede, G. (2001) *Culture's Consequences: Comparing Values, Behaviours, Institutions and Organizations Across Nations* (2nd edn), Thousand Oaks, CA: Sage Publications.

Holliday, A. (1999) Culture as constraint or resource: essentialist versus non-essentialist views, *IATEFL Language and Cultural Studies SIG Newsletter Issue* 18: 38–40.

Inglehart, R. (2006) *Inglehart-Wezel Cultural Map of the World* from the World Values Survey website, online at: www.worldvaluessurvey.org/ (accessed on 9 Sept 2008).

Inglis, D. (2005) *Culture and Everyday Life*, Abingdon: Routledge.

Jonietz, P. L. and Harris, D. (eds) (1991) *World Yearbook of Education: International Schools and International Education,* London: Kogan Page.

Jordan, A., Carlile, O. and Stack, A. (2008) *Approaches to Learning: A Guide for Teacher*, Glasgow: Open University Press.

Kohls, L. R. and Knight, J. M. (1994) *Intercultural Awareness: A Cross-Cultural Training Handbook* (2nd edn), Maine: Intercultural Press.

Kotrc, P. (1994) International schools – shared values? the role of schools philosophies in international schools. MA Dissertation: Oxford Brookes University.

Krober, A. L. and Kluckhohn, C. (1952) *Culture: A Critical review of Concepts and Definitions*, Cambridge, MA: Harvard University Press.

Kusuma-Powell, O. (2004) Multilingual, but not making it in international schools, *Journal of Research in International Education* 3(2): 157–72.

Langford, M. (1998) Global nomads, third culture kids and international schools. In M. Hayden and J. Thompson (eds) *International Education: Principles and Practice,* London: Kogan Page, pp. 28–43.

Langford, M., Pearce, R., Rader, R., Sears, C. (2002) *The Essential Guide for Teachers in International Schools,* Saxmundham: John Catt Educational Ltd.

Leach, R. (1969) *International Schools and their Role in the Field of International Education,* Oxford: Pergamon Press.

Lee, W. O. (2001) Moral perspectives on values, culture and education. In R. Gardner, J. Cairns and D. Lawton (eds) *World Yearbook 2001: Values, Culture and Education,* London: Kogan Page, pp. 27–45.

McCaig, N. M. (1996) Understanding global nomads. In C. D. Smith (ed.) *Strangers at Home: Essays on the Effects of Living Overseas and Coming 'Home' to a Strange Land,* New York: Aletheia, pp. 99–120.

Mackenzie, P., Hayden, M. and Thompson, J. (2001) The third constituency: parents in international schools, *International Schools Journal* 20(2): 57–63.

Mackenzie, P., Hayden, M. and Thompson, J. (2003) Parental priorities in the selection of international schools, *Oxford Review of Education* 29(3): 299–314.

Mattern, G. (1990) The best of times, the worst of times – and what to do about it on Monday morning, *International Schools Journal* Spring 19: 35–47.

Matthews, M. (1988) The ethos of international schools. MSc Dissertation, University of Oxford.

Mclachlan, D. A. (2007) Global nomads in an international school: families in transition, *Journal of Research in International Education* 6(2): 233–49.

Mead, M. (ed.) (1951) *Cultural Patterns and Technical Change,* Paris: UNESCO.

Mejia, A. M. de (2002) *Power, Prestige and Bilingualism: International Perspectives on Elite Bilingual Education,* Clevedon: Multilingual Matters.

Moscovici, S. (1981) On social representation. In J. P. Forgas (ed.) *Social Cognition: Perspectives on Everyday Life,* London: Academic Press, pp. 181–209.

Munro, J. (2007) Learning internationally in a future context. In M. Hayden, J. Thompson and J. Levy (eds) *Handbook of Research in International Education,* London: Sage, pp. 113–27.

Murphy, E. (ed.) (1990) *ESL: A Handbook for Teachers and Administrators in International Schools,* Clevedon: Multilingual Matters.

Murphy, E. (ed.) (2003) *The ISJ Compendium Vol 1. ESL: Educating Non-Native Speakers of English in an English-Speaking Medium,* Suffolk: Peridot Press Publications.

Murphy, E. (ed.) (2004) *The International Schools Journal Compendium. Vol. 3: The International School Classroom: Adapting Lessons for a Culturally Diverse Student Body,* Saxmundham: John Catt Educational.

Nisbett, R. E. (2005) *The Geography of Thought,* London: Nicholas Brealey Publishing.

Paris, P. (2003) The International Baccalaureate: A case study on why students choose to do the IB, *International Education Journal* 3(2): 232–43.

Pasternak, M. (1998) Is international education a pipedream? A question of values. In M. Hayden and J. Thompson (eds) *International Education: Principles and Practice,* London: Kogan Page.

Pearce, R. (1994) International schools: the multinational enterprises' best friends, *Relocation News* 32 October: 8.

Pearce, R. (1998) Developing cultural identity in an international school. In M. Hayden and J. Thompson (eds) *International Education: Principles and Practice*, London: Kogan Page, pp. 44–62.

Peterson, A. D. C. (1987) *Schools Across Frontiers*, La Salle, IL: Open Court.

Pollock, D. C. and Van Reken, R. E. (2001) *Third Culture Kids: The Experience of Growing Up Among Worlds*, Yarmouth: Nicholas Brealey/Intercultural Press.

Ponisch, A. (1987) Special needs and the International Baccalaureate. MSc Dissertation, Oxford University Department of Educational Studies.

Potter, D. and Hayden, M. (2004) Parental choice in the Buenos Aires bilingual school market, *Journal of Research in International Education* 3(1): 87–111.

Robottom, I. and Norhaidah, S. (2008) Western science and Islamic learners: when disciplines and culture intersect, *Journal of Research in International Education* 7(2): 148–63.

Ross, I. (1977) The intuitive psychologist and his shortcomings: distortion in the attribution process. In L. Berkowitz (ed.) *Advances in Experimental Social Psychology*, *Vol. 10*, New York: Academic Press, pp. 173–220.

Rousseau, J. (1762/1991) *Emile or On Education*, Allan Bloome (ed.) London: Penguin.

Samovar L., Porter, R. and McDaniel, E. (2007) *Communication between Cultures* (6th edn), Belmont, CA: Wadsworth/Thomson Learning.

Sapir, E. (1958) *Culture, Language and Personality* (ed. D. G. Mandelbaum), Berkeley: University of California Press.

Schwartz, S. H. (1997) Values and culture. In D. Munro, S. Carr and J. Schumaker (eds) *Motivation and Culture*, New York: Routledge, pp. 69–84.

Sears, C. (1998) *Second Language Students in Mainstream Classrooms*, Clevedon: Multilingual Matters.

Skinner, B. F. (1969) *Contingencies of Reinforcement: A Theoretical Analysis*, Englewood Cliffs: Prentice-Hall.

Smith, P. B., Bond, M. H. and Kağitçibaşi, Ç. (2006) *Understanding Social Psychology across Cultures: Living and Working in a Changing World* (3rd rev. edn), London: Sage.

Snowball, L. (2007) Becoming more internationally-minded: international teacher certification and professional development. In M. Hayden, J. Thompson and J. Levy, (eds) *Handbook of Research in International Education*, London: Sage, pp. 247–55.

Spencer-Oatey, H. (2000) *Culturally Speaking: Managing Rapport through Talk across Cultures*, London: Continuum.

Sternberg, R. J. (1999) *Cognitive Psychology* (2nd edn), Orlando: Harcourt Brace College Publishers.

Stobie, T. (2007) Coherence and consistency in international curricula: a study of the International Baccalaureate diploma and middle years programme. In M. Hayden, J. Thompson and J. Levy (eds) *Handbook of Research in International Education*, London: Sage, pp. 140–51.

Tao, L., Yuan, H., Zuo, L., Qian, G. and Murray, B. (2006) Teacher expectations of student reading in middle and high schools : A Chinese perspective, *Journal of Research in International Education* 5(3): 269–99.

Terwilliger, R. I. (1972) International schools – cultural crossroads, *The Educational Forum* XXXVI(3): 359–63.

Thomas, W. P. and Collier, V. P. (2002) *A National Study of School Effectiveness for Language Minority Students' Long-Term Academic Achievement*, Santa Cruz, CA: Center for Research on Education, Diversity and Excellence, University of California-Santa Cruz.

Thompson, J. J. (1998) Towards a model for international education. In M. Hayden and J. J. Thompson (eds) *International Education: Principles and Practice*, London: Kogan Page, pp. 276–90.

Tsolidis, G. (2002) How do we teach and learn in times when the notion of 'global citizenship' sounds like a cliché? *Journal of Research in International Education* 1(2): 213–26.

Trompenaars, F. and Hampden-Turner, C. M. (1997) *Riding the Waves of Culture* (2nd edn), London: Nicholas Brealey.

Useem, J., Donoghue, J. D. and Useem, R. H. (1963) *Human Organizations*, Englewood Cliffs: Prentice Hall.

Van Oord, L. (2005) Culture as a configuration of learning: hypotheses in the context of international education, *Journal of Research in International Education* 4(2): 173–91.

Van Oord, L. (2008) After culture: intergroup encounters in education, *Journal of Research in International Education* 7(2): 131–47.

Van Oord , L. and den Brok, B. (2004) The international teacher: students' and teachers' perceptions of preferred teacher–student interpersonal behaviour in two united world colleges, *Journal of Research in International Education* 3(2): 131–55.

Vygotsky, L. (1986) *Thought and Language*, Cambridge, MA: MIT Press.

Walker, G. (2004) *To Educate the Nations: Reflections on an International Education*, Saxmundham: John Catt Educational Ltd.

Ward, C. A., Bochner, S. and Furnham, A. (2001) *The Psychology of Culture Shock* (2nd edn), Hove: Routledge.

Willis, D. B., Enloe, W. M. and Minoura, Y. (1994) Transculturals, transnationals: the new diaspora, *International Schools Journal* XIV(1): 29–42.

7   International curriculum

James Cambridge

What should be the focus of inquiry in the study of 'international curriculum'? It would seem logical to break up the discussion into two parts, by first addressing the question 'What is the curriculum?' and then by considering the question 'What is the international context for implementation of the curriculum?' One response to the former question would be to propose that the curriculum consists of what is taught or learned in school. This is to argue that the curriculum comprises school subjects such as science, mathematics, languages and so on. From this perspective, the curriculum refers to knowledge and its acquisition by the learner. However, such a view may be criticised as being simplistic because it may also be argued that curriculum refers not only to *what* is taught or learned but *how* it is taught or learned. Such considerations point to the need to think about theories relating to the nature of knowledge and the nature of learning. Do the subjects in the curriculum stand apart from each other, or are there linkages and interconnections between them? There is also the need for a sociological approach to curriculum if it is assumed that learning constitutes a shared, social activity. Furthermore, theories about the curriculum are likely to be influenced by ideas concerning the aims and purposes of education and schooling. What is school for? Is it to socialise the child? To reproduce national or societal culture? To transmit specific knowledge and skills? To prepare the learner for higher education or paid employment? Or is it to inculcate a love of learning and to encourage the individual to develop as a lifelong learner? Such arguments are made more complex by the implementation of a curriculum in an international context. For example, to what extent is knowledge universal and common across all cultures, or are certain aspects of knowledge particular to specific cultures? How should knowledge be selected for inclusion in the curriculum? By what criteria should that selection be made? If it is acknowledged that important purposes of schooling include the socialisation of the child and the reproduction of culture, then it needs to be clear *whose* culture has been identified as worthy of reproduction, and on what grounds. Hence, the study of 'international curriculum' requires a critical perspective that questions not only the decisions that are made about selection and implementation, but also questions the assumptions underlying those decisions.

This chapter will review a variety of approaches to inquiry into curriculum. It will not be possible to give an exhaustive account in the restricted space allocated here. However, it is intended that the arguments presented will acquaint the readers with theory such that they will be able to evaluate critically examples of curriculum development and implementation drawn from their own school contexts and experience.

The content of this article will be presented in three parts, moving from the general to the particular. There will be a progressive focus on curriculum issues starting with a discussion of how curriculum issues may be theorised, then looking at aspects of international curriculum, and leading on to an account of grouped baccalaureate-type qualifications and continuity between pro-grammes for different age groups of learners. In conclusion, there will be a summary discussion that draws the various lines of argument together.

Theorising curriculum

What is education for? Three alternative goals have been identified for education comprising democratic equality (schools should focus on preparing citizens), social efficiency (they should focus on training workers), and social mobility (they should prepare individuals to compete for social positions) (Labaree 1997). These goals represent the educational perspectives of the citizen, the taxpayer, and the consumer respectively. Whereas the first two goals look on education as a public good, the third goal sees it as a private good. It is evident that these contrasting goals will have a profound impact on curriculum design and development, each with a particular focus. For example, it may be expected that education for democratic equality will attempt to give equal entitlement and access to the same curriculum for all, whereas education for social efficiency will concentrate on narrow vocationalism and the acquisition of specific skills. The goal of education for positional com-petition is likely to produce a curriculum that strongly differentiates between categories of learners through mechanisms identified with selection, streaming and tracking, according to context or location.

Schubert (2008) identifies a variety of 'contemporary venues of curriculum inquiry' including:

- intended curriculum, which specifies explicit goals to shape outlooks and capacities;
- taught curriculum, which specifies the curriculum as it is implemented – or recreated – in school.
- experienced curriculum, consisting of the thoughts, meanings and feelings of students as they encounter the curriculum;
- embodied curriculum, which constitutes 'a reading and writing of the self in relation with the world' (Schubert 2008: 409);
- hidden curriculum, consisting of that which is learned in school but not specified in the official curriculum;

- tested curriculum, consisting of that which is subject to educational assessment. This embodies the view of school as a sorting mechanism. 'Testing is the universal joint in that machine, having been critiqued as measured lies, official knowledge, standardized mandates, and contradictions' (Schubert 2008: 410);
- null curriculum, consisting of that which is not subject to educational assessment. However, non-assessed subjects become non-subjects because 'commodification of curriculum in tests and state standards makes topics not represented on tests seem unnecessary . . . This term refers to that which is minimised or excluded due to priority and budget . . . Policy-makers (state, federal, and corporate) buy test scores as the "profit margin" indicator of curricular success' (Schubert 2008: 410);
- outside curriculum, consisting of the wider domain of curriculum to be encountered in contexts beyond school, including 'homes, families, peer groups, mass media (e.g. the Web, videogames, television, movies), and non-school organizations (e.g. church, sports, music, dance, museum, gangs, scouts, workplaces)' (Schubert 2008: 410). However, Schubert points out that 'just as school curriculum has intended, taught, embodied, hidden, tested, and null dimensions, so do curricula outside of school'.

Schubert (2008) identifies four approaches to curriculum inquiry comprising empirical-analytic, hermeneutic, critical and postmodern approaches.

- Empirical-analytic inquiry serves technical interests (e.g. designing instructional materials, developing a curriculum, testing for results) and requires the social organization of workplace hierarchies to accomplish its tasks of production and accountability for predicted outcomes (as done in industry, business, corporate planning, and technology). Key dimensions of its mode of rationality assume that success rests on achievement of control and relative certainty and that law-like propositions exist and can be applied and tested. Empirical-analytic rationality fits the dominant press in schools to demonstrate accomplishment of standards by meeting goals as revealed on standardised tests. This assumes that standards of knowledge, skill, and disposition can be defined objectively and that items on tests credibly indicate the extent to which the standards have been met (Schubert 2008: 400).
- Hermeneutic inquiry originates in the Judaic tradition of text interpretation, wherein subsequent generations of scholars (before the printing press) wrote interpretive commentary on religious texts. Metaphorically, text (in phenomenological literature) can be any idea or event that is transformed by exchange of ideas over time. Or a text can be perspectives embodied within persons, continuously transformed via interpersonal encounter. Thus, the interest served is practical – that is, deriving situational meaning and insight that improves decision and action in actual

states of affairs. The social organization of hermeneutic inquiry is interaction among persons and situations. The mode of rationality acknowledges humans as subjective beings who construct understandings through
intersubjective relationships. Such understandings can reveal insight
beneath the flurry of everyday life by attending carefully to meanings
embedded in metaphors (Schubert 2008: 400).

- Critical inquiry serves emancipatory interests, assuming that inequities
  pervade social life shaped to benefit dominant groups. While critical
  theorists respect the hermeneutic or practical ideal of interaction, dialogue,
  or deliberation as genuine communication without hierarchy, they assert
  that such an ideal cannot occur in contemporary society unless the social
  organization overcomes hierarchies of race, class, gender, ethnicity, appearance, language, nationality, sexuality, reputation, religion or belief, place,
  membership, and other sources of inequity. Critical inquiry problematizes
  and challenges assumptions situated in prevailing practices through *praxis*
  (critical inquiry embodied in action) aimed to overcome false consciousness, repression, and oppression by dominant ideologies (Schubert 2008:
  400–1).

- Postmodern inquiry decries master narratives, condemning the empirical-
  analytic, hermeneutic and critical as such. The interest served is deconstruction, the delineation and interrogation of multiple meanings. It
  involves listening to many narratives, voices appreciated as worth hearing
  in any phenomenon studied. The social organization is the signifier (or
  symbol). Deconstruction assumes that relationships between the signifier
  and that which is signified (i.e. meaning) are unstable. Further, the
  signifieds (attributes signified) are actually signifiers that move in and out
  of relationships. Thus inquiry becomes a reading of the world as multiple
  texts, deconstructing texts, and reflecting on and relating to meanings of
  floating signifiers (Schubert 2008: 401).

Scott (2008) reviews the history of curriculum development in terms of a series
of contrasting curriculum episodes. He proposes that seven such episodes may
be identified, comprising scientific curriculum-making, intrinsic worthwhile
knowledge, innovative pedagogical experimentation, socio-cultural learning,
critical pedagogy, instrumentalism, and school effectiveness/school improvement.

Scientific curriculum-making refers to the specification of behavioural
objectives for learning advocated by theorists such as Franklin Bobbitt and
Ralph Tyler. That is to say,

> curriculum-making was understood as a linear process which starts with
> the development of clear objectives or goals, proceeds to the selection of
> content which is specified in behavioural terms – that is, its acquisition

must be an observable and testable process – and finishes with the evaluation of that process to see if those objectives have been met.

(Scott 2008: 7)

Curriculum development from this perspective may be termed 'scientific' because

> using this approach, we tackle curriculum development as a *problem-solving* exercise. We follow steps not unlike those of the scientist who begins by identifying a problem, then comes up with a hypothesis to solve it or explain it, and who finally performs some test or experiment that allows him [sic] either to accept that hypothesis or else reject it in favour of an alternative which he then puts to the test in the same way.
>
> (Rowntree 1982: 8, italics in original)

The behavioural objectives approach to curriculum development may be criticised in a variety of ways. For example, it may be argued that learning is trivialised by concentrating on those behaviours that are testable (Stenhouse 1975). In this way, there is a danger of assuming that if something cannot be measured, then it cannot be assessed and therefore should not be part of the learning process. Furthermore, the linear design model adopted by this approach in theory may be unrelated to the ways in which learners learn in practice. Nevertheless, elements of this theory of curriculum development may be found inscribed in the assessment policy of an international curriculum such as the International Baccalaureate Diploma Programme (International Baccalaureate 2004) in which learning outcomes are specified in terms of behaviours to be demonstrated by the learner.

The view that the curriculum should contain and express intrinsically worthwhile knowledge has been identified with foundationalist epistemology. This is associated with, for example, the educational thought of Paul Hirst. It acknowledges that curriculum is always a selection from the total of human knowledge. Foundationalism offers three types of reasons for including some forms of activities in a curriculum while excluding others, comprising 'logical delineations between domains of knowledge, distinctive mental and cognitive operations, and cross-cultural social distinctions' (Scott 2008: 9). Different forms of knowledge, for example logico-mathematical, empirical, inter-personal, moral, aesthetic, religious and philosophical, represent logical delineations between domains of knowledge. In some cases, these forms have been constructed by deduction with reference to reason or theory. In other cases they have been constructed by induction with reference to empirical observation. Gardner's (1983) seven forms of intelligence (linguistic, logical-mathematical, spatial, musical, bodily kinaesthetic, interpersonal and intra-personal) are examples of distinctive mental or cognitive operations identi-fied in individual psychology. Cross-cultural social distinctions have been identified in claims that contrasting approaches to teaching and learning can be observed across different societal cultures (Hofstede 1986, 2001). Policy documents published by the International Baccalaureate such as the IB *Learner Profile* (International Baccalaureate 2006) make reference to foundationalist curriculum theories about different forms of knowledge.

The view of curriculum development as innovative pedagogical experimentation has been identified with the process model (Stenhouse 1975). This approach offers a critique of the behavioural objectives model discussed above while conceptualising curriculum development as the role of teachers as curriculum experimenters and action researchers. School-based curriculum development, for example in peace and conflict studies particularly in schools associated with the United Nations and member institutions of the United World Colleges movement, may be identified with this perspective (Thomas 1998; Van Oord 2006, 2007). In such examples of curriculum development, the courses themselves and the methods of teaching them are subject to continuing inquiry and critique. Teachers implementing the IB Primary Years programme are encouraged to develop school-based curricula that may be interpreted as hypotheses to be validated through practice.

Socio-cultural models of learning are associated with theorists such as Lev Vygotsky. This expresses the view that mind, cognition and memory can only be understood as functions that are carried out with other people and in society. Constructivist learning theories address 'inter-subjective interchange in which learners construct knowledge in the light of experiences they have in and outwith the classroom, and in the process create meanings for themselves and others' (Scott 2008: 12). Policy documents published by the International Baccalaureate (e.g. International Baccalaureate 2008) make reference to pedagogy based on constructivist learning theories.

Critical pedagogy 'seeks, through pedagogic means, to surface and in the process disrupt conventional forms of understanding which serve to reproduce undemocratic, racist, sexist and unequal social relations' (Scott 2008: 14). Arguments pertaining to education for social justice may be seen with respect to access to international education (Wilkinson 1998; Hahn 2003; Whitehead 2005; Doherty 2009), the contrasting 'inclusive' and 'encapsulated' missions of international school (Sylvester 1998), and the impact of differential salary scales on international school staff (Hardman 2001; Knapp 2001; Cambridge 2002a; Bunnell 2009). It may also be argued that a commitment to action and service in the context of experiential learning, which may be interpreted as the legacy of Kurt Hahn's educational thought (Price 1970; Röhrs 1966, 1970), is an important component of education with an emphasis on international values. This position is exemplified by the statement that: 'unlike some post-modern viewpoints, critical pedagogy is predicated on a clear ethical position with regard to society and the way society reproduces itself' (Scott 2008: 14).

Instrumentalism in education frequently refers to the transmission of knowledge and specialised skills (Bernstein 1975, 2000). Nevertheless, Scott

(2008) argues that instrumentalism constitutes an approach to curriculum that argues that

> it is possible to provide a justification for the contents of a curriculum in terms of certain virtues or experiences that children should have in order to lead a fulfilled life. The project is clearly normative and redefines the notion of instrumentalism away from economism.
>
> (Scott 2008: 16)

The term 'away from economism' in this context refers to the idea that education can be not only a preparation for the instrumental end of employment alone but also for leisure. However, this approach may be criticised in two ways. First, it is difficult to define what exactly constitutes 'a fulfilled life' and, second, the experiences required to cultivate such virtues are equally hard to define and select. Scott (2008) links instrumentalist views of curriculum to discourses of personal autonomy, the capacity to reflect and make choices. Hence, there is a linkage with lifelong learning, a concept that is identified as part of the mission of the International Baccalaureate (International Baccalaureate 2009).

Although school effectiveness and school improvement constitute discrete discourses, they are frequently coupled together. The linkage between curriculum and school improvement assumes 'a technicist model which is at odds with critical, innovative and reflexive views of curriculum' (Scott 2008: 17). In the North American context, appeals are made to arguments relating to school improvement in justification for adopting the programmes of the International Baccalaureate (International Baccalaureate 2005).

Basil Bernstein has contributed to theorising the sociology of knowledge in three areas comprising language and social class, the construction of the curriculum, and knowledge development (Scott 2008). The relationship between language and social class is inscribed in the acquisition by the learner of codes that make explicit the recognition and realisation rules that operate in pedagogic discourse. Recognition rules are the means by which learners 'are able to recognise the specialty of the context they are in' (Bernstein 2000: 17). That is to say, learners need to be able to recognise the codes underlying communication in the classroom. Bernstein argues that the distribution of recognition rules in society is determined by power relations. Realisation rules enable the learner to use appropriate forms of language in the classroom, that is, to 'speak the expected legitimate text' (Bernstein 2000: 17).

The construction of the curriculum is based on relations between different forms of knowledge. In some contexts, there are strong boundaries insulating the different subjects. What goes on in the Mathematics classroom, for example, is separate from and unrelated to what goes on in the Modern Foreign Languages classroom. There is strong classification between the subjects. In other contexts, classification between curriculum contents, and the boundaries insulating the different subjects, is weak. The internal organisation of school subjects is also variable. In some subjects, knowledge is hierarchically ordered such that learning needs to be sequential. Selection, sequencing, and pacing of curriculum contents are indicators of strong framing. Bernstein (2000) proposes two ideal codes that describe the curriculum. The 'collection code' demonstrates strong classification and strong framing, whereas the 'integrated code' demonstrates weak classification and weak framing. The curricula implemented in international schools may be evaluated in terms of whether they are collection or integrated codes. This comparison may be made between programmes of study serving the same age group (for example, a state curriculum and an international curriculum for students aged 16–18) or between programmes of study serving students of different ages in phases of education (for example, primary, junior secondary and upper secondary students).

The structure of the curriculum has an impact on school management and organisation. A linkage is proposed between the structures of 'the formal organization of the school and the disciplinary organization of knowledge' (Siskin 1994: 37). The strong framing of collection codes means that pedagogic discourses and practices may vary between subjects, and that individual teachers may operate with considerable autonomy and have divergent ways of addressing their particular subjects in terms of selection of content, order, pacing and assessment. Bernstein (1975: 101) argues that the integrated code, with weaker classification and weaker framing, 'will not permit the variations in pedagogy and evaluation that are possible within collection codes'. He suggests that 'there will be a pronounced movement towards a common pedagogy and a tendency towards a common system of evaluation. In other words, integrated codes will, at the level of the teachers, probably create homogeneity of teaching practice' (Bernstein 1975: 101).

Moreover, 'integrated codes may require a high level of ideological consensus, and this may affect the recruitment of staff' (Bernstein 1975: 107). This can be observed in the implementation of International Baccalaureate programmes. Implementation of IB programmes requires values and attitudes about curriculum and pedagogy to be shared between teachers. The IB has an explicit Mission Statement that refers to its 'internationally minded' values. The IB Learner Profile (International Baccalaureate 2006) describes the attributes expected of students pursuing IB programmes. There is a process of authorisation for schools aspiring to offer IB programmes, and schools are strongly urged to send teachers to professional development training workshops accredited by the IB. These processes all contribute to strengthening shared understandings, values and attitudes relating to the curriculum.

Two contrasting models of pedagogic practice may be identified with a focus on performance and competence respectively. A performance model of pedagogic practice 'places the emphasis upon a specific output of the acquirer [i.e. the learner], upon a particular text the acquirer is expected to construct and upon the specialised skills necessary to the production of this specific output, text or product' (Bernstein 2000: 44). Fitz *et al.* describe the performance model as

> the dominant, established model . . . with the focus upon acquirers' past and future accomplishments, with strong apparent progression and pacing, evaluation focused on what was missing from their texts in terms of explicit and specific criteria of which they were made aware.
>
> (Fitz *et al.* 2006: 6)

By contrast, the acquirers in a competence model of pedagogic practice 'apparently have a great measure of control over selection, sequence and pace . . . The emphasis is upon the realisation of competences that acquirers already possess, or are thought to possess' (Bernstein 2000: 45). Competence models may be identified with 'liberal/progressive' education (Fitz *et al.* 2006: 7). However,

> there is a range of hidden costs if the competence model is to be successful in its own terms. The hidden costs are time-based. The teacher often has to construct the pedagogic resources; evaluation requires time in establishing the profile of each acquirer; and in discussing projects with groups, socialising parents into the practice is another requirement; establishing feedback on the acquirer's development (or lack of it) is a further time cost.
>
> (Bernstein 2000: 49)

The third aspect of Bernstein's (2000) theorisation of educational relationships is the pedagogic device, comprising the rules for the distribution, recontextualisation and evaluation (i.e. assessment) of knowledge. Knowledge, as it is created in universities and other places of research and knowledge production, must be selected, sequenced and paced in order to be made available to learners in schools. This process is pedagogic recontextualisation or pedagogisation of knowledge (Singh 2002). Curriculum and assessment organisations such as the International Baccalaureate are centres of pedagogic recontextualisation. The recent history of educational reform in many parts of the world has traced a shift in control over pedagogic recontextualisation, away from decentralised bodies independent of direct governmental control, such as examination boards, towards increasing centralisation and direct government control (Ball 1990; Fitz *et al.* 2006). Such centralised control of the curriculum is identified with the 'Official Recontextualisation Field' (Singh 2002). Curriculum development in the international context is becoming increasingly complex, particularly with regard to interactions with the multiplicity of Official Pedagogic Fields in different states, all of which have to be negotiated with in order to gain official recognition for international programmes of study.

To sum up, Scott (2008: 141) identifies a series of questions for curriculum designers comprising:

- What items of knowledge should be included in a curriculum and what items excluded?
- What reasons can be given for including some items of knowledge and excluding others?
- How should those items of knowledge be arranged in the curriculum?
- What is the relationship between items of knowledge within a curriculum and skills or dispositions that are taught as part of the curriculum?
- What is the relationship between disciplinary or academic knowledge and pedagogic knowledge?
- What types of arrangements in schools are suitable for delivery of the curriculum?
- What should be the strength of the insulations between different types of children, teachers and learners, teachers and educational managers, different types of knowledge, different types of skills, different educational purposes, different teaching episodes, different parts of the policy cycle and different organisational units?

Scott (2008: 141) comments that the last of these questions is 'pivotal to an understanding of the curriculum'. He argues that:

> We need . . . to think through the implications of understanding the world of education in a Bernsteinian manner. By describing a curriculum in terms of the strength of the relationships between the different parts, there is a ready-made conceptual framework for analysing the different parts of the curriculum as they are enacted in different parts of the world.
>
> (Scott 2008: 141)

The discussion that follows in this article will take account of this argument, and it will be useful to keep in mind Scott's list of questions. Scott identifies the enactment of the curriculum in different parts of the world as a focus of study. The next section will address the 'international context' for education and curriculum development.

Aspects of international curriculum

What constitutes 'international education'? How does international education differ from, say, 'multicultural education'? One way of contrasting these constructs may be to identify the sites in which they are practised. It may be proposed that international education takes place in international schools, whereas multicultural education may take place in a variety of school contexts including those in national educational systems. However, an increasing number of independent schools and schools in national education systems, as well as many international schools, offer an international curriculum such as the programmes of the International Baccalaureate. Consequently, it cannot be stated categorically that international schools are where international education (however that is defined) takes place uniquely, because an international school may offer an education that has no claims to be international. International education may be experienced by a student who has not attended a school that claims to be international (Hayden and Thompson 1995).

Definitions of international education are dependent upon context. International education is a contested field of educational practice involving the reconciliation of economic, political and cultural-ideological dilemmas, which may be identified as the competing 'globalist' and 'internationalist' perspectives (Cambridge 2003; Cambridge and Thompson 2001, 2004). The globalist approach to international education is influenced by and contributes to the global diffusion of the values of free market economics, expressed in terms of an ideology of meritocratic competition combined with positional competition. This is accompanied by quality assurance through international accreditation and the spread of global quality standards that facilitate educational continuity for the children of the globally mobile clientele. Globalised international education serves a market that requires the global certification of portable and transferable educational qualifications. This arrangement also facilitates educational continuity for the children of the host country clientele with aspirations towards social and global mobility. It is a view of international education as a globally branded product, 'a reliable product conforming to consistent quality standards throughout the world' (Cambridge 2002b: 227). The internationalist approach to the practice of international education is founded upon international relations, with aspirations for the promotion of peace and understanding between nations. It embraces a progressive, person-centred existential and experiential educational philosophy that values the moral development of the individual and recognises the importance of service to the community and the development of a sense of responsible citizenship. Internationalist international education celebrates cultural diversity and promotes an internationally minded outlook. It is 'a transformative discourse which locates all fields of enquiry in a supra-national frame of reference and upholds the cause of peace' (Rawlings 2000: 365).

From this account of the discourses of international education, it is evident that the construction and development of international curriculum is disrupted by competing positions that attempt to reconcile the instrumental needs for matriculation and university entrance with the expressive order values associated with progressive, person-centred education. While 'international education' is applied to the theory and practice of education for international-mindedness in international schools and other institutions, the term is also used in the related field of 'international and comparative education'. Comparative education emerges from a strong theoretical tradition of academic studies making comparisons between national systems, but international education is 'more explicitly applied and action-oriented' (Crossley 1999: 255). This frequently places international education in the context of international development aid and the transfer of expertise between national systems of education. Nonetheless, it may be argued that it is from this 'international and comparative' perspective that Thompson (1998) presents a typology of ways in which international curriculum is developed comprising processes of exportation, adaptation, integration and creation.

Exportation of curriculum refers to the marketing abroad of existing national curricula and examinations in which little attempt has been made to change the curriculum for an international clientele.

> The value system is unapologetically that of the national country from which it is exported, but it does depend on an assumption of society identity between national country and receiver country . . . Concession to any overt form of internationalism is slight, and is confined to the notion that the curriculum may be called 'international' only in the sense that it is used in a geographically dispersed market.
>
> (Thompson 1998: 279)

Lave (2003) gives a vivid account of how such exportation of curriculum has been used in the service of cultural reproduction in a 'British community school' in an expatriate enclave.

Adaptation of curriculum takes place when

> an acknowledgement is made in the selection of elements for the curriculum of the different contexts in which the curricula and examinations may be used . . . Although content elements may constitute the major focus for the adaptation process, acknowledging context differences, the inherent value system may not change at all. Thus, the 'international value system' is automatically equated with the value system built into the national programme, so running the risk of a frequently unwitting process of cultural imperialism.
>
> (Thompson 1998: 279)

Examples of adapted curricula include the Cambridge International General Certificate of Secondary Education (IGCSE) and Advanced International Certificate of Education (AICE).

Integration of curriculum occurs when 'best practices' from a range of 'successful' curricula are brought together to determine a curriculum that may be operated across a number of systems or countries. Thompson (1998) identifies this eclectic approach with the formation of the European Baccalaureate, to be found in European Schools in the European Union, and the early development of the International Baccalaureate. However, 'whatever the benefits of bringing together examples of good practice in pedagogy for a sharing of ideas across a number of systems, the dangers of confusing strategies from quite different, and often inconsistent, values or ideological positions are manifest' (Thompson 1998: 279).

Creation of curriculum is the process that attempts to create a new programme from first principles.

> Those principles will need clear exposition at the outset, a task that will be among the most challenging in the development of the whole programme. That is certainly true in the case of an international curriculum, for which value positions, agreement on the basis for selection of content, and a view of the nature of international society are likely to be contentious.
>
> (Thompson 1998: 280)

It is proposed that the programmes of the International Baccalaureate may be identified with this category.

Thompson (1998) identifies the contribution of foundationalist curriculum theorists who discuss curriculum in terms of 'an initiation into forms of knowledge or cognitive structures' (Scott 2008: 42).

> [F]rom quite different ideological positions Phenix (1964) in the USA, and Hirst and Peters (1970) in the United Kingdom, offered ways in which a curriculum may be constructed based on an epistemological approach involving 'realms of meaning' and 'forms of knowledge' respectively, a perspective which was adopted, to a great extent, in the creation of the International Baccalaureate programme.
>
> (Thompson 1998: 278)

Thompson (1998) proposes a 'brick wall' metaphor for international education in which 'whole institutional learning' constitutes the entire wall constructed from 'within subject learning' in discrete subjects that constitute the bricks, and 'interstitial learning' extending beyond the subjects that constitutes the mortar binding all the other components together. Interstitial learning provides

> opportunities for international learning that takes place *between* the subjects of the curriculum, and that arises from the various styles of inter- and transdisciplinary processes that are part of the planned and unplanned experience for the students and teachers. Such 'interstitial learning' is likely to involve not only those academic subjects that cross the boundaries between traditional interpretations of schools subjects, but also to include learning associated with such structures as pastoral care, guidance, discipline codes, approaches to individual special needs, and what has become known as the hidden curriculum, all of which can make a contribution to the generation of an international attitude.
>
> (Thompson 1998: 286)

Thompson (1998) makes no explicit reference to the theories of Basil Bernstein, so it is unclear whether or not it is valid to interpret the references above to transdisciplinary process and boundaries between subjects in terms of concepts such as classification and framing (Bernstein 1975, 2000). However, it may be argued that 'international values' or 'international mindedness' provide an overarching construction in the curriculum that weakens the classification (i.e. boundary strength) between the academic subjects. Walford (2002) proposes a similar idea in his discussion of classification and framing of the curriculum in Evangelical Christian and Muslim schools in England and the Netherlands. In the case of some Evangelical Christian schools:

> There still may be a collection code of subjects, but there is an attempt to integrate these subjects at a deeper level by relating them back to belief in a Biblical view of God, creation and the role of human beings in that creation. To the extent that teachers are successful in making each of the subjects and topics examples of God's creation, humanity's fall and redemption, they produce an integrated code with an 'overarching weak classification' between contents. It is a way of linking all subjects through the superimposition of one master-viewpoint on all.
>
> (Walford 2002: 416)

Do international values constitute a similar 'master-viewpoint'? To what extent might international values and religious values have an analogous impact on the implementation of the curriculum in different contexts? The means by which an ideology of international values contributes an 'overarching weak classification' to relations between curriculum contents in international education, as outlined by Walford (2002), would be an interesting topic for further school-based inquiry.

Wylie (2008: 7) contends that international education is 'the internationalization of message systems and formal educational knowledge'. Informed in part by Bernstein, he proposes that

> the message systems of international education such as curriculum, pedagogy and assessment along with mechanisms for learning and control can be defined from the theoretical perspectives of colonialism, post-colonialism, the emergence of global economic imperialism, global ideology and the hope for a global civil society.
>
> (Wylie 2008: 7)

These ideologies are identified as mechanisms of social control. Wylie (2008: 11) proposes that 'relationships between the practical aspects of international education, such as the message systems and the mechanisms of learning and control, and the theory associated with a trajectory from colonialism to global civil society can be constructed as a matrix'.

Wylie (2008: 12) identifies 'colonialism' with a colonial perspective of history, Western science and religion. The colonial curriculum increases and reinforces power and social control. The 'post-colonial' discourse of curriculum privileges 'Western' curriculum models, with colonial curriculum taught in a colonial context that maintains the *status quo*. The 'global economy' discourse presents a colonial perspective on culturally diverse curriculum that broadens the scope and frames of reference of the curriculum. Freedom is identified with a Western, capitalist expansionist ideology of economic development. The 'global ideology' discourse produces a critical and culturally aware curriculum based on multiple perspectives and social change. Wylie identifies the IB mission with this transnational discourse. The 'global civil society' discourse is associated with a curriculum that defines and maintains local culture and recognises cultural and social differences with a perspective that is critical of neoliberal globalisation. Wylie proposes that the global civil society discourse is for 'decolonising the mind'.

In what may be regarded as a contentious statement, Wylie argues that the matrix

> theoretically frames the relationship between ideological intentions and practical outcomes of international education. Reading across the table, international education is seen as moving closer to an ideology of global citizenry in a theoretical shift from colonialism to global civil society.
>
> (Wylie 2008: 11)

It is proposed that this is contentious because it makes an assumption of social progress between the various discourses of international education that may be unwarranted. While it is conceded that international education does contain the potential to disrupt the existing social order and create opportunity for social mobility, in practice it remains a potent means of reproduction of social and economic privilege. However, this point of view may be considered unacceptably pessimistic. Nonetheless, Wylie (2008) offers a framework for the description and analysis of curriculum, pedagogy, assessment, teachers and use of information and communications technology in an international context that may function as a valuable heuristic device.

Grouped Baccalaureate-type programmes and continuity between programmes

Having considered curriculum in an international context, this section will discuss grouped qualifications such as a 'baccalaureate model' of curriculum in general, followed by consideration of the International Baccalaureate Diploma Programme and other IB programmes in particular. This is because, perhaps as an accident of historical contingency, the development of international curriculum in terms of grouped baccalaureate-type qualifications has been intimately linked to arguments about the reform of upper secondary education particularly in terms of replacing 'a highly selective, narrow and elective curriculum' (Young and Leney 1997: 43) with a curriculum with greater breadth and balance. It is worth pointing out here that A.D.C. (Alec) Peterson, who was the founding Director General of the International Baccalaureate (1968–77), was pre-eminently a campaigner for the reform of secondary education and the replacement of GCE Advanced Level (A-levels) in England and Wales (Peterson 1965, 1972, 1977, 1987).

Working from published sources, including data from selected national systems listed in the *International Review of Curriculum and Assessment Frameworks Internet Archive* (www.inca.org.uk) and a variety of 'international' and 'non-national' curricula (e.g. International Baccalaureate Diploma Programme, European Baccalaureate, Cambridge International Examinations Advanced International Certificate of Education, and Advanced Placement Advanced Diploma for Overseas Study), Thompson *et al.* (2003: 43) characterise the features of a 'baccalaureate-type' curriculum in terms of:

- a curriculum or programme of study for upper secondary education that may be used as a school leaving qualification;
- a qualification for admission to higher education, for entry into employment, and as a foundation for learning throughout life;
- a programme of study that constitutes a broad and balanced curriculum;
- a compulsory core element offering learners a common experience, in addition to optional or elective elements.

With reference to the statement that a baccalaureate qualification can be used as a school-leaving examination, Thompson *et al.* (2003: 34) comment that 'if it is accepted that a curriculum is more than a series of intended learning outcomes, then an examination alone will not be sufficient to constitute a curriculum'. They then cite Young (1998: 119) with reference to GCE A-levels in England and Wales:

> A-levels are subject examinations and the Examining Boards examine subjects, not the curriculum. For the Examining Boards there is no such thing as the A-level curriculum. The term 'A-level curriculum' refers to the programmes of study that a school or college can offer and a student can choose, based on A-level subject examinations. The A-level curriculum is the responsibility of individual schools and colleges, and for each school and college it is different.

Hence, rather than simply being a collection of examined subjects, it is proposed that a baccalaureate-type curriculum displays structure and coherence. Such qualities may arise out of how combinations of subjects are selected to give breadth and balance, and out of the possibility of cross-curricularity in the form of building connections between subjects. From a Bernsteinian perspective, this suggests that baccalaureate-type curricula represent a weakening of classification (i.e. the boundaries) between subjects. Finegold *et al.* (1990) criticised GCE A-level in England and Wales for offering an 'early selection, early specialisation' programme of study that closes down options at too early a stage in the learner's career. The breadth and balance of a baccalaureate-type qualification offers the prospect of 'late selection, late specialisation' that enables learners to keep their educational options open for as long as possible. However, baccalaureate-type qualifications have, in turn, been criticised for their paternalistic 'you are not getting down from this table until you have finished your dinner' attitude to subject choice by learners (Smith 2003: 6). This point of view arguably represents a strong and valid challenge to the implementation of baccalaureate-type curricula in an increasingly market-oriented environment in which customer choice is considered more important than the philosophical concerns of the educational service provider.

It may be argued that the most important structural aspect of a baccalaureate-type curriculum that confers breadth and balance is the mix of compulsory and elective or optional subjects taken by the learner. This model offers the possibility of a common core curriculum experienced by all learners combined with the flexibility of subject choice determined by the needs and interests of the individual learner. However, the choice of elective or optional subjects may – or may not – be constrained by selection from subject groups such that the learner must pursue a second language and a science, each chosen from a menu of options, and so on. This constitutes the difference between a closed 'selection of options from subject groups' and an open 'free selection of options'. Thompson *et al.* (2003) present a typology of baccalaureate-type curricula in the form of a two-dimensional matrix (see Table 7.1) representing contrasting approaches to the common core and selection of optional or elective subjects.

Table 7.1 A general typology of curricula

	Selection of options from subject groups	*Free selection of options*
Compulsory common core subjects	Type A	Type B
No compulsory common core	Type C	Type D

Source: Thompson *et al.* 2003: 43

This matrix generates a typology of four ideal types of curriculum, comprising:

- selection of optional or elective subjects from subject groups with a compulsory common core (type A);

- free selection of options with a compulsory common core (type B);
- selection of optional or elective subjects from subject groups with no compulsory common core (type C);
- free selection of options with no compulsory common core of subjects (type D).

Thompson *et al.* (2003: 43) add that 'the possibility needs to be acknowledged that a curriculum model may exist which comprises compulsory core subjects only with no options, but in practice this is not found'. Variations in the composition of the common core may be observed across different educational systems. In some systems specific subjects, such as citizenship or religion, form the compulsory core. Other systems focus on 'key skills' such as literacy, numeracy or information and communications technology skills. In the case of the International Baccalaureate Diploma Programme, the common core comprises participation in the Theory of Knowledge course and Creativity, Action, Service (CAS) and the completion of a 4,000-word extended essay (International Baccalaureate 2009).

In conclusion, Thompson *et al.* (2003: 44) propose that

> In terms of the summary characteristics identified, it is clear that models A and B represent possibilities for structures applicable to baccalaureate programmes. The observation that such programmes should include a common experience for all students in order to qualify as a true bacca-laureate in such a classification would lead us to suggest that models C and D should be treated as quasi-baccalaureate structures.

The IB Diploma Programme for upper secondary students is not the sole programme of study offered by the International Baccalaureate. The IB Primary Years and Middle Years programmes are also available for learners in younger age groups (International Baccalaureate 2009). An apparently perennial topic of debate seems to be the extent to which the IB Middle Years programme, relative to other available programmes, constitutes a good preparation for learners aspiring to pursue the IB Diploma Programme. Reimers (2004) reports an attempted statistical comparison between outcomes of the IB Middle Years Programme and other programmes expressed in terms of achieved IB Diploma grades but, as Caffyn and Cambridge (2005) argue, the inferences drawn from this study are not valid because the research is flawed by methodological problems.

Attention is also drawn to the exchanges in the *International Schools Journal* between Ellwood (1999) and Guy (2000, 2001) concerning whether it is possible, or desirable, to teach the Cambridge International GCSE and the IB Middle Years Programme concurrently in the same classroom. Ellwood (1999) outlines the differences between a two-year programme of discrete subjects undertaken in preparation for externally assessed formal examinations, and the five-year holistic programme which is internally assessed and externally moderated. She concludes that there is sufficient overlap in their respective philosophies and modes of delivery that makes them 'not incompatible'. Guy (2000, 2001) argues that the IB MYP and Cambridge IGCSE are fundamentally incompatible in their respective philosophies and purposes. She rebuts Ellwood's (1999) proposition that there is sufficient overlap in the two programmes to enable them to be taught together. In Guy's view, attempting to provide a dual programme places an additional, unnecessary and perhaps even harmful burden on students as they wrestle with the demands of the MYP Personal Project and other innovative assessment schemes while, at the same time, they prepare themselves to pass the formal and more traditional examinations of the Cambridge IGCSE.

Another focus of inquiry is the need for continuity between programmes of study, for example in the transition of learners between the IB Middle Years and Diploma programmes. What are the similarities and differences between programmes encountered by learners? Stobie (2007) compares and contrasts these two IB programmes of study by asking the question 'What characterizes a coherent and consistent international curriculum?' One attribute of coherence is that 'the intended and experienced curriculum should share a consistent set of values' (Stobie 2007: 141). However, empirical research findings in a national education system identify more concrete characteristics that influence curriculum continuity.

Researching the implementation of the National Curriculum in England, Schagen and Kerr (1999) identify three aspects of 'cross-phase liaison' between schools, that is liaison between schools serving different age ranges of children in order to facilitate successful transition of learners from one school to the next. They comprise marketing, pastoral and curriculum-focused approaches. They observe that secondary schools 'in areas where there is competition for pupils may work hard at improving pastoral links because this can be an indirect but highly effective method of marketing' (page 85). Schagen and Kerr (1999: 86) propose that curriculum-focused liaison between schools comprises two components, namely curriculum continuity and individual progression. Continuity refers to consistency in terms of curriculum content and classroom practice, with the aim of avoiding unnecessary repetition of work and abrupt changes in learning styles. Individual progression refers to 'building on children's prior attainment so they do not "mark time" or revert to a lower level' (Schagen and Kerr 1999: 5). The authors propose that factors operate at three levels to influence, positively and negatively, curriculum continuity and individual progression, comprising:

- system-level factors, including the National Curriculum itself, national assessment tests, value-added analysis, league tables of schools, the burden on teachers' time, open enrolment policies, and the availability of funding for liaison activities;

- school-level factors, including competition between schools, the priority assigned to cross-phase continuity, autonomy between schools, autonomy between subject departments, and communications between and within schools;
- classroom-level factors, including teachers' use of transfer documentation from the child's previous school.

Notwithstanding such considerations, Stobie's (2007) perspective on transition and continuity appears to concentrate on curriculum continuity and the intended curriculum exclusively. Perhaps this focus on curriculum continuity is understandable in the light of the knowledge that, at the time of publication of his work, he had recently been appointed by the International Baccalaureate as Head of Diploma Programme Development (Hayden *et al.* 2007: xv). While conceding that concepts such as breadth, depth, balance and ideology are important when considering curriculum coherence, Stobie argues that they are inadequate by themselves. Instead, Stobie (2007: 142) argues that

> for an intended curriculum to be considered 'coherent and consistent' it must have an identifiable philosophy as well as clearly specified aims and objectives. These should indicate the values base, involving the assumptions about the nature of knowledge and learning, against which the prescribed programme syllabuses and broader planned activities can be compared for consistency and coherence.

Stobie (2007) also compares and contrasts the IB Diploma and Middle Years programmes. In two tables of comparisons, he attempts to demonstrate evidence found in IB curriculum documents in support of assertions made concerning features shared by both programmes (page 146) and examples of aims, objectives and content found in the curriculum guides that support the assertion that 'the MYP and Diploma promote International Understanding and World Citizenship' (pages 147–8). However, notwithstanding the degree of similarity between programmes evinced by his study, Stobie (2007) also draws attention to contrasting positions.

> The historical origins of the Diploma and MYP give a good insight into the ideological basis of the intended curricula. In considering factors that shaped the Diploma in the 1960s and 1970s, Hill's description (2001) of three forces is illuminating. These are utilitarian (a school leaving programme facilitating university entrance), ideological (development of international perspectives to promote understanding and peace) and pedagogical (the promotion of critical thinking and problem-solving and a balanced and broad-based curriculum educating the whole person).
>
> (Stobie 2007: 144)

On the other hand,

> the fact that the MYP was not conceived as school leaving certificate was viewed by Gerard Renaud (1989), one of the most influential thinkers behind its development as an opportunity to make [it] more progressive, visionary and internationally focused than the Diploma.
>
> (Stobie 2007: 145)

The contrast between the Middle Years and Diploma programmes is exemplified by the statement that

> The significance of this distinction is important in understanding the orientation, structure and development of the two programmes. The need for acceptance by universities of the Diploma required external examinations and the prescription of a good deal of content. It forced subjects to be essentially treated as 'discrete' and constrained the development of holistic learning. By contrast, the MYP expected teachers and schools to take a more active role in school-based curriculum development, through school development of cross-curricula [sic] themes that were infused in subject teaching called 'Areas of Interaction': Approaches to Learning, Community Awareness and Service, Homo Faber (the creative genius of humans), Environmental Education and Health and Social Education.
>
> (Stobie 2007: 145)

This point of view, contrasting the discourses inscribed in the IB Middle Years and Diploma programmes respectively, appears to express a common theme in the key differences between phases of education. A similar perspective is expressed by Fitz *et al.* (2006: 100):

> As Bernstein noted . . . the strong preference, particularly of the new middle class, was for primary classrooms where boundaries between work, play and the subjects were weak and pedagogy 'invisible', aiding teacher discovery of the multiple talents of their progeny while, for secondary schools, their preference, given that their abilities had now been made explicit, was for strong subject boundaries in traditional knowledge domains, as found in grammar schools and in the [National Curriculum].

Hence, whereas the IB Diploma Programme may be inscribed with a discourse of weaker classification and framing when compared with other upper secondary programmes of study, it is inscribed with a discourse of stronger classification and framing when compared with the IB Middle Years Programme. However, although Stobie (2007) makes reference to a variety of curriculum theorists in his article, Bernstein is not among the sources he cites. It may be proposed that this omission weakens Stobie's arguments by not giving him access to an important body of scholarship that addresses pedagogic discourse, even though he identifies issues and points of contrast that would gain clarity from analysis in terms of Bernstein's theoretical perspective.

Summary

This chapter has discussed international curriculum by focusing progressively on theories about curriculum and curriculum inquiry in general, the nature of international curriculum in particular, and specific examples of international curriculum including the nature of grouped qualifications and issues relating to portability and transferability of curriculum with respect to cross-phase liaison. It may be argued that international curriculum should also be considered in the contexts of national systems and their reactions to the processes of multiculturalism and globalisation.

The role of education in the reproduction of societal culture constitutes a recurrent theme in discussions about curriculum. Generally, this is in the context of national societal cultures. How can education be used to produce, say, good Australians? In post-colonial settler societies in particular, there is perceived to be a need to forge a sense of national identity from disparate multicultural populations formed by historical or more recent immigration. This education for diversity may also be coupled with responses to economic, political and cultural globalisation in the form of education for cosmopolitan citizenship. The concept of cosmopolitan citizenship is central to the discourse of international education. It suggests a world community to which all of humankind belongs, with mutual interests, and with a consciousness of human rights as universal entitlements. Cosmopolitan citizenship in a liberal democracy is not an alternative to national citizenship, nor is it even in tension with it. However, a limited understanding of citizenship as a function of nationality is no longer adequate because 'globalisation has enabled the development of a consciousness that identity is multiply situated' (Osler and Starkey 2005: 21).

Construction of a curriculum requires the selection, sequencing and pacing of content. The criteria for implementing such processes may be implicit or explicit, and are invariably sites of political struggle particularly where there is reproduction of social and economic position through participation in education. International education is no different from education in a national context because it has been argued that it 'encourages positive attitudes to community service, global citizenship and meritocratic competition while it is used as a means of enhancing positional competition and personal economic advancement' (Cambridge and Thompson 2004: 172).

Doherty (2009: 76) asks how the International Baccalaureate curriculum, in particular,

> articulates with these patterns and flows of relative advantage/disadvantage
> orchestrated through the social distribution of school curricula; whether
> the IB can deliver citizenship of a new order relating to more global

collectives lived beyond the nation; or whether it has been enlisted and/or recontextualised locally to serve middle-class strategy.

Doherty (2009) argues that, between them, structural reproduction and global citizenship act as drivers to select who gets access to the 'more globally disposed' IB curriculum.

In the Australian context, it is evident that the International Baccalaureate programmes may be interpreted as curricula that reinforce existing economic and social privilege of new middle class elites (Hahn 2003; Whitehead 2005; Doherty 2009). Nevertheless, this interpretation may be local and contingent. Different interpretations may prevail in other locations. In the United States, for example, rather than acting as reinforcements of class privilege, the IB programmes may be interpreted as drivers for the implementation of school improvement policies, and promoters for inclusion in education of the children of 'underserved' communities (Kugler and Albright 2005). Consequently, the sociological impact of international education is by no means universal or evenly spread. Such a view is exemplified by Cambridge and Thompson (2001: 6), who propose that international education may be identified with a variety of constructs including:

- a transplanted national system serving expatriate clients of that country located in another country;
- a transplanted national system serving clients from another country;
- a simulacrum of a transplanted national educational system, for example the programmes of the International Baccalaureate Organization, serving expatriate clients and/or host country nationals; and,
- an ideology of international understanding and peace, citizenship and service.

It may be noted that these constructs address not only *instrumental* order values associated with transmission of knowledge and specialist skills but also *expressive* order values associated with transmission of conduct, character and manner (Bernstein 2000).

Consequently, scholarship and inquiry into curriculum in the international context has the potential to be wide-ranging and diverse. There are numerous approaches that could be adopted, as the multiplicity of 'contemporary venues for curriculum inquiry' identified by Schubert (2008) suggests. There are technical issues associated with the selection, sequencing and pacing of curriculum content, but these also constitute foci for economic, political and sociological inquiry. The complexity of international education from the perspective of the interactions between pedagogic recontextualising agencies, such as the International Baccalaureate, and the Official Recontextualisation Fields (Bernstein 2000; Singh 2002) of national jurisdictions would make a fertile area of inquiry.

To conclude, it would be salutary to inquire into the extent to which international curriculum is an integrated global construct that is the same everywhere – or does it constitute a collection of segmented curricula specific to a variety of local contexts?

References

Ball, S. J. (1990) *Politics and Policy Making in Education: Explorations in Policy Sociology*, London: Routledge.

Bernstein, B. (1975) *Class, Codes and Control, Vol. 3: Towards a Theory of Educational Transmission*, London: Routledge & Kegan Paul.

Bernstein, B. (2000) *Pedagogy, Symbolic Control and Identity: Theory, Research, Critique* (revised edition), Lanham, MD: Rowman & Littlefield.

Bunnell, T. (2009) *International Schools as Organizations: A Population Ecology Approach*, Saarbrücken: VDM Verlag Dr. Müller.

Caffyn, R. and Cambridge, J. (2005) From Middle Years Programme to Diploma Programme: A critical response to Candice Reimers *IB Research Notes* 5(2): 2–9. Online at: www.ibo.org/programmes/research/publications/documents/notesjuly05.pdf (accessed 18 February 2009).

Cambridge, J. (2002a) Recruitment and deployment of teaching staff: a dimension of international school organization. In M. C. Hayden, J. J. Thompson and G. Walker (eds) *International Education in Practice*, London: Kogan Page, pp. 158–69.

Cambridge, J. (2002b) Global product branding and international education, *Journal of Research in International Education* 1(2): 227–43.

Cambridge, J. (2003) Identifying the globalist and internationalist missions of international schools, *International Schools Journal* XXII(2): 54–8.

Cambridge, J. and Thompson, J. J. (2001) 'A Big Mac and a Coke?' Internationalism and globalisation as contexts for international education. University of Bath: Unpublished paper. Online at: http://staff.bath.ac.uk/edsjcc/intedandglobaldoc.pdf (accessed 18 February 2009).

Cambridge, J. and Thompson, J. J. (2004) Internationalism and globalisation as contexts for international education, *Compare* 34(2): 157–71.

Crossley, M. (1999) Reconceptualising comparative and international education, *Compare* 29(3): 249–67.

Doherty, C. (2009) The appeal of the International Baccalaureate in Australia's educational market: a curriculum of choice for mobile futures, *Discourse: Studies in the Cultural Politics of Education* 30(1): 73–89.

Ellwood, C. (1999) IGCSE and the IB Middle Years Programme: how compatible are they? *International Schools Journal* XIX(1): 35–44.

Finegold, D., Keep, E., Miliband, D., Raffe, D., Spours, K. and Young, M. (1990) *A British 'Baccalauréat': Ending the Division Between Education and Training*, London: Institute for Public Policy Research.

Fitz, J., Davies, B. and Evans, J. (2006) *Educational Policy and Social Reproduction*, London and New York: Routledge.

Gardner, H. (1983) *Frames of Mind*, New York: Basic Books.

Guy, J. (2000) IBMYP and IGCSE: Are they really compatible? A response to Caroline Ellwood (Part I) *International Schools Journal* XX(1): 10–17.

Guy, J. (2001) IGCSE and IB MYP: How compatible are they? (Part II) *International Schools Journal* XXI(1): 11–18.

Hahn, A. M. (2003) The Intersection of Language, Power and International Education: A Critical Discourse Analysis of the International Baccalaureate Organization, New York, New York: Columbia University Teachers College, EdD dissertation.

Hardman, J. (2001) Improving recruitment and retention of quality overseas teachers. In S. Blandford and M. Shaw (eds) *Managing International Schools*, London: Routledge Falmer, pp. 123–35.

Hayden, M. C. and Thompson, J. J. (1995) International schools and international education: a relationship reviewed, *Oxford Review of Education* 21(3): 327–45.

Hayden, M. C., Levy, J. and Thompson, J. J. (2007) List of contributors, *The SAGE Handbook of Research in International Education*, London: Sage.

Hill, I. (2001) Early stirrings: the beginnings of the international education movement, *International Schools Journal* XX(2): 11–21.

Hirst, P. H. and Peters, R. S. (1970) *The Logic of Education*, London: Routledge & Kegan Paul.

Hofstede, G. (1986) Cultural differences in teaching and learning, *International Journal of Intercultural Relations* 10(3): 301–20.

Hofstede, G. (2001) *Culture's Consequences* (2nd edn), Los Angeles and London: Sage.

International Baccalaureate (2004) *Diploma Programme assessment principles and practice*, Cardiff Gate: International Baccalaureate. Online at: http://ibo.org/diploma/assessment/documents/d_x_dpyyy_ass_0409_1_e.pdf (accessed 18 February 2009).

International Baccalaureate (2005) *A Look at North American IB Legislation*, available from IBO website at: www.ibo.org/ibna/documents/ibnalegislation.pdf (accessed 27 February 2007).

International Baccalaureate (2006) *IB learner profile booklet*, Cardiff, UK: International Baccalaureate. Online at: www.ibo.org/programmes/documents/learner_profile_en.pdf (accessed 18 February 2009).

International Baccalaureate (2008) *Towards a Continuum of International Education*, Cardiff Gate: International Baccalaureate. Online at: http://occ.ibo.org/ibis/documents/general/g_0_iboxx_amo_0809_1_e.pdf (accessed 18 February 2009).

International Baccalaureate (2009) Website, online at: www.ibo.org (accessed 18 February 2009).

Knapp, R. (2001) The implications of a two-tier salary scale on teacher relations: a case study, *International Schools Journal* XXI(1): 57–68.

Kugler, E. G. and Albright, E. M. (2005) Increasing diversity in challenging classes, *Educational Leadership* 62(5): 42–5.

Labaree, D. F. (1997) Public goods, private goods: the American struggle over educational goals, *American Educational Research Journal* 34(1): 39–81.

Lave, J. (2003) Producing the future: getting to be British, *Antipode* 35(3): 492–511.

Osler, A. and Starkey, H. (2005) *Changing Citizenship: Democracy and Inclusion in Education*, Maidenhead: Open University Press.

Peterson, A. D. C. (1965) Secondary reorganisation in England and Wales, *Comparative Education* 1(3): 161–9.

Peterson, A. D. C. (1972) *The International Baccalaureate: An Experiment in International Education*, London: George Harrap.

Peterson, A. D. C. (1977) Applied comparative education: the International Baccalaureate, *Comparative Education* 13(2): 77–80.

Peterson, A. D. C. (1987) *Schools Across Frontiers*, La Salle: Open Court.

Phenix, P. H. (1964) *Realms of Meaning*, New York: McGraw Hill.

Price, T. (1970) Some aspects of character-building. In H. Röhrs (ed.) *Kurt Hahn*, London: Routledge and Kegan Paul, pp. 80–91.

Rawlings, F. (2000) Abstract of doctoral thesis. Globalisation, curriculum and international communities: a case study of the United World College of the Atlantic, *International Journal of Educational Development* 20(4): 365–6.

Reimers, C. (2004) From MYP to Diploma: an investigation into the impact of the International Baccalaureate Middle Years Programme on International Baccalaureate Diploma candidates, *International Schools Journal* XXIV(2): 11–18.

Renaud, G. (1989) Approaches to learning. Unpublished paper presented to the International Schools Association.

Röhrs, H. (1966) The realm of education in the thought of Kurt Hahn, *Comparative Education* 3(1): 21–32.

Röhrs, H. (1970) Responsibilities and problems of international education, *Comparative Education* 6(2): 125–35.

Rowntree, D. (1982) *Educational Technology in Curriculum Development* (2nd edn), London: Paul Chapman Publishing.

Schagen, S. and Kerr, D. (1999) Bridging the gap? The National Curriculum and progression from primary to secondary school, Slough: National Foundation for Educational Research. Online at: www.nfer.ac.uk/publications/other-publications/downloadable-reports/pdf_docs/Gap.pdf (accessed 18 February 2009).

Schubert, W. H. (2008) Curriculum inquiry. In F. M. Connelly *et al.* (eds) *The SAGE Handbook of Curriculum and Instruction*, Los Angeles: Sage, pp. 399–419.

Scott, D. (2008) *Critical Essays on Major Curriculum Theorists*, London and New York: Routledge.

Singh, P. (2002) Pedagogising knowledge: Bernstein's theory of the pedagogic device, *British Journal of Sociology of Education* 23(4): 571–82.

Siskin, L. S. (1994) *Realms of Knowledge: Academic Departments in Secondary Schools,* Washington, DC and London, UK: Falmer Press.

Smith, G. (2003) Is there 'too much maths' in schools? *Insider* (University of Bath magazine) June 2003, pp. 6–7. Online at: www.bath.ac.uk/pr/insider/jun03.pdf (accessed 18 February 2009).

Stenhouse, L. (1975) *An Introduction to Curriculum Research and Development*, Oxford: Heinemann Educational.

Stobie, T. (2007) Coherence and consistency in international curricula: a study of the International Baccalaureate Diploma and Middle Years Programmes. In M. C. Hayden, J. Levy and J. J. Thompson (eds) *The SAGE Handbook of Research in International Education*, London: Sage, pp. 140–51.

Sylvester, R. (1998) Through the lens of diversity. In M. C. Hayden and J. J. Thompson (eds) *International Education: Principles and Practice,* London: Kogan Page.

Thomas, P. (1998) Education for peace: the cornerstone of international education. In M. C. Hayden and J. J. Thompson (eds) *International Education: Principles and Practice*, London: Kogan Page, pp. 103–18.

Thompson, J. J. (1998) Towards a model of international education. In M. C. Hayden and J. J. Thompson (eds) *International Education: Principles and Practice*, London: Kogan Page, pp. 276–90.

Thompson, J. J., Hayden, M. C. and Cambridge, J. (2003) Towards a structural typology for Baccalaureate-style curricula. In T. Pound and G. Phillips (eds) *The Baccalaureate: A Model for Curriculum Reform*, London: Kogan Page, pp. 29–46.

Van Oord, L. (2006) Peace and conflict studies: the first three decades, *International Schools Journal* XXV(2) 8–13.

Van Oord, L. (2007) To Westernize the nations? An analysis of the International Baccalaureate's philosophy of education, *Cambridge Journal of Education* 37(3): 375–90.

Walford, G. (2002) Classification and framing of the curriculum in Evangelical Christian and Muslim schools in England and the Netherlands, *Educational Studies* 28(4): 404–19.

Whitehead, K. (2005) *Advertising Advantage: The International Baccalaureate, Social Justice and the Marketisation of Schooling*, Paper WHIO5426, presented to Australian Association for Research in Education Annual Conference, Parramatta, New South Wales, 27 November–1 December 2005. Online at: www.aare.edu.au/05pap/whi05426.pdf (accessed 18 February 2009).

Wilkinson, D. (1998) International education: a question of access. In M. C. Hayden and J. J. Thompson (eds) *International Education: Principles and Practice*, London: Kogan Page, pp. 227–34.

Wylie, M. (2008) Internationalizing curriculum: framing theory and practice in international schools, *Journal of Research in International Education* 7(5): 5–19.

Young, M. F. D. (1998) *The Curriculum of the Future*, London: Falmer.

Young, M. F. D. and Leney, T. (1997) From A levels to an advanced curriculum of the future. In A. Hodgson and K. Spours (eds) *Dearing and Beyond: 14–19 Qualifications, Frameworks and System*, London: Kogan Page, pp. 40–56.

8 Assessment and international schools

Richard Bates[1]

In a totally pedagogised society, schooling appears to see much of its relevance confined to its function of accreditation, of distributing diplomas.

(Magalhaes and Stoer 2009: 245)

Perhaps the most important consideration in encouraging the spread and development of multilateral international schools is the prospect that graduates of such institutions be assured of university placement.

(Leach 1969: 45)

Opportunity, access and credentials

The second half of the twentieth century saw a steady increase in the aspirations of parents and their children in developed and, latterly, developing countries alike. These aspirations were fed and consolidated mid century through substantial economic development and a significant expansion of employment opportunities in business, government and, perhaps most of all, in transnational corporations. Many of these jobs demanded high-level skills that could only be produced through expanded secondary and then tertiary educational institutions. As the size of the middle class increased through access to mass education and employment growth, it appeared for a while that the demo-cratisation of education would lead to middle class jobs for everyone.

However, simultaneously with this increase in aspirations and hopefulness, inequalities in income and wealth were also increasing, particularly towards the end of the century. The result is that while the coming of the 'knowledge society' has indeed resulted in increased demand for 'knowledge producers' and 'symbolic analysts' at some levels, the reorganisation of work on a global basis has, despite its enlargement of the middle class, led to only modest transformation of opportunity for large numbers of populations in both developed and developing countries.

As Michael Young observes:

> global changes towards more flexible economies have not turned out to be as progressive and evenly distributed as predicted by political economists such as Priore and Sabel (1984) and Reich (1991). The majority

of people in work still stay in the same field if not the same company or organization for most of their working lives. The new industries of the e-economy with their new learning demands have had much publicity, but quantitatively they create remarkably few jobs. Furthermore, not only has the transformative capacity of the new technologies, at least in the short term, been vastly exaggerated, but some of the most characteristic jobs of the new economy are in call centres and the fast food and security industries, none of which require many highly qualified 'knowledge workers'. In other words, the increasingly mobile and qualified society on which the claims for qualification frameworks are based bears little relationship to the realities of modern economies.

(Young 2008: 133)

Nonetheless, (and while this may be a particularly Western viewpoint), qualifications frameworks are springing up everywhere and present a new form of control of both knowledge and individuals. As Bernstein has observed, within the emerging knowledge-based economy where information and expertise are coded, stored and made available electronically, knowledge becomes literally disembodied and dehumanised. In this form it 'flows like money' (Bernstein 1996: 86). Moreover, qualifications frameworks are increasingly tied to competencies that codify and certify the knowledge and performance required by particular employment categories – categories that shift and alter as institutions and occupations are continuously restructured, thus giving a new meaning to the idea of lifelong learning.

Such frameworks are transforming traditional demands on education systems in two significant ways. First, the role of education in *socialising* the individual into the adult role of citizen as broadly conceived (Durkheim 1965 in Brown 2006) is being altered to a narrowed focus on socialisation for work. This is particularly the case where qualifications frameworks are focused on the production of specific competencies and performance. Here

Knowledge . . . instead of qualifying the individual, transforms the individual into a set of cognitive-driven competencies. Knowledge no longer educates the individual and society, rather it becomes a tool for positioning individuals on (or excluding them from) the labour market. One of the results of this transformation is a process of individualisation where individuals are reduced to their 'performance'.

(Magalhaes and Stoer 2009: 236)

This leads to the second of Durkheim's educational roles – that of the *selection* and *allocation* of individuals in various hierarchies of talent on the basis of common examinations. Credentials valorise a supposed hierarchy of talent through which individuals are allocated to various positions within the credentialed society. This function is particularly important where there is a mismatch between supply and demand for particular competencies.

This mismatch is important at two levels. First, in terms of high-level skills, (both technological and cultural), there is currently a war for talent. As economies shift towards reliance on knowledge-based industries 'the differential value of highly talented people continues to mount' (Michaels in Lauder 2007: 445). Simultaneously, as processes of internationalisation and globalisation proceed it is clear that 'those who have a strong multilingual (including English) and cultural background will have a head start in this war for talent' (Lauder 2007: 445). The implications for schools are an increased emphasis on high level knowledge-based curricula combined with cross-cultural and multilingual studies, specifically including English. These are particularly important concerns for international schools.

Second, as Brown (2006) points out, educational credentials are positional goods, goods that are significantly affected by the availability of and access to particular forms of education. As availability of and access to general education increases, (as was the case in advanced economies during the last century), the competition for positional advantage intensifies, leading to both an inflation in the demand for credentials at more and more advanced levels and to increasingly desperate measures through which families attempt to ensure positional advantage through access to elite education.

The difficulty here is that governmental attempts to increase educational opportunity and reduce inequalities forces previously privileged individuals and their families to try to find ways out of the social congestion that builds up around popular institutions at all levels. The paradox however, is that if there is an insufficient increase in available high-level employment, competition intensifies as opportunity calcifies. But few can afford to withdraw from the competition for a livelihood; a competition that continues to intensify in what Brown (2006) calls the 'Opportunity Trap'.

In such a situation

> Absolute performance is not sufficient, because cashing in one's opportunities depends on access to scarce credentials, jobs and networks. For societies, this means that what can be offered to the winners cannot be offered to the population as a whole. There are simply not enough good jobs to go around. An important part of the attraction of elite universities or blue-chip companies is the fact that they offer social status and lifestyles that are in short supply. They are sought after because they are exclusive rather than inclusive.
>
> (Brown 2006: 387)

This is not only an issue within nation states, but also increasingly an issue within the globalised economy. In particular the globalisation of higher education is changing the nature of educational hierarchies, which are themselves becoming globalised. As Lauder observes: 'Higher education systems are becoming increasingly global, coalescing in a hierarchy based on reputation and starting to form a winner-takes-all global market (Lauder 2007: 444).

In this situation Leach's (1969) observation at the head of this chapter is particularly pertinent: one of the reasons for the spread of international schools is that their assessment processes are seen to increase the chance of admission to university and often to elite universities. Lowe endorses this view:

> One interpretation of the rapid expansion in many countries of the numbers of schools offering 'international' qualifications is that they are a response by local elites to a stiffening of the local positional competition on the one hand and a globalization of that competition on the other. As more people gain local educational qualifications, those who can afford to do so seek a new competitive edge by taking qualifications that they hope will give them a local advantage. At the same time, it is hoped that these international qualifications will give access to a labour market that is becoming increasingly globalised – for the most advantageous occupations at least.
>
> (Lowe 2000: 24–5)

One key element of such an international education is that it includes and is often conducted partially or wholly in English. This is not exclusively characteristic of international schools. For instance, as Member States of Europe move towards a common European policy in education, approximately 90 per cent of pupils at upper secondary levels learn English, regardless of whether it is compulsory or not (Enever 2009: 187). While this move provides competition for international schools, the fact that many international schools offer a curriculum in English as well as other frequently used international languages such as French, German and Spanish as well as local national languages suggests that 'education at an elite international school may provide a head start not only in access to the top universities but also for subsequent entry to the fast track management systems of the [Multinational Corporations]' (Lauder 2007).

International schools and access to higher education

Top universities and elite international schools have a tendency, therefore, to articulate their assessment/examination systems and admissions policies through a number of specific mechanisms. Some of these arrangements provide for direct admission to universities from individual schools that are seen to produce 'good' students. However, many international schools rely upon more systematic arrangements brokered by international organisations. For instance, the IBO has agreements with nearly two thousand universities that the IB Diploma will be accepted as an entry level qualification, and, in some instances, will also gain students credit within the first year of their degree. Moreover, of the 1,837 universities listed as having such agreements with the IBO in the 2007 *Yearbook* an overwhelming number (1,243) were located in English-speaking countries including the USA (986), Canada (126), the United Kingdom (91), and Australia and New Zealand (40). Japan was the only other individual country, and the only non-English speaking country, with a significant number of such agreements (305).

Not surprisingly, the examinations offered by international schools reflect this orientation towards English-speaking universities. Some 518 schools provide details of the examinations they offer in the *ECIS International Schools Directory 2008/2009*. As many schools offer access to more than one examination some 943 examinations were available from major internationally recognised examining authorities. Within this total, 306 schools offered the IB Diploma (IBDP); 289 offered the Scholastic Achievement Test (SAT) (USA); 118 offered the Advanced Placement Program (AP) (USA); and 230 offered the International General Certificate of Secondary Education (IGCSE) (UK). Small numbers of schools offered particular examinations relevant to the national origins of their students (German, French, Spanish, Canadian, Australian, etc.) or examinations required by the host country.

Clearly, the majority of these key examinations are conducted in English and are oriented towards the overwhelming number of English-speaking universities mentioned above.

Such an orientation towards particular examinations and destinations presents international schools with both advantages and challenges. The advantage is that the schools are clearly responding to parental demand for English/American examinations and destinations. But there are significant differences between the American tests and English examinations which are both norm referenced and without articulation to a whole school curriculum, and the IBO Diploma which is both criterion referenced and articulated with curricular programmes designed for Primary (PYP) and Middle (MYP) years.[2]

The complexity facing schools attempting to provide students oriented towards different destinations with appropriate certification is exemplified in Ramalho's case of an international school where

> All students . . . were to receive on completion, a high school diploma from an official accredited institution. At the same time, some students needed to be able to merge back in any U.S. school at any grade level, and benefit from transferable diplomas. In addition, some students were seeking preparation to enrol in U.S. colleges and universities, as well as local universities . . . . Because of the different students' needs the school granted local diplomas for students planning to attend local colleges and universities, an American diploma for students planning to attend U.S. colleges and universities, as well as an International Baccalaureate (IBO) diploma aimed at facilitating the mobility of international students (from one country to the next) while at the same time, providing students with college-preparatory advanced diplomas.
>
> (Ramalho 2007: 3)

But complexity does not reside solely in the requirements of individual students and their destinations, nor in the different principles of assessment of particular American and English norm referenced examinations and the criterion referenced IBO Diploma. It also lies in the curricular principles that underlie the various examinations.

Curriculum, assessment, examinations and tests

For instance, The IBO offers a three-level programme starting at the Primary Years (PYP), then the Middle Years (MYP) and finally the last two years of high school the Diploma Programme (DP). Each of these levels has an explicit curriculum framework that provides the scaffolding upon which schools and teachers build their approach to learning.[3]

In the *Primary Years Program* (PYP) six trans-disciplinary themes of global significance provide the framework for exploration and study: *who* we are; *where* we are in place and time; *how* we express ourselves; *how* the world works; *how* we organise ourselves; and *sharing* the planet. Teachers are guided by these six trans-disciplinary themes as they design units of inquiry that both transcend and articulate conventional subject boundaries.

The programme can be illustrated by a hexagon with the six trans-disciplinary themes surrounding six subject areas: language, social studies, mathematics, arts, science, and personal, social and physical education. The trans-disciplinary themes and subject areas form the knowledge element of the programme.

These themes and subject areas are linked with five 'essential elements', which guide the pedagogy of the programme, emphasising concepts, know-ledge, skills, attitudes, action, so that students are given the opportunity to:

- gain knowledge that is relevant and of global significance;
- develop an understanding of concepts, which allows them to make connections throughout their learning;
- acquire trans-disciplinary and disciplinary skills;
- develop attitudes that will lead to international-mindedness;
- take action as a consequence of their learning.

The result is a highly articulated framework of academic subjects, trans-disciplinary themes and pedagogical principles.

The *Middle Years Programme* (MYP) offers a similarly integrated approach to curriculum through five areas of interaction: Approaches to Learning; Community and Service; Homo Faber; Environments; Health and Social Education. These five areas of interaction serve to integrate the learning of particular subjects as they

- are embedded in the subjects and developed naturally through them;
- provide both an organisation and an extension of learning within and across the subjects, through the exploration of real-life issues;

- inspire special activities and interdisciplinary projects;
- form part of the framework for student inquiry and take investigative learning further than subject boundaries;
- are a vehicle for refining conceptual understanding through different perspectives;
- guide reflection and lead from knowledge to thoughtful action.

Subject curricula are offered in nine areas, all of which must be covered by the student. These are: Language A, Language B, Humanities, Technology, Mathematics, Arts, Sciences, Physical Education and Personal Project. The curriculum as a whole is underpinned by an emphasis on the fluidity of the curricular framework and the interrelatedness of the subjects. Aspects of the areas of interaction are addressed naturally through the distinct disciplines. In particular, the framework is flexible enough to allow a school to include other subjects not determined by the IB but which may be required by state or national authorities.

The overall philosophy of the programme is expressed through three fundamental concepts that support and strengthen all areas of the curriculum. These concepts are based on: intercultural awareness, holistic learning and communication.

Similarly the *Diploma Program* (IBDP) is constructed as an integrated curriculum, this time around three core components. The *Extended Essay*, with a prescribed limit of 4,000 words, offers students the opportunity to investigate a topic of individual interest and acquaints them with the independent research and writing skills expected at tertiary level. The interdisciplinary *Theory of Knowledge* (TOK) course is designed to provide coherence by exploring the nature of knowledge across all disciplines, encouraging an appreciation of other cultural perspectives.

Participation in the school's *Creativity, action, service (CAS)* programme encourages students to be involved in artistic pursuits, sports and community service work, thus fostering their awareness and appreciation of life outside the academic arena.

Surrounding these three core areas are the six subject areas of which three are studied at 'standard' level and three at 'advanced'. They are: Language A1, Second Language, Individuals and Societies, Experimental Sciences, Mathematics and Computer Science, and The Arts.

Associated with each of these three integrated curricula is a written assessment policy that is available to all sections of the school community. The policy is a lengthy series of guidelines and rules that are available for individual subjects and programmes of the IBO through the Online Curriculum Centre (OCC). All participating schools have access to the OCC and their staff are expected to stay in touch with their teaching areas through the internet. The website is updated regularly. The various curriculum groups that decide what is to be taught meet on a regular basis and are constantly fine-tuning the content and assessment criteria for their subject area. The members of these various groups are selected by the IBO on the basis of regional balance, experience in the subject area and willingness and ability to take part in regular meetings both nationally and internationally.

The IBO encourages schools to view assessment as being integral with planning, teaching and learning. Learning expectations and integral assessment strategies are made clear to students and parents. The school uses a balanced range of strategies for formative and summative assessment, which are reviewed regularly. Learning at the school involves students in both peer- and self-assessment. The levels of students' current knowledge and experience are assessed before embarking on new learning. Students are provided with regular and prompt feedback to inform and improve their learning. Assessment at the school provides students with regular opportunities for reflection on their own learning.

The assessment process allows for meaningful reporting to parents about students' progress. Assessment data is analysed to provide information about the individual needs of students. There are efficient systems for recording data about student learning, which are in keeping with the requirements of the programme. Assessment data is analysed to inform the evaluation and subsequent modification of teaching and learning strategies.

Assessment within the PYP addresses all the essential elements of the programme. Data, including evidence of development in terms of the IB learner profile, is reported to all participants in the learning process: students, parents, teachers and school administrators, and other schools at the time of transfer. Assessment at the school requires the storage of and easy access to student work showing evidence of the process of learning and progress over time. While the IBO has guidelines for schools offering the PYP, individual schools have a degree of independence as to just how to provide feedback (reporting) to parents. The summation of the PYP is an exhibition at the end of the academic year where students show a particular project they have been working on all year. This is a method used to prepare students for later work within the MYP and DP.

Assessment within the MYP is a continuous process and is designed to address the MYP objectives in each of the eight subject groups and the personal project, according to a criterion-referenced approach. The assessment focuses on process as well as product. Teachers/supervisors participate in the standard-isation of assessment, where appropriate. Schools have the option of choosing to moderate the MYP on their own or by selecting a range of projects and course work from their student body, are able to have certificates provided by the IBO.

Student learning within the Diploma Program is regularly assessed against the objectives and assessment criteria specific to each subject. Student work is criterion-referenced rather than norm-referenced. Teachers provide an estimated grade list to IBO and any deviation over two grade points is referred to central assessment centres and is reassessed.

The IBO is moving to replace its single assessment centre in Cardiff with a network of assessment centres as the demand for their services has made it impossible to administer all aspects of their programmes through the Cardiff examinations centre. The centre at Cardiff will be replaced by centres at three other locations: The Hague, Washington and Singapore. The replicated centres will have the task of ensuring that all IBO schools worldwide have the same standards and offer the same criteria for assessing student's work.

Another international assessment system, and arguably the oldest, is that offered by Cambridge University. Cambridge International Examinations (CIE) formerly known as the University of Cambridge Local Examinations Syndicate (UCLES), was set up in 1858. It is a non-teaching department of the University of Cambridge, and a not-for-profit organisation. Its mission is 'to work in partnership with education providers worldwide to deliver high-quality and leading-edge assessment services' (www.cie.org.uk).

Cambridge International Examinations (CIE) is the world's leading provider of international qualifications for 14–19 year olds. Qualifications include IGCSEs, which were pioneered by CIE over 20 years ago, O Levels, A and AS Level, and business qualifications in disciplines such as ICT, management and office administration. CIE's qualifications are recognised by universities, education providers and employers across the globe. CIE provides assessment and related syllabi for some sixty-eight subjects at both IGCSE and A Level examinations. It also provides assessment and reporting services at various levels of primary and middle years in key areas such as literacy and numeracy.

However, unlike the IBO programmes, the CIE does not provide an integrated curriculum, but is focused upon assessment and examination in various subjects at various levels. Associated with these examinations in a wide range of subject areas are syllabi, but these are not grounded in an integrated theory of curriculum, teaching or learning. Indeed, CIE is focused almost exclusively upon processes of summative assessment, leaving issues of curricular and pedagogical integration to individual schools. If the IBO operates on the basis of an *integrated* code, then the CIE operates on the basis of a *collection* code (Bernstein 1971).

Running parallel with the CIE examinations are the Cambridge ESOL Examinations (www.cambridgeESOL.org). Cambridge ESOL (English for Speakers of Other Languages) exams are the world's leading range of certificates for learners of English. Each year they are taken by over 1.75 million people, in 135 countries.

Again, as with the IB Diploma the important thing about the CIE and CESOL qualifications is that they are recognised for entry to higher education institutions across the world. They provide summative assessment in particular subject areas that is standardised against a huge population, a process capable of providing data on comparative performance within and between schools and countries.

Admission to American universities is governed by a significantly different process: a process of testing that seems to be divorced from curricular or

pedagogical processes and relies for its validity on standardisation of performance against large student populations. While, because of this process, such
tests can claim statistical validity and reliability, it is a moot point as to their
face (or content) validity across complex curricular differences. The tests most
often used are the SAT and AP tests which are conducted by the American
College Board (www.collegeboard.com/). These tests are explicitly 'curriculum
free' in that:

> Students take the SAT Subject Tests to demonstrate to colleges their
> mastery of specific subjects such as English, history, mathematics, science,
> and foreign languages. The content of each test is not based on any one
> approach or curriculum but rather evolves to reflect current trends in high
> school course work (www.professionals.collegeboard.com/testing/sat-
> subject/about).

Hour-long tests are available in some twenty subjects in multiple choice format
and are machine scored. In this they differ significantly from both the IBO
assessments and those of the CIE. They are supported by a Subject Tests
Preparation Center and a variety of publications that assist students to prepare
for the tests. But while students are encouraged to prepare for the format of
the tests they are explicitly advised that they cannot study specific content
for the DSAT or AP examinations. So, while it is a popular programme among
United States colleges and hence students trying to gain access to them, it is
not an integrated curriculum like that provided by the IBO or even the syllabus-
based programme offered by CIE. Indeed, it might well be called a curriculum-
free assessment system.

Difference, contradiction and assessment in international schools

In the face of such different assessment and examination systems, international
schools are presented with some rather difficult choices. Clearly the curricular
and pedagogical demands of the various assessment and examination systems
are quite different, making the internal provision and coordination of teaching
and learning problematic. The resolution of tensions between curricula and
related assessment procedures may well depend upon the location of the school
and the composition of its staff. For instance, Hayden notes that

> Based on quite different philosophies (holistic, reflective and constructivist
> in the case of the MYP, and more compartmentalised, prescriptive and
> skills-based in the case of IGCSE) the MYP assessment structure is more
> likely to be familiar to those with a background in countries of, for example,
> continental Europe while their British counterparts, for instance, are
> more likely to identify more strongly with the external examinations and
> certifications of the IGCSE.
>
> (Hayden 2006: 143)

Ellwood has argued that such differences can be overcome and that some work at school level and 'some adjustment' might 'provide a possibility of synthesis' (1999: 36). On the other hand, Guy argues that an 'examination driven programme' such as the IGCSE works *against* the fundamental goals of student-centred learning and constructivist pedagogies that are fundamental to the MYP where 'assessment procedures should reflect precisely the aims of the pedagogy' (Guy 2001: 14).

Moreover, while the IB programmes were designed from the start as curricula aimed at developing international-mindedness, the IGCSE programmes are adaptations of the English GCSE. So while IGCSE examinations and syllabi are international in terms of offering and access, they are not international in a curriculum sense.

The attempt to develop assessment techniques and structures that are truly 'international' is however a very challenging process as Roger Brown (2002) makes clear. Using the work of Hofstede (1991, 2001), Brown argues that the values embedded in particular national cultures shape both what knowledge is thought to be worthwhile (the problem of curriculum) and the processes by which that knowledge is evaluated (the problem of assessment). Brown takes the issue of national/cultural differences as the starting point for arguing that the most appropriate form of 'international' assessment would be one that relied to a substantial degree upon internal rather than external assessment in that 'if an assessment system has sufficient flexibility within it, then it may be able to be adapted to match more closely the values of a particular group' (2002: 76).

This is not only a superficial issue related to the technical construction of assessment procedures, but one that addresses the issue of substantive (deep structural) epistemological and valuational differences between cultures (Van Oord 2007). A truly international assessment process would need to reflect the differences in curriculum and pedagogy that such epistemological and valuational differences call for. As Brown suggests 'An internal assessment component can provide flexibility for the matching of cultures and assessment, in a way that is not possible with the necessarily more standardised approach of external assessment' (2002: 76).

Such assessment goes, however, against the grain of rapidly developing systems of international assessment based upon comparisons of national performance such as TIMSS and PIRLS run by the International Association for the Evaluation of Educational Achievement (www.iea.nl/) and PISA run by the OECD (www.pisa.oecd.org/). Such programmes of comparative assessment are designed to allow policy makers to adapt their educational systems so as to improve relative performance. While such comparisons are highly problematic in a technical sense and open to varied and contradictory interpretations (Torrance 2006), they are a crucial component in the political process of ensuring international economic competitiveness (Benveniste 2002; Bonal and Rambla 2009). Moreover, such tests are increasingly used by nation states to define measurable objectives or benchmarks that education systems must achieve. In this they have

> contributed to globalising the explanatory and normative frameworks for education and development . . . [and had] an interesting effect on the convergence of the means . . . countries are planning to use to improve the quality of their education systems.
>
> (Bonal and Rambla 2009: 154)

Associated with such tests are measures directed towards the setting of standards in all curriculum areas and at all levels of schooling. While the development of such standards is more often than not the preserve of state agencies, and concerned with key subject areas such as literacy, numeracy and science, and while 'the development of standards for K-12 international education has . . . lagged behind the national school process' (Oden, 2006: 179) attempts are also being made to develop international standards for 'international mindedness'. The argument here is that

> If schools are to promote . . . global awareness, then they should develop standards and benchmarks that reflect an international multicultural perspective. Students should be able to demonstrate their understanding that there are valid perspectives other than their own and that there is a relationship between our dispositions and behaviour.
>
> (Lewis 2005 in Oden 2006: 179)

However, such attempts to develop standards for international mindedness are rare and stand rather outside the international press towards the development of standards and assessment (especially in areas of international competitive achievement such as English, Mathematics and Science) and the articulation of national development policies directed towards increasing national performance and international competitiveness.

Such developments quite understandably create a sense of unease in international schools. If those sending their children to such schools are seeking positional advantage in their own communities as well as access to international employment opportunities as argued above, then they are likely to also demand proof of performance. As MacClelland suggests 'Quality control issues in assessment are essential in marketing the school; parents will want to know that the assessment results are reliable and hold up well to schools of similar standing' (2001: 49).

This is a particular problem for international schools in remote communities, operating in countries where local performance standards are not high and where linguistic and cultural custom is foreign to the cultures to which the graduates aspire.

'International schools often feel quite vulnerable about assessment as they are frequently isolated schools trying to ensure that the standard of education they provide is the same quality as that in national systems possibly thousands of miles away' (MacClelland 2001: 54).

Adding to this sense of vulnerability is the discontinuity felt by many schools due to the high turnover of staff, students, parents and often governing bodies. This may provide for continuous challenges to curriculum, pedagogy, assessment and performance as the diverse aspirations and destinations of students mix and re-mix within the school.

In order to provide continuous reassurance (or possibly to confirm the extent of the problem!) various commercial agencies provide international schools with services that allow comparisons to be made between schools, classes and individuals against national and international norms. One such organisation is the *International Schools Assessment* (ISA) service developed by the Australian Council for Educational Research and used by 28,000 students from 174 international schools in 70 different countries.[4]

Based upon the OECD's Programme for International Student Assessment (PISA) it is a 'high quality' test that international schools may use to monitor student performance in mathematical literacy, reading and writing and to confirm that their internal assessments are aligned with international expectations of performance. The ISA allows schools to compare the mathematics, reading and writing performance of individual students, class groups and grade levels within their school and with all other ISA international schools and students. ISA reports also provide schools with detailed diagnostic information about student performance.[5] Similar services are provided by the Curriculum, Evaluation and Management Centre, (CEMC) at Durham University (www.cemcentre.org/).

Choice and compromise in international school assessment policies

Thus assessment is a complex but crucial issue for international schools, particularly as it structures their association with prestigious examination bodies, standardised assessment organisations and, perhaps especially, higher education institutions. As Cambridge argues, such attachments are part of 'global product branding' for international schools where

> schools act as the retailers of products (i.e. academic qualifications) that are 'manufactured' by the examination boards. Schools and examination boards are joined in a symbiotic relationship giving mutual benefit, because the examination boards require schools' knowledge of local markets while schools derive benefit from their association with the name and reputation of the branded product that they are retailing . . . . The establishment of quality standards through accreditation constitutes an important part of the franchising process.
>
> (Cambridge 2002: 231)

The issue for international schools is at least in part one of choosing the particular franchise to which it wishes to belong and also of gaining accreditation from the franchising body. In the case of schools that are overseas outposts of national systems (such as some British and American schools abroad, military schools and company schools) the preferred franchise is fairly unproblematic. The assessment system that is current in their home country is preferred. For other schools that attract multiple nationalities or parents who want 'additional opportunities' (Theresa 2008: 80) on a world-wide basis the choice is more difficult as Cambridge makes clear:

> These contrasting curricula and associated assessment systems appeal to different sections of the client population for international education, depending on whether they require a qualification that is specific to college entry in the USA, as in the case of the College Board examinations, or one that has wider currency (e.g. IBO, CIE).
>
> (Cambridge 2002: 239)

Some schools, as Ellwood (1999) suggests, may attempt to integrate various curricular, pedagogical and assessment options. But combining different curricular, pedagogical and assessment principles may produce inconsistencies and contradictions (Guy 2000, 2001). Moreover, while international schools may brand themselves as 'internationally minded' parents who choose an international school for their children do not necessarily do so because of its proclaimed international-mindedness. Indeed, Theresa, for instance, reports that students and parents in her case study school were not at all interested in the international orientation of its IB programme

> I anticipated more favourable responses about international-mindedness in the IB Program and curriculum, but my findings produced an unexpected outcome: the stakeholders at AISS-E shared a view of the IB curriculum that was not at all reflective of the IB mission statement of international-mindedness. The stakeholders generally did not link the IB with international-mindedness. . . . [S]tudents all experienced IB curricula, and yet not one of them viewed their IB courses as internationally-minded . . . . [For] parents the difficulty level of the curriculum was more significant than its international outlook or global ethos. These findings pointed to IB curricula that provided academic rigor and not international-mindedness.
>
> (Theresa 2008: 79)

Matthews and Sidhu (2005) report similar findings from Australian schools in which 'international students do not experience Australian schools as sites for sponsoring new forms of global subjectivity and imagination' (2005: 62). Quite the contrary: international students in the schools they studied 'do not experience schools as culturally dispassionate institutional spaces . . . but as sites of racialization, prejudice and racism' (2005: 61). Despite (perhaps because of) these findings Matthews and Sidhu go on to argue the need for an international education that is not solely driven by attempts at market and positional advantage, but are truly driven by 'intercultural sensitivities, including identification with a global community, [as] important preconditions for effective participation in 21st century civic life' (2005: 63).

The question of assessment in international schools can, therefore, be seen to be driven by more than one impulse and by attachments to various contradictory curricular, pedagogical and assessment practices. How these are resolved in practice depends very much upon the particular circumstances, clientele and personnel of individual schools. But perhaps those schools that use the term 'international' in their title as more than simply a marketing, positioning or global branding exercise might need to consider carefully whether their assessment practices (and their associated curricular and pedagogical practices) do indeed promote international mindedness and identification with the global community, for schools can surely only legitimately call themselves international if they are committed to the encouragement of global citizenship and if their curricular, pedagogical and assessment practices demonstrate such commitment.

Notes

1   Nigel Bagnall of the University of Sydney helped with an earlier version of this paper.
2   For instance the IB Diploma grading system is criterion referenced and anyone achieving 75 per cent against the criteria for a particular subject will be awarded a 'perfect' pre-tertiary score of 7. This is quite different from other norm referenced examinations where regardless of score only a predetermined percentage can achieve a 'perfect' pre-tertiary score.
3   The following description is adapted from the IBO website www.ibo.org/general/what.cfm.
4   The following description is derived from www.acer.edu.au/isa.
5   The use to which such data can be put may be examined by the Principal's Report to Parents at the Swiss International School available at: www.swissinternationalschool.ch/fileadmin/basel/pdf/ISA_SIS_RESULTS_2008.PDF.

References

Benveniste, L. (2002) The political structuration of assessment: negotiating state power and legitimacy, *Comparative Education Review* 46(1): 89–118.

Bernstein, B. (1971) *Class Codes and Control*, London: Routledge & Kegan Paul.

Bernstein, B. (1996) *Pedagogy, Symbolic Control and Ideology*, London: Taylor and Francis.

Bonal, X. and Rambla, X. (2009) 'In the name of globalisation': southern and northern paradigms of educational development. In R. Dale and S. Robertson (eds) *Globalisation and Europeanisation in Education*, Oxford: Symposium, pp. 143–58.

Brown, P. (2006) The opportunity trap. In Lauder *et al.* (eds) *Education, Globalization and Social Change*, Oxford: Oxford University Press.

Brown, R. (2002) Cultural dimensions of national and international educational assessment. In J. Hayden, G. Thompson and G. Walker (eds) *International Education in Practice*, London: Routledge, pp. 66–79.

Cambridge, J. (2002) Global product branding and international education, *Journal of Research in International Education* 1(2): 227–43.

Dale, R. and Robertson, S. (eds) (2009) *Globalisation and Europeanisation in Education*, Oxford: Symposium.

Ellwood, C. (1999) IGCSE and the IB Middle Years Programme; how compatible are they? *International Schools Journal* 19(1): 35–44.

Enever, J. (2009) Languages, education and Europeanisation. In R. Dale and S. Robertson (eds) *Globalisation and Europeanisation in Education*, Oxford: Symposium, pp. 179–92.

European Council of International Schools (ECIS) (2008) *The ECIS International Schools Directory*, Melton, Suffolk: John Catt Educational.

Guy, J. (2000) IBMYP and IGCSE – are they really compatible? A response to Caroline Ellwood Part I, *International Schools Journal* 20(1): 10–17.

Guy, J. (2001) IGCSE and IB MYP: how compatible are they? Part II, *International Schools Journal* 21(1): 11–18.

Hayden, M. (2006) *Introduction to International Education: International Schools and Their Communities*, London: Sage.

Hofstede, G. (1991) *Cultures and Organizations*, London: Harper & Collins.

Hofstede, G. (2001) *Cultures Consequences: Comparing Values, Behaviours, Institutions and Organizations Across Nations*, Thousand Oaks: Sage Publications.

International Baccalaureate Organization (2007) *IB World Schools Yearbook 2007*, Saxmundham, Suffolk: John Catt Educational.

Lauder, H. (2007) International schools, education and globalization: towards a research agenda. In M. Hayden, J. Levy and J. Thompson (eds) *The SAGE Handbook of Research in International Education*, London: Sage Publications, pp. 441–9.

Lauder, H., Brown, P., Dillabough, J. and Halsey, A. (eds) (2006) *Education, Globalization and Social Change*, Oxford: Oxford University Press.

Leach, R. (1969) *International Schools and their Role in the Field of International Education*, Oxford: Pergamon Press.

Lowe, J. (2000) Assessment for educational quality: implications for international schools. In M. Hayden and J. Thompson (eds) *International Schools and International Education*, London: Kogan Page, pp. 15–28.

MacClelland, R. (2001) Managing assessment in the international school. In S. Blandford and M. Shaw (eds) *Managing International Schools*, London: Routledge, pp. 48–62.

Magalhaes, A. and Stoer, S. (2009) Performance, citizenship and the knowledge society. In R. Dale and S. Robertson (eds) *Globalisation and Europeanisation in Education*, Oxford: Symposium, pp. 233–60.

Matthews, J. and Sidhu, R. (2005) Desperately seeking the global subject: international education, citizenship and cosmopolitanism, *Globalisation, Societies and Education* 3(1): 49–66.

Oden, T. (2006) The role of standards in K-12 international education. In H. Lauder, P. Brown, J. Dillabough and A. Halsey (eds) *Education, Globalization and Social Change*, Oxford: Oxford University Press, pp. 176–88.

Ramalho, E. (2007) Combined Policies and Ideologies in an American International School, *Journal of Cases in Educational Leadership* 10(2–3): 1–9.

Theresa, H. (2008) *International-mindedness in Education: A Case Study of an International School*, Milton Keynes: Lightning Source.

Torrance, H. (2006) Globalizing empiricism: what, if anything, can be learned from international comparisons of educational achievement? In H. Lauder, P. Brown, J. Dillabough and A. Halsey (eds) *Education, Globalization and Social Change*, Oxford: Oxford University Press, pp. 824–34.

Van Oord, L. (2007) To westernize the nations? The International Baccalaureate's philosophy of education, *Cambridge Journal of Education* 37(3): 375–90.

Young, M. (2008) *Bringing Knowledge Back In*, London: Routledge.

9 The International Baccalaureate

Its growth and complexity of challenges

Tristan Bunnell

Introduction to the challenges

The Geneva-registered International Baccalaureate Office (IBO) celebrated its fortieth anniversary in October 2008. The International Baccalaureate (IB) now conceivably forms a continuum of international education for 3–19-year-olds; the initial Diploma Programme (DP) was joined in 1994 by the Middle Years Programme (MYP), and three years later by the Primary Years Programme (PYP). The year 2010 began with the IB involving a very diverse body of 2,800 schools in 138 countries worldwide offering a combination of 3,400 programmes to 800,000 children. The IB, with its philosophical foundation of 'liberal education for human rationality' (see Sobulis 2005), has undeniably been central to the development of international schooling in practice. It is argued that the IB is overtly international at the content level but thoroughly 'western' at the epistemological level (see Van Oord 2007).

The IB initially underwent slow growth, mainly within the largely hidden world of 'international schools'. Until the late 1970s there was no guarantee of its survival, and the story has been well told since 2001 by Ian Hill (Deputy Director General of the IBO) within numerous copies of the *International Schools Journal*. The fall of the Berlin Wall facilitated rapid expansion, especially in the USA, Canada, England (*not* Britain), and Australia, and although maintained national schools there have joined the fray in large numbers, the body of schools worldwide continues to be a rather exclusive and elite grouping. The 'big four' countries mentioned above accounted for no less than 60 per cent of all IB schools at the beginning of 2010. Furthermore, they contained 51 per cent of PYP schools, 53 per cent of DP ones, and 70 per cent of all MYP schools. What this reveals, aside from the obvious 'Western' and 'Anglocentric' bias, is the fact that the IB finds it much easier to expand into countries where there is not a rigid national curriculum, or national system of education. England has a National Curriculum until post-16 schooling, where the curriculum provision is now quite crowded. Furthermore, this shows the IB tends to grow in areas where it already has a large presence.

The IB has always been a difficult and complex educational product to study and analyse. There has been a frenetic pace of change and rapid growth over the past four decades. Obtaining a holistic overview of developments is not an easy task. Much of the analysis is still mainly held within the context of an internal discourse, and articles in journals such as the *International Schools Journal* are difficult to obtain in the public domain. Relatively little critical discourse has occurred, while most of the major authors are IB protagonists, and much of the more critical literature is contained within the 'IB World' through work such as the now-defunct *IB Research Notes*. Furthermore, much of the literature has lately been concerned with the history and early development of the IB rather than current or future developments. This helps to explain the dearth of material on the IB within the general educational field of scholarly publication, and this means the researcher must tread carefully through the literature for signs of bias or exaggeration. It is important in particular to separate the 'facts' from the 'myths', and the IB has its fair share of the latter. The IB has always been open to external attack. For some it is too elite, too academic, too 'Western', too idealistic, too much linked to the United Nations (UN), and growing too fast. The IB has also always been open to internal angst. Even in 1972, Alec Peterson, a key architect of the IB, was unhappy with the direction the programme was taking, and asking 'Is the IB an elitist project?' (Peterson 1972). Its lack of activity in Africa, for example, has always been an issue of concern although speeches by the former Chair of the IB Board of Governors (see Seefried 2006, 2008) reveal optimism for the future.

In short, the growth and development of the IB has always been problematic. The early years of the IB were focused on recognition and growth per se whilst funding and survival were major issues (see Fox 1998, Hill 2002). The period since the late 1990s has seen the IB focus much more on consolidating its image and corporate identity, and this has seen the IB emerge as a global brand, comparable to other symbols of hyperglobalisation (see Cambridge 2002). A by-product of this corporate development is that schools are increasingly viewed as *customers* rather than *members*. The rapid growth of the IB is understandably fundamentally altering the *relationship* it has with its schools.

After four decades of rapid growth the IB began to undertake a strategic planning exercise in 2004 seeking to prepare for one million children by 2014 (IBO 2004). By 2007 this was already looking an underestimate and the IB has since pushed this projection forward to educating 2.5 million children in 10,000 schools by 2020. What this reveals is that the IB is always desperately trying to keep its infrastructure and plans ahead of the growth curve; trying to be 'fit for purpose'. The growth between 2004 and 2005 alone was larger than the IB body had been in 1987.

Out of this planning process has come a more critical discourse. It has been discussed (Doherty *et al.* 2009) how IB graduates in Australia are utilizing their capacity to cross national borders (this is termed 'border artistry'), and how the IB offers them a competitive edge with which to strategically pursue economic and cultural capital. However, the IB has in many ways become its own biggest critic. What has been revealed through documentation (e.g. IBO 2006) and presentations (e.g. Beard 2006) is that the IB faces a number of incredibly complex dilemmas and challenges. It always did, but the rapid and largely unplanned growth of the past four decades has created a situation where the IB is keen to direct its further expansion and wishes to widen its access beyond the global elite, who it arguably still largely serves. At the same time it has created over time a brand, with logo, that carries a strongly academic image, and the IB is keen to protect both the integrity and quality assurance of its 'product'.

This complex set of challenges is made all the more difficult by the fact that the IB is unique in having at its heart a radical Mission Statement to 'create a better and more peaceful world through intercultural understanding and respect', whilst also possessing a publically quoted value-system and a set of idealistic outcomes; this emerged in April 2006 in the format of the 10-point 'IB Learner Profile'. This chapter presents a background to studying this complexity of challenges. First, the reader must learn a little about the history and growth of the IB as this creates a context for understanding the current situation.

The early challenges

The IB as a programme of study had been in existence beyond 1968. The UNESCO-convened Conference of Internationally minded schools had organized in 1950 a four-week long course for teachers interested in inter-national schooling, and fifty people had met up at the United Nations-linked International School of Geneva. This school had been formed in 1924 by employees of the League of Nations, and the International Labour Office, and along with the one in Yokohama, had formed the first 'modern' type of international school. It is possible that some of the teachers from 1950 were involved in the development of the first IB course, the impetus for which came out of a conference of social studies teachers in Geneva in 1962. It was here that the name 'International Baccalaureate' was first used. Using material developed by UNESCO in geography, and in history, the first course appeared in Contemporary History, and was sat by four students at Geneva in June 1963.

As well as giving the IB a longer timeline than many imagine, this story reveals two things. First, the IB has its roots in the Cold War, in 1962, at the peak of the Cuban missile crisis and this partly explains its radical Mission Statement. Second, the IB has historical links with the UN and this has helped create a number of 'myths' and exaggerations, as seen in the vociferous attack on the IB in the United States (see Bunnell 2009). Interestingly, the IB had wished for a more formal link with the UN. At a conference in France in 1974 it had been suggested that the IB be integrated with UNESCO, but the offer was rejected. The story of the 'early stirrings' also reveals another fact about the IB, and one that has symbolized its growth and development ever since.

The IB came about through conflicting reasons and thus involves a fundamental compromise. On the one hand there was the desire for a more internationalist curriculum. At the same time, the school in Geneva required a
pragmatic solution to the fact that the students there operated within different
sections. There was a need to 'unite' the school. Hence, the IB came about
ultimately for both ideological and pragmatic reasons.

A further pragmatic need was to serve the globally mobile international
community (diplomatic and corporate), who required in the 1960s a transferable qualification that offered the opportunity of repatriation into elite
Colleges and Universities 'back home'. It was being stated in the late 1970s
(e.g. Hymer 1979) that an 'international capitalist class' had emerged, spear-
headed by a social class operating within multinational corporations (Goldfrank
1977). Two decades later the term Transnational Capitalist Class (TCC)
appeared, identifying a deliberate project of institutionalizing globalization,
beginning in the late 1960s. Significantly, this is the period in time (1967
to be exact) that the IBDP emerged in its trial-exam phase, giving a clear
indication of its links with the TCC. Robinson and Harris (2000) argue the
TCC is a global ruling class since it controls the levers of an emerging transnational state apparatus and of global decision making. This places the IB at
the forefront of educating the global elite, within its 'core' base of 'international
schools'.

The IB therefore from the outset was inextricably linked with a dichotomy
of type of school, and the educating of the children of the TCC. The first DP
trial-exam in June 1967 had involved the United World College of The
Atlantic, in south Wales. This had been formed in 1962 by the German
educationalist Kurt Hahn, and is now one of a network of thirteen United
World Colleges (UWC) on five continents. Students are selected for scholarship
by national committee, and this type of school fits within a hyperglobalist
thesis viewpoint of globalization given that it transcends national borders.
Other IB pioneers include the Copenhagen International High School, a form
of 'market-led' institution catering primarily for the globally mobile children
of diplomatic or transnational corporation personnel. This type of school is
also linked with the hyperglobalist thesis, serving employees of the global
economy. By definition, this type of school has to conform to common
standards worldwide as it seeks to serve a transient body of parents looking
for a familiar product.

International schooling in general has always involved a fundamental
dilemma, and the reconciling of differing approaches. On the one hand, the
IB can be seen to be promoting an ideal of behaviour and character and universal
values. In this sense it serves a civic purpose and is arguably worthy of public
funding either by individual governments or by the UN. The notion of the
IB as a global public good is a novel yet viable one especially given its stated
mission of facilitating global peace. On the other hand, the IB can be viewed
as a provider of a global quality-assured and branded certification process

to an elite group of candidates. In this sense, it is a facilitator of economic supremacy, operating within a global unregulated system of education. In this context the IB might be seen as undermining the national interest and therefore not worthy of any public funding.

Of course, in practice most IB schools probably lie somewhere between the two approaches which helps to explain the rich diversity of schooling that has emerged. Perhaps the body of IB schools should be viewed within a continuum of activity rather than a fundamental dichotomy. However, it is this fundamental dilemma, of reconciling the idealistic mission of the IB with the demand from elite schools for a pragmatic, quality-assured, and economically advantageous product that acts as a constant theme to any study of the IB. It is also the key to understanding the potential for future tension within the broad 'movement'.

The growth of the International Baccalaureate

The IB can be viewed through a 'lifetime' analogy. The period until 1983 can be regarded as the stage of 'infancy' and the IB began to move beyond its initial Northern European nexus. This period saw the IB have two Directors General (Alec Peterson 1968–77; and Gérard Renaud 1977–83). The IBDP was a low-key experiment until 1976 with exam entrants purposively limited to a controlled sample of 500 students. The May 1970 examination involved just 29 students undertaking the full diploma. By 1972, there were twenty-two schools in fourteen countries authorized to enter candidates for the DP examination. The year 1975 saw St Stephen's, in Rome, become the first DP School in Italy. Kodaikanal International School in 1976 became the first in India and New York's Francis Lewis School became the first American high school to come on board the project.

At the second Inter-Governmental Conference in London, 15–16 February 1978, it was recommended the IB undertake a 'carefully controlled expansion', beyond its present fifty schools. There were fifty-eight IB schools worldwide when the Narrabundah College in Canberra became the first in Australia in 1979, and there were seventy-three when the International School Moshi (Tanzania) in 1980 became the first in Africa. The 100 mark was hit in 1982, the twenty-fifth anniversary of the first trial examination. The following year saw Spanish join French and English as 'working' languages of the DP. Roger Peel became the third IB Director General in 1984. There were 128 IB schools at this time. The 200-mark was hit in 1987. There were 345 schools worldwide when the International School of Beijing Shunyi became the first IB school in China in 1991. The fifteen-year period that saw Peel as Director General (1984–99) was the 'youthful' period, and this saw the IB grow from 130 to 800 programmes.

Towards the end of the 1990s, commentators began to talk of the 'coming of age' of international schooling. It did appear that something major was occurring within the field at this time, and deliberate attempts were certainly being made to create a greater sense of structure and purpose. The International Education System Pilot Project had appeared in 1996, as an attempt to create an international school 'system'. The DP in 1997 formed a 'continuum of international education'. The IB Council of Foundation (now called the Board of Governors) met in Bucharest in May 1999 and was given advice by consultants that the IB required greater strategic planning. A five-year strategic plan duly appeared that year.

Not surprisingly, it was during this period that commentators talked of the shift from the early role of the IB in creating something for a niche group of mobile students, and being a provider of good programmes for international schools, towards a role of convincing others who are not international of the value of the IB. This period in time is a fundamentally important one for the IB; a period of consolidation was taking place after three decades of ad hoc growth and development. Several commentators have since reflected back on this change in 'era'. Walker (2007) stated the IB had successfully passed its short-term aim of providing an international qualification, and while the first era had involved 'contact' the next one will involve 'connection' and 'impact'. What Walker seemed to imply was that the short-term aim of the IB, of creating 'schools across frontiers' designed for globally mobile students, had been superseded in the late 1990s by an aim of greater influence among a broader body of students and a deeper scope of activity. This was problematic for the IB as it required a deliberate shift away from its 'international school movement' base towards more involvement with 'national schooling', and elite private schooling. This helps to explain why the latter two types, in early 2010, helped form almost 90 per cent of the 'IB World'.

Much had occurred since the previous plan in 1999. The 'IB World' doubled from 1,000 to 2,000 schools between the years 2000 and 2004. There were several key catalysts for this. One was the tumultuous events of September 2001 which led immediately afterwards towards a move to putting 'the world into American classrooms'. Another stimulus was the emergence of the popular 'world is flat' paradigm which placed pressure on countries such as the US and England to educate the next generation for working in a more competitive world. As result of this, the IB began in the US to receive federal funding, which has proven problematic.

The period of rapid expansion under Director General George Walker's guidance (1999–2006) can now be viewed as the 'adulthood'. Any reader who has studied development economics will be familiar with Walt Whitman Rostow's model of economic growth which states countries undertake five stages. Stage 3 of the Rostow Model is the 'Take-Off' stage. In terms of the IB this coincides with the 'adulthood' period. Stage 4 of the Rostow Model is the 'Drive to Maturity' stage and this is arguably the current stage of the IB lifetime, beginning in 2006. This is the period of one's life when one begins to reflect on the past and plan for the future as the IB did in 2004 when it produced a comprehensive ten-year strategic plan.

The International Baccalaureate in 2010

The IB in 2006 began to show less concern over growth per se and more concern over its overall level of access. This is a tremendously complex area for the IB, involving at least nine different dimensions. There is a desire to open up to parents who cannot afford the fees, the *economic* access challenge. There is a further wish to widen the programmes in languages other than English, the *linguistic* access challenge. The DP in Spanish continues to grow but the programme in French is essentially moribund and presumably economically unviable (only twenty-eight schools were following the DP in French in 2009). What this reveals is that the IB stands accused of trying to 'fight on too many fronts'. As the *Copenhagen Consensus* conferences, organized by the Danish 'sceptical environmentalist' Bjørn Lomborg, have shown, the world faces many problems but not all can be attained at once. There needs to be a prioritizing of problems based upon what is most feasible. The IB arguably needs to start applying a similar sort of discussion.

The embracing of a less elite client might be deemed a priority by some. The appeal of the IB to the global and national elite is now very evident. In December 2008, Wellington College announced its plans to offer the MYP, and several of England's top scoring examination result schools are now 'IB World Schools', for example, Sevenoaks, Oakham, North London Collegiate Girls', and King's College Wimbledon. Together, these four schools accounted for almost half of the top grades (45 points) awarded in the May 2008 DP examination.

At first glance, the appeal of the IB to the rising economic elite seems to override any overtly idealistic tendency. However, the IB involves a remarkably diverse grouping of schools and the ones mentioned above should in no way be supposed as 'typical'. In the USA, where 38 per cent of all IB schools are located, the vast majority (92 per cent) are state-funded, and half the primary ones are Title 1 Category (i.e. has typically around 40 per cent or more of its students from low-income families), revealing their inner-city locations (Connor 2008). In fact, almost 60 per cent of IB schools are maintained national ones, although there are huge regional variations. In the Middle East, for example, all the IB schools are private, and they can definitely be classified as an elite grouping. This region of the world offers a good case study of the growth and development of the IB (see Bunnell 2008a).

The rather crude 'growth chart' statistics mask an enormous geographical disparity of IB involvement and this could be deemed by some educators as being another priority area. The raw statistics hide a multitude of discrepancies, all of which undermine the notion of the IB as a 'global player'. In early 2010, just some dozen countries accounted for 75 per cent of the 'IB World' (in rank order: USA, Canada, UK, Australia, Mexico, India, Spain, China, Germany, Sweden and Ecuador). At the other extreme, eighty-five nation states, representing 62 per cent of all countries with an IB schools, had less than five apiece. Only 2 per cent of IB schools were in Africa, a figure largely unchanged since the 1980s. The May 2008 DP examination revealed that 54 per cent of students were US citizens, whilst fifty-eight countries had less than ten of their citizens registered for the exams. This immediately raises the point that the IB could do much to widen its *geographical* access.

In early 2010, large parts of the world remain relatively untouched by the IB, including countries such as Italy (20 schools), Japan (17 schools), France (10 schools), Nigeria (3 schools). The point to observe here is that the IB is an *international* player but it is not a truly *global* one. The IB programmes have centres of activity and areas such as Warsaw and Buenos Aires might be deemed 'cores'. There are as many IB schools in Buenos Aires as there are in the whole of China. There are the same number in South Australia as in the whole of Africa, and as many in Toronto as Japan. Warsaw has the same number as New Zealand. There are more MYP schools in Chicago than in China.

The IB looks set for much further growth facilitated by online curriculum development or the further internationalizing of national curricula, and continuing outsourcing of English-speaking services. A report from the British Council in 2006 has estimated that by 2015 half the world's population will be speaking or learning English, and this may propagate further IB growth. The BRIC economies (Brazil, Russia, India, and China) accounted for only 5 per cent of the IB World in early 2010 and there is potentially room for enormous future expansion here. Furthermore, the Middle East accounted for just 2 per cent of IB activity yet international schooling in general is growing rapidly there.

The year 2020 seems an incredibly long time away in terms of the IB and its developments, but it seems highly likely the goal of educating 2.5 million children will be reached. The current compound growth of 14 per cent should see the IB reach out to 3,000 schools during 2010 while this should double to 6,000 by 2015. In this context, the goal of 10,000 schools should easily be reached four or five years later on. Stage 5 of the Rostow Model, the final one, is the 'High Mass Consumption' stage. The IB is seemingly heading rapidly towards this stage. A total of 36,000 students undertook the full DP examination in May 2007, an increase of 160 per cent since year 2000. The PYP alone saw a 23 per cent rise in school numbers during 2009, and saw a 213 per cent rise since 2005. The DP saw a 67 per cent rise in school providers between 2005 and 2009. The issue to discuss therefore is what paths will the IB take over the next ten years and what challenges will it incur? The aim of growing in a more directed manner within a wider access paradigm yet maintaining quality assurance is a difficult conundrum to solve.

Future challenges

There are several major challenges to be faced that have not yet been openly discussed. First, the continued growth of the IB stands to dilute the power of the brand. The DP is seen as an expensive programme to buy into (e.g. Sen 2001) and its role as a facilitator of marketing advantage has been identified as an important one (e.g. McGee 2003). Part of the problem is that the IB is heavily reliant on school examination fees and the 'annual fee' which is the same for each school irrespective of size. Schools presumably obtain some cache and image enhancement by offering the DP, which now stands as a globally branded, seemingly quality-assured, educational product untainted by 'grade inflation' like the English Advanced Levels, where 27 per cent of grades in 2010 were a Grade A. The IB still only gives out full marks in the May DP examination to about 0.2 per cent of students.

Here lies a complex dilemma for the IB; how to expand the IB programmes within a wider access paradigm yet still maintain the image of an exclusive product. One answer would be to expand mainly within the realms of reputable national and private schools. The IB has a strong base here already. *Newsweek* magazine in May 2009 published its annual list of 'America's Best High Schools' in which thirty-four out of the top 100 schools offered the DP. In 2004, just 6 per cent of the prestigious Headmasters' and Headmistresses' Conference (HMC: a grouping of 250 leading private schools, mainly in Britain) offered the DP. By early 2010 this number had risen another 11 per cent (to involve 17 per cent or thirty-five schools). Put another way, more than one in six of the 'IB World Schools' in Britain in late 2009 was a HMC member, and that number is expected to double by 2012. In Australia, six members (out of eleven) of the prestigious grouping of the 'Associated Public Schools of Victoria' are IB schools.

Another challenge linked with increased access is that of maintaining quality assurance. By quality, the IB means 'reliability' and 'consistency'. As the IB grows it becomes more difficult to ensure that support and in-service training, for example, meet the usual or expected standards. This is important as the IB relies heavily upon word-of-mouth marketing and has never advertised its programmes. Future growth depends on the IB maintaining its image as a standardized high-quality product. The appointment in 2006 of Ohio-born Jeffrey Beard, a former businessman and charity fund-raiser, as Director General was a very significant development in consolidating the IB image. The IB immediately underwent a move towards capturing its presence as a global product. The IB Learner Profile, as noted earlier, made its appearance in 2006 and a new corporate visual identity appeared in April the year after (replacing the 2001-designed one). This is a controversial area. As the IB offers a reliable product conforming to consistent quality standards throughout the world it can be compared to other branded products such as hamburgers or soft drinks.

A third major challenge is to continue growing yet maintain the image of a cohesive 'IB World'. Many international schools worldwide are isolated from the local and national community. The sense of belonging to a global community is presumably a powerful and reassuring one. At the same time, the 'international school movement' is becoming increasingly marginalized within the 'IB World' and may be tempted at some point to re-create its own separate product. It was becoming clear in late 2009 that the 'international school movement' takes exception to being seen as 'customers' (see Matthews 2009). We might expect this tension to accelerate in the near future.

The IB unveiled in July 2008 its radical plans for reorganization into three separate inter-competing regions; Singapore, The Hague and Montgomery County, Maryland. This may propogate further North American expansion. The IB unveiled in April 2007 its first three-year 'community' theme, 'Sharing our Humanity'. This was based upon six topics adapted from the book *High Noon: 20 Global Problems, 20 Years to Solve Them* written in 2002 by the World Bank's vice-President for Europe, Jean-Francois Rischard. This move seemed symptomatic of a wider attempt to consolidate the diversity of the 'IB World' and at the same time ensure a more consistent and standardized product. But, another three topics will be needed by 2020.

The IB faces a challenge in bringing a sense of order and 'system' to the globally branded 'IB World'. This is an incredibly complex and multilayered one, reflecting the unplanned growth and development over four decades. The German School Beirut has been offering the DP since 2004 and the Toronto French School since 1990. As the 'IB World' grows in size, and diversity, the task of maintaining a sense of 'community' gets harder and more complex. Although the IB is assessed and governed from Cardiff and Geneva, its marketing and authorization process has always operated at a regional level. The IB is not a 'Swiss-based' organization as implied by opponents in the US. The first regional office to appear, in 1977, was IB North America (IBNA), located in New York. There were six IB schools in the US at this time. IBNA has always been a separate entity from the IB, and in June 2008 the two bodies merged. In 1982, the IB established a regional office in Buenos Aires (IB Latin America, or IBLA). That same year it created an office in Singapore (IB Asia Pacific, or IBAP). The Africa, Europe, and Middle East regional office (IBAEM) first opened in London in 1978. After several interim moves, IBAEM settled in Geneva in 1994. What this shows is that establishing a more ordered global presence has always been a challenge for the IB.

The IB schools themselves have pragmatically grouped together at a regional and local level, forming a bewildering array of acronyms. Indeed one on-going development concerning international schooling is the creation of an 'alliance'. The Alliance for International Education (AIE) met for its fifth conference in Melbourne in July 2010 and its ten 'patrons' include the IB. A myriad of sub-regional IB associations exist, especially in North America. The Guild of International Baccalaureate Schools of the Northeast (GIBS) is just one of twenty groupings, and involves schools in New York, New Jersey, Rhode Island, Massachusetts, Connecticut, and Pennsylvania. The IB Schools and Colleges Association (IBSCA) has been a key catalyst for growth in England.

Another major challenge for the future concerning growth is that more areas of the world will reach a 'critical mass' (see Seefried 2006). This rather vague concept has not been fully elucidated upon by the IB but it can be viewed within economies of scale context. It has become clear that 'critical mass' (identified by the IB as a bloc of about fifty schools in a country) also brings with it critical attention, especially when the IB moves into national schooling and receives tax-payer funding. In early 2010, only about ten areas of the world statistically had this situation (the Mid-Atlantic of the USA, California, Florida, Canada, Australia, Mexico, Argentina, India, Spain and England). In the 107 countries where there are fewer than ten IB schools, this is presumably less of an issue at present. The US government was one of only five worldwide that supported IB expansion in state schools that year, alongside England, Ecuador, Australia and Canada. Consequently, the IB has come under parental and wider tax-payer scrutiny in the US, and come under vociferous political attack (see Bunnell 2009). Questions began to be asked about the origins and mission of the IB. One school in Pittsburgh dropped the IB in 2006 and the resulting debate revealed much about the controversies surrounding the IB in the US (see Walters 2006).

Lastly, the IB has so far operated in a largely monopolistic situation with regard to international curricula, while in many parts of the world there is a sole IB school, giving it an automatic monopoly situation. However, there were signs in early 2010 that this is radically beginning to change. The Cambridge International Primary Programme (CIPP) was launched in April 2003. In 2008, the UK's largest examination body, the Assessment and Qualifications Alliance (AQA) launched its 'AQA Baccalaureate', deliberately intended as a home-grown and 'cheaper' option than the DP. Moreover, Fieldwork Education Ltd, a subsidiary of The World Class Learning Schools and Systems Group, has created the International Primary Curriculum (IPC). It was intended initially for the small bloc of Shell Company Group of Schools yet involved 530 schools in fifty countries in September 2008. Of these, 386 were state-funded primary schools in England, compared to the eight PYP schools there at that time. The IPC was described in the *Primary Leadership Today* journal in July 2008 as 'an international education within a national system'. The point to observe here is that the market is becoming a more crowded and competitive one. International schooling now involves more than just the IB.

Future paths

One glaringly obvious path forward is for the IB to expand internally. This might be deemed a 'low-risk' path. In January 2010, the statistics revealed that only 139 schools (5 per cent of total) undertook the 'continuum' as such, while 59 per cent of schools offered merely the DP. In fact, 83 per cent of schools do just one of the three programmes (interestingly, these three percentage figures have remained fairly stable since 2004). If all current IB schools were to do the 'continuum' this would expand the total number of programmes by almost 150 per cent. In the US alone in 2010 there is room for another 2,000 programmes. These are big figures. What we also know is that many schools offer the DP programmes to few students. The elite and highly academic image of the DP has led to it being offered in most schools worldwide to only the highest achievers. In fact, 48 per cent of schools offer it to only half their students. Only 36 per cent of schools offer it to all, and 31 per cent offer it to less than a quarter (IBO 2006). The Middle East is a good example of this. Qatar has five DP schools yet only thirty-three students were entered for the 2005 examinations from this country. Saudi Arabia's two schools, on the other hand, entered 115 students.

The 'IB World' is growing fast but in some parts of the world it is growing slower than the 'international school movement'. In a sense, this shows how the two have taken a slightly different course. According to an article in 2007 in the *International Schools Journal* there were 205 'international schools' in Dubai alone in April 2007, plus a further sixty-three in Qatar. However, only fifteen schools in these countries undertook the IB programmes. The moral of the story here is that the IB could go back to its 'roots' and cater more for its original client base, the 'international schools', who in early 2010 accounted for just 12 per cent of the 'IB World'. This figure had been 18 per cent seven years ago (Walker 2003), and can thus be expected to fall to around 3 or 4 per cent by 2020. According to the online database *ISC Research*, though, there were 5,500 of these schools in early 2010, spread across 236 countries. It is estimated, given the 11 per cent annual growth rate between 2006 and 2009, that there will be 10,000 'international schools' by 2015 and 15,000 in 2020 (although this growth figure had fallen to 7 per cent in early 2010). The downside of this move, of course, is that it will simply reinforce the view that the IB is a peripheral educational player, and will diminish any 'impact' that the programmes might have on national education. The upside is that it will give the 'international school movement' a bigger say than at present and may help dissipate any further 'growth tensions'. Here lies a major future dilemma for the IB.

A 'high-risk' path would be to widen access in parts of the world so far largely untouched by the IB. The IB has always been keen to gain greater access into Africa and the wider Islamic world, but this is difficult given the current political situation and the cultural values espoused by the IB, such as critical thinking, which is not a universal value. The involvement of the IB with the Aga Khan Academies is symbolic of the move, especially since 2006, towards widening access to parts of the world by working *through* organizations, in partnership and close alignment. The IB has realized it cannot attain all of its access goals alone and has embarked on partnerships and alliance-building. This is symbolic of international schooling in general.

In 2000, His Highness the Aga Khan had initiated a programme for the establishment of an integrated network of nineteen schools, called Aga Khan Academies, planned for locations in Africa and Asia and with admission based solely on merit. His Highness delivered the 2008 Peterson Lecture (see Aga Khan 2008). There is much to be learned about the IB and its philosophy from these lectures as they reveal honesty and idealism that is rarely evident beyond the internal IB discourse and this is also true of the Aga Khan's speech. The first Academy began operating in Mombasa in 2003 and it is intended they will all eventually offer the 'continuum'. The path of widening access through partnerships is a pragmatic but problematic one. Directed growth through partnerships is a risky strategy. The IB risks compromising its quality assurance and autonomy, plus the attack on the IB in the US partly involved the association the IB has with other organizations such as UNESCO and the Earth Charter.

Another way forward is to offer online provision of the DP, which seems logical for a pre-Higher Education qualification, yet this is also fraught with difficulty. So far the IB has trod carefully. There have been two pre-pilot DP online experiments involving six schools in five countries. September 2008 saw the start of a four-year pilot phase, involving initially seventy-five students from a minimum of thirteen schools worldwide. The IB has identified a potential demand in the future of about 6,000 students. But, there is no guarantee that the programme will continue beyond 2012. As shown in Bunnell (2008b) the task of maintaining quality provision is a concern as is the extent to which an 'IB experience' can be offered online.

In particular, online provision of IB courses could lead to a 'fake' product appearing. Schools could be tempted to pretend they offer the IB when in fact they have not been authorized and do not offer the full Diploma. The IB has suggested that perhaps another term be offered, the 'IB Partner' school, with separate logo, to differentiate these schools from the authorized 'IB World' schools. The notion of a new class of 'IB Partner' schools, buying online courses from approved 'IB Open' schools may introduce a two-tier system of schools, which might further dilute the sense of community and existence of an 'IB World'.

Conclusions

The speeches made by the IB leadership and governance bodies, since 2006 in particular (see Beard 2006, and Seefried 2008), have three major themes in common. First, they present openly and honestly the issues facing the IB as it adjusts to the huge growth of the past two decades. This involves a formidable set of complex challenges and dilemmas. At the same time, the IB seems to have rediscovered through the strategic planning process its idealistic sense of mission which adds another set of challenges to the equation. Third, these speeches reveal the degree of internal optimism by the IB. There is no doubting that the IB is presenting a 'brave face' on the issue of handling huge growth and yet maintaining its aims and meeting the diverse sets of demands. However, some commentators and educators are sceptical about the ability of the IB to meet many of its challenges especially its goal of wider access in parts of the world such as Africa, and its ambitious pursuit of online provision. Moreover, the IB is now made up of numerous 'constituencies', each with their own agenda. Continued 'unity' is not guaranteed. It is also not clear, in early 2010, how the three 'global centres' will operate, or compete.

In short, the 'IB World' is fast becoming a bewilderingly diverse and problematic one. The IB has grown in such a way that there is a huge dispersal of power and authority which adds a considerable challenge to the IB plan of directed growth within a more inclusive access paradigm. Furthermore, not only is this organisation structure a drain on resources, with overlapping and inter-competing areas of activity, but it considerably dissipates any sense of an IB 'community'. This is important since the notion of an 'IB World' is a key marketing tool. From the very outset in 1962 the IB has involved the challenge of meeting a dichotomy of demands and the need for compromise. In many ways this is symbolic of the field of 'international schooling' in general. Even within its initial International School of Geneva setting, the IB was torn between offering a radical internationalist curriculum committed to education for global peace, and the pragmatic need to offer what Alec Peterson termed an educational 'Nansen passport'. Indeed, even the name 'IB' suggests compromise. Why not call it the Global Diploma, or the International School Leaving Certificate?

This constant need for reconciling the fundamental dilemma between the ideological and the pragmatic demands has imposed severe limitations on both the scale and scope of the IB over its four decades of existence. As shown by the strategic planning documents (IBO 2004, 2006), the IB involves a frustrating impasse; the IB Mission Statement implies a need for inclusive and broad access, yet this might compromise the quality of the curriculum, which now stands as a globally branded quality-assured product bought into by schools in the expectation of a standardized package. It seems crude to say this, but the IB in some ways stands as a cold war relic, and its ambitious, even idealistic Mission Statement gives it a unique marketing niche among curricula offerings, yet at the same time it imposes severe restrictions and tensions.

The IB entered a distinct 'second era' around the late 1990s, as did the field of international schooling in general. This proves the historical linkage between the two. The first era of the IB had been undeniably problematic – the DP was technically an experiment until the mid 1970s and there was no guarantee that the programme would be funded or recognized on the scale needed. It was inevitable that this first period should focus on growth per se. The current wave of globalization has facilitated the rapid growth of the IB from a bloc of 300 schools in 1990 to the current one encompassing eight times more. By 2015 it should be sixteen times more.

The growth and development of the IB has always been problematic and never more so than at present. In particular, the IB is inextricably linked to the forces of globalization and is prone to attack particularly from a hyperglobalist lens, although a sceptical reality exists in practice. The IB has emerged as a seemingly elite product, offering economic and social advantage. The attack in the US since 2004 shows how the expansion of the IB can meet resistance, and gives evidence of how its depth in any one country will be constrained by the need to compromise with political opposition. The IB has always desired access to more schools in remote areas of the world, such as sub-Saharan Africa, although again there is concern that this might compromise the need to maintain a high quality product. The Middle East shows how limited an impact the IB makes in parts of the world. The growth in England shows how far it can make an impact on national curriculum, but also shows how the path might be a 'divisive' one (see Bunnell 2008c).

Questions can be raised about how the IB can possibly manage this set of complex issues. The emerging 'growth-access' dilemmas are especially difficult. The IB wishes to maintain growth yet maintain its integrity and image of quality. The online provision of the DP raises many issues here. The IB wishes to make more inroads into national education yet is sensitive and prone to tax-payer and political opposition. The attack in the US has proved how potentially damaging this can be. The IB wants to improve its level of access and meet its ambitious mission yet is aware that much of its growth is for pragmatic not idealistic reasons, plus the only way this can happen is for the IB to move beyond its 'Western' operational paradigm. The Middle East shows how difficult this task is. The IB is acutely aware of its image as an elite product yet is unwilling to compromise the quality of its programmes. The IB in England reveals how it is settling into an elitist, and potentially divisive, pattern of activity in some countries. The intended reorganization into three autonomous regions may give the IB much more of a regional presence and may help to dissipate the notion of a Geneva-centric organization, a theme of attack in the US. What it might also do is create a sense of regional community, arguably lacking at present. This author worked in an IB school in London for fourteen years and was not conscious of any overt sense of a British, or European, 'IB community'. However, it could also dilute the image of an 'IB World'.

The IB is condemned to working within a fundamental dichotomy of mission, one idealistic and the other pragmatic, each placing considerable demands on its role and direction. At some point the dam may burst. The IB has worked hard to produce its global brand and so far it has maintained its integrity and quality appearance. But, it has become very clear to those involved within the 'IB World' that rapid growth is creating a considerable amount of stress and strain. The IB is trying very hard to keep the system 'fit for purpose', and keep ahead of the growth curve, but it is fighting a tough battle on a number of difficult fronts. In particular, it faces a challenge holding its disparate 'constituencies' together. The 'international school movement' appears especially uneasy with the current situation, while any compromising of the quality might force other groupings (e.g. the elite English private schools) to seek alternative programmes of study. A key challenge for the future seems one of simply holding the 'IB World' together. International schooling has become a complex area of education, attracting a diverse clientele. It is not guaranteed that they can be permanently 'allied'. The future path for the IB looks as unpredictable as the 'first era' was, maybe even more so.

References

Aga Khan, His Highness the (2008) Global education and the developing world, lecture delivered by His Highness the Aga Khan to the Annual General Meeting of the IB marking its 40th Anniversary, Atlanta, Georgia, 18 April 2008, available at: www.ibo.org/council/peterson/documents/AgaKhanspeech.pdf (accessed 20 January 2010).

Beard, J. (2006) Where the IB is heading, speech delivered by Jeffrey Beard at IB Asia-Pacific Regional Conference 6–9 October 2006, available at: www.ibo.org/dg/speeches/documents/jeff_beard061006.pdf (accessed 20 January 2010).

Bunnell, T. (2008a) The International Baccalaureate and its Middle East challenge, *Education, Business and Society: Contemporary Middle Eastern Issues* 1(1): 16–25.

Bunnell, T. (2008b) The International Baccalaureate and its Diploma Programme online: the challenges and opportunities, *Journal of Research in International Education* 7(3): 325–43.

Bunnell, T. (2008c) The International Baccalaureate in England and Wales: the alternative paths for the future, *Curriculum Journal* 19(3): 151–60.

Bunnell, T. (2009) The International Baccalaureate in the USA and the emerging 'culture war', *Discourse* 30(1): 61–72.

Cambridge, J. (2002) Global product branding and international education, *Journal of Research in International Education* 1(2): 227–43.

Connor, J. (2008) From international schools to inner-city schools: the first principles of the International Baccalaureate Diploma Program, *Teachers College Record* 110(2): 322–51.

Doherty, C., Mu, L. and Shield, P. (2009) Planning mobile futures: the border artistry of International Baccalaureate Diploma choosers, *British Journal of Sociology of Education* 30(6): 757–71.

Fox, E. (1998) The emergence of the International Baccalaureate as an impetus for curriculum reform. In M. Hayden and J. Thompson (eds) *International Education: Principles and Practice*, London: Kogan Page, pp. 65–76.

Goldfrank, W. (1977) Who rules the world? Class formation at the international level, *Quarterly Journal of Ideology* 1(2): 32–7.

Hill, I. (2002) The history of international education: an International Baccalaureate perspective. In M. Hayden, J. Thomson and G. Walker (eds) *International Education in Practice: Dimensions for National and International Schools*, London: Kogan Page, pp. 18–29.

Hymer, S. (1979) *The Multinational Corporation: A Radical Approach*, Cambridge, England: Cambridge University Press.

IBO (2004) *Strategic Plan of the International Baccalaureate Organisation*, IBO, Geneva, Switzerland, available at: www.ibo.org/mission/strategy/documents/sp2004.pdf (accessed 20 January 2010).

IBO (2006) *From Growth to Access: Developing an IBO Access Strategy*, IBO, Geneva, Switzerland, available at: www.ibo.org/mission/strategy/documents/FromGrowthtoAccess.pdf (accessed 20 January 2010).

Matthews, M. (2009) Challenging the IB: a personal view post-Seville, *The International Educator* 24(2): 19–20.

McGee, R. (2003) Implementing the International Baccalaureate Diploma Programme in UK schools – Rationales and Challenges, *IB Research Notes* 3(2): 3–8, available at: www.ibo.org/programmes/research/publications/documents/notesapril03.pdf (accessed 2 January 2010).

Peterson, A. (1972) Is the IB an elitist project? *IBO Annual Bulletin* 8: 1–2.

Rischard, J-F. (2002) *High Noon: 20 Global Problems, 20 Years to Solve Them*, New York: Basic Books.

Robinson, W. and Harris, J. (2000) Towards a global ruling class? Globalisation and the Transnational Capitalist Class, *Science and Society* 64(1): 11–54.

Seefried, M. (2006) Access all areas, *IB World* 48: 10–12, available at: www.ibo.org/ibworld/sep06/seefried.cfm (accessed 20 January 2010).

Seefried, M. (2008) The IB, educating hearts and minds to meet the challenges of today's world, lecture delivered by Monique Seefried, Chair of the IB Board of governors, International School of Geneva, January 2008, available at: www.ibo.org/council/members/seefried/speeches/documents/educating_hearts_minds_en.pdf (accessed 20 January 2010).

Sen, G. (2001) Can the IB strengthen the local, globally? *IB World* May 27: 12, available at: www.ibo.org/ibworld/documents/may01.pdf (accessed 20 January 2010).

Sobulis, H. (2005) The philosophical foundations of the International Baccalaureate Curriculum, *IB Research Notes* 5(3): 2–5.

Van Oord, L. (2007) To westernize the nations? An analysis of the International Baccalaureate's philosophy of education, *Cambridge Journal of Education* 37(3): 375–90, available at: www.informaworld.com/ (accessed 20 January 2010).

Walker, G. (2003) IBO: Now for the stage of influence, *International Schools Journal* 14(2): 11–18.

Walker, G. (2007) International education: from contacts to connections, lecture delivered at IB Asia-Pacific Regional Conference 4 January 2007, available at: www.ibo.org/dg/emeritus/speeches/documents/george_walker040107.pdf (accessed 20 January 2010).

Walters, J. (2006) All American trouble, *The Guardian*, 14 March, available at: www.ntua.gr/posdep/MME/media/2006-03-14_Guardian.pdf (accessed 20 January 2010).

10 Education for global citizenship

Reflecting upon the instrumentalist agendas at play

Harriet Marshall

Introduction

One of the central claims of International Schools is that they have the capacity and the commitment to develop ideas and predispositions towards global citizenship among their pupils. But it is often unclear just what might be meant by global citizenship, both in theory and in practice. This chapter sets out to explore and expose the tensions between different agendas and calls for what is loosely called 'global citizenship education'. While readers might be more familiar with related terms – such as international education, global education, development education, education for sustainable development and global understanding, or cosmopolitan learning – the term global citizenship education is used in part because it is increasingly visible in a number of educational fields and traditions (for a more in-depth discussion on this terminology debate see Marshall 2007). The arguments presented here are located within a UK context and many of the references reflect this, though much of what is said will also have resonance for those working in other international contexts.

This chapter is structured so that the reader is first introduced to the idea of global citizenship education, then to the instrumentalist agendas at play, before being provided with a set of theoretical tools to more effectively engage with these tensions (which might be useful for any related future empirical research). Throughout the chapter the reader is also invited to re-engage with sociological questions relating to the purpose of education and schooling, and the associated role of knowledge through this lens of global citizenship education.

Global citizenship education

Calls for the development of global citizenship education, global education, international education, cosmopolitanism or a form of 'global mindedness' in schools come from a wide range of different organisations – from inter-governmental bodies, national governments, non-governmental organisations (NGOs), the media and the voluntary and business sectors. These calls cover a wide range of different agendas, including sustainability, internationalisation, economic integration, skills and knowledge for the global economy, and social justice and equality. Demands for post-national citizenship in schools are also connected with the view that the social is no longer just local, so that, in this respect, schools are always part of global networks and flows of information, goods and people (Urry 2000). All of these calls must be contextualised with care – historically, politically, culturally and geographically – and situated among wider instrumentalist agendas.

In the UK the idea of global citizenship education is increasingly familiar to schools and to organisations and individuals that work with them (such as the specifically appointed international education officers in local government authorities). An oft referenced source is Oxfam's curriculum for global citizenship (2006), where it is viewed as enabling 'pupils to develop the knowledge, skills and values needed for securing a just and sustainable world in which all may fulfil their potential', giving 'children and young people the opportunity to develop critical thinking about complex global issues in the safe space of the classroom' and fostering a global citizenry ideal based on respecting and valuing diversity, acting responsibly and being 'outraged' by social injustice (Oxfam 2006: 1–3). While some, such as Andreotti (2006), have criticised the lack of theorisation of global citizenship education (in the UK in particular), a body of work is emerging. There are, for instance, those who theorise and engage with global citizenship education in relation to the philosophy of cosmopolitanism, extending models of cosmopolitanism and Kantian cosmopolitan democracy offered by those such as Held (1995). This discourse often talks about those whose loyalties, values, knowledge and norms go beyond the national towards transnational commonalities (Roth 2007), though there are recognisably different types of cosmopolitanism out there (Beck 2006; Rizvi 2008). For example, Nussbaum (2002) contrasts cosmopolitan universalism and internationalism with 'parochial ethnocentricism' and 'inward-looking patriotism'. Advocates of this sort of global or cosmopolitan citizenship education argue that 'citizenship education should also help students to develop an identity and attachment to the world' (Banks 2008: 134).

Weenink (2008) also outlines two arguments within cosmopolitan theory that, in turn, can sometimes be observed in global citizenship education or what he calls international educational activity – the idea of 'awareness of global connectedness' and the idea of 'an orientation of open mindedness towards the Other' (2008: 1089–90). His argument is that a number of upper-middle class parents in the Netherlands aspire to a model of cosmopolitan education for their children based on notions of global connectedness as part of their social reproduction strategy, providing them with knowledge, skills and assets that 'give their offspring a competitive edge in the globalizing social arenas' (ibid.: 1093). Such a position may, or may not encourage 'open-mindedness towards the Other'. His useful conceptualisation of 'cosmopolitan capital' will be revisited later in this chapter.

Another way of engaging with global citizenship education may be found in recognising the existence of multiple global citizenships (or cosmopolitanisms). For example, Urry (1998) considers the existence of several possible global citizenships: global capitalists 'who seek to unify the world around global corporate interests which are increasingly "de-nationalised"'; global reformers, global environmental managers and earth citizens 'who seek to take responsibility for the globe through a distinct and often highly localised ethics of care'; and global networkers 'who set up and sustain work or leisure networks constituted across national boundaries' (1998: 4). Urry goes on to identify a fourth category of 'global cosmopolitans' who develop 'an ideology of openness towards "other" cultures, peoples and environments' and who are concerned about developing an 'orientation' to other 'citizens, societies and cultures across the globe' (ibid.). This plurality of global citizenships could mean that some global citizenships may clash with others (if they have opposing agendas). It is therefore very important to recognise the situatedness and imaginary or socially constructed nature of different forms of global citizenship education (Marshall 2009). Schools have to develop pedagogical and curricular responses to this plurality of global citizenships, global agendas, and identify ways in which individuals can choose to respond or relate to the global. Different advocates of global citizenship education (e.g. NGO workers or governmental officials) prioritise certain global citizen 'types' over others, according to their particular agendas. It is to these agendas we must now turn.

Instrumentalist agendas at play

Having recognised the existence of a plurality of different types of global citizenships and therefore global citizenship educations, it is also important to place these various forms within the context of powerful economic or what are sometimes called 'technical' instrumentalist agendas. Technical-economic instrumentalism reminds us that 'the curriculum has always been, albeit selectively, related to economic changes and the future employability of students' (Young 2008: 22). Technical instrumentalists are most often the dominant group in education policy creation, 'for them the curriculum imperative is not educational in the traditional sense, but directed towards what they see as the needs of the economy', in other words 'preparing for the global more competitive knowledge-based economy of the future' (ibid.: 20).

The technical-economic instrumentalist agenda of much of the global citizenship education policy requires of students (and teachers) a pragmatic and arguably neo-liberal understanding of legal structures, rights and responsibilities. There seems to be plenty of evidence for the dominance of the technical-economic instrumentalist agenda in schools. Keeping our focus upon education for global citizenship, a good illustration of the dominance of the economic agenda in global citizenship education policy in the UK can be found in the document *Putting the World into World Class Education* (DfES

2004) (and its follow-up action plan DfES 2007). Despite the need to 'instil a strong global dimension into the learning experience of all children and young people' and to 'support the improvement of education and children's services worldwide, particularly in Africa', the overarching goal advocated by this document is to equip young people and adults 'for life in a global society and work in a global economy' and to ensure that the EU becomes 'the most competitive and dynamic knowledge-based economy in the world' (DfES 2004: 3). Learning in a global context is therefore understood by the UK government as being about equipping 'employers and their employees with the skills needed for a global economy', involving the learning of economically useful languages (a much talked-about aspiration among parents as well as reported by Weenink, 2008), and the move towards 'mutual recognition and improved transparency of qualifications' (DfES 2004: 6). This is a good illustration of what Rizvi (2008) describes as an intercultural and cosmopolitan education 'within the logic of consumption', one placed firmly within existing global economic conditions.

Another manifestation of the economic-instrumentalist agendas of some forms of global citizenship or international education can be seen in Whitehead's study of the marketing practices of international schools and their selective marketing of the benefits of the International Baccalaureate (Whitehead 2005) to prospective parents. From the advertisements of forty South-Australian schools offering the IB (International Baccalaureate), Whitehead discovered that the schools were 'selling social advantage rather than social justice' where the IB was presented as 'a commodity which enhances the former' (2005: 2–3). In other words, 'pragmatic realism overrides the IB's humanitarian and socially just ideals' with the result that 'student identities are being reconstructed along individualistic lines as these schools teach the skills required of the entrepreneurial individual in the corporate workplace rather than a socially responsible citizen' (Whitehead 2005: 10). A possible critique of this chapter can be found in the uncritical way in which Whitehead engages with the neo-liberal ideals of the school as a place to transmit certain values and civic ideals – a position about which Fish (2008), Rizvi (2008) and Andreotti (2006) would raise serious concerns.

We may be generally familiar with the discourse of 'instrumentalism' in relation to efforts to raise standards in schools and where educational policy is increasingly directed to achieve political and economic goals. Working in a UK context, Young (2008) has argued that the two main expressions of instrumentalism in educational policy are marketisation and regulation (or what is sometimes called 'quality assurance') – and that these trends have received criticism from both the political right and left. Indeed, we should remember that the technical-instrumentalist agendas of educational policies and practice can be critiqued from both the political right by neo-conservatives who wish to retain traditional curricular structures and subjects, as well as by the left, who might, for example, engage in more of a neo-Marxist critique of hegemonic capitalist economic models.

An instrumentalist agenda sees education, the curriculum and knowledge as a means to an end, not as ends in themselves. As Young argues 'it is the curriculum's role in making a particular form of society that is stressed' (Young 2008: 21). However, the technical-economic instrumentalist discourse is not the only one apparent among calls for global citizenship education in schools and their associated ideal form of society. Many of those more on the political left (and in some religious groups) engaged in education for global social justice and human rights for example, are also overtly or covertly engaged in their own instrumentalist agenda. While the term instrumentalism has more often been associated with an economic agenda, I argue that it is also an appropriate term to apply to the work of some of those engaged in promoting education for a 'particular type' of active and impassioned global citizenship – that which, for example, intends for young people to join particular ideologically driven global causes and agendas.

The global social-justice instrumentalism that requires an emotional (and arguably active) commitment to, and understanding of, particular inter- pretations of economic, political, legal or cultural injustice can also be found in global citizenship education policy and practice – even though its status may in fact be extremely marginal in schools. Oxfam (2006), for example, advocates that young people become 'outraged by social injustice', but its model of the ideal global citizen appears to be situated in a Western, neo-liberal and arguably economically stable country context. Some advocates of education for sustainable development (ESD) have also described the purpose of ESD as the development of 'positive attitudes and behaviour', the realisation of sustainability indicators, and delivery of 'relevant knowledge' as outlined in particular policy documents (Huckle 2004). In other words, the instru- mentalism of some global citizenship education policy is intended to 'balance the economic or instrumental values that modern society places on (and extracts from) nature with ecological, aesthetic, scientific, existence and spiritual values' (ibid. 2004: 7).

Dobson (2003) has considered the complexities associated with the idea of education *for* ecological, environmental, or global citizenship as opposed to education through or about global citizenship education – just as Beck differentiated more generally between education *for* and education *about* citizenship (Beck 1998). The notion of education 'for' global citizenship (or indeed sustainable development, as Dobson also considers), implies that there is an agreed understanding of global citizenship or sustainable development that educationalists can work towards, and with this an agreed knowledge base. However, I would argue that it is currently impossible to identify any such agreement in any form unless you examine particular (and 'exceptional') curricular programmes like that of the International Baccalaureate. A different articulation of education for or through global citizenship comes from Huckle who references the work of Michael Bonnett to argue that rather than viewing sustainability 'as policy designed to achieve a certain state of affairs' (and one could apply this to the more generic idea of global citizenship as well), that teachers should instead 'conceive of sustainability as a frame of mind that involves respect for human and non-human nature seeking their own fulfilment through a process of co-evolution' (2004: 6). In other words, Huckle suggests that education for sustainable development (and again, I believe that in this situation this could be interchanged with the idea of global citizenship education) should aim to develop 'a frame of mind' as opposed to developing 'positive attitudes and behaviour', realising sustainability indicators, and delivering particular knowledge as outlined by policy documents – where the instrumentalism of the latter appears more overt than the former. This 'frame of mind' might be likened to Arnot's discussion of 'global conscience collective' (2008).

Recognising that other instrumentalist agendas might be at play and that these two (the technical-economic and the global social justice) are in themselves highly complex and increasingly indistinguishable, it is interesting to explore the tensions related to their coexistence in global citizenship education – although of course by examining research featuring the dominance of the knowledge-economy discourse (contained in a number of forms in Lauder *et al.* 2006) and the economic-instrumentalist agendas in education around the world, we would be wise to re-emphasise the comparatively reduced powers of the social justice agendas. The above-mentioned document *Putting the world into World Class Education* (DfES 2004) interestingly lists the eight key concepts – diversity, interdependence, social justice, sustainable development, and so forth – which originate from the NGO-produced (DfES-endorsed) document *Developing the Global Dimension in the School Curriculum* (DfES 2005). But of course the DfES, a governmental department, clearly sees these concepts in quite a different light from the way in which, for example, a development education NGO such as Oxfam or Save the Children (with more overt social justice agendas) may view them.

From a research perspective it will be interesting to see how schools negotiate the tensions between these two agendas. It is also important to observe and investigate to what extent schools and educationalists are aware of the particular ideological, cultural, political and historical context out of which these drivers for global citizenship arise. Whether it is Weenink's articulation of cosmopolitan capital, the Welsh Assembly's idea of education for sustainable development and global citizenship (DCELLS 2008) or UNICEF-UK's promotion of global citizenship and human rights education, such calls for these types of education in schools need to be historically, culturally, geographically and politically situated.

Tools for engaging with these agendas and tensions

There are a number of sociological tools to help us engage in reflective critique of the different types of instrumentalist agendas and their situatedness at this level, three of which are briefly surveyed and introduced in this section.

Understanding the underlying notion of cosmopolitan capital

A common governmental answer to a perceived growing level of disconnection with civil society, whether at a local, national or international level, is to provide people with a form of 'social capital' which it is hoped may, in turn, remedy certain societal problems. Social capital is a sociological concept that has been largely attributed to the work of Coleman, Bourdieu and Putnam (explored and compared in O'Brien and O Fathaigh 2004), whereupon social capital is about acquiring and mobilising certain resources and social connections for a particular end (in Bourdieu's perspective, a means to maintain class structures (Grenfell 2007), or from Putnam's perspective, a tool to foster civic engagement (Putnam 2000)). An example of this thinking can be seen in the underlying drivers for the introduction of the Citizenship Curriculum in England and Wales (QCA 2007). Here the concept of social capital clearly motivated key actors involved in the introduction of citizenship in schools. The so-called 'third way' political and ideological approach of the New Labour Government in the UK from the late 1990s onwards (Giddens 2000), relied heavily on the cultivation of social capital to enhance levels of social trust and health, lower levels of crime and improve national economic performance and growth. Kisby (2006) provides evidence for his social capital thesis with regard to citizenship education in the UK by quoting a previous Secretary of Education, David Blunkett, as saying that 'it is clear that weak civic engagement and an absence of social capital deprives democracy of its vitality, health and legitimacy' and that social capital and citizenship 'weave together' as 'those who volunteer in their communities tend to be more likely to vote' (Kisby 2006: 155, quoting David Blunkett). Citizenship education in England and Wales can therefore be seen as 'an attempt to increase both young people's knowledge of politics . . . and their ability to engage in political processes' (ibid.). There are parallels here with some governmental and non-governmental calls for global citizenship education.

The theoretical constructs of social capital (linked to the benefits of being in certain groups, networks or relationships of influence and support), and cultural capital (linked to forms of knowledge, skills, education and advantages giving people a higher societal status) are useful for theorising and analysing global citizenship education. For example, articulations of 'cosmopolitan capital' (Weenink 2008) and 'critical ecological capital' (Huckle 2004) can now be discovered in global citizenship education theory and research. In the context of cosmopolitanism, cosmopolitanisation theory and talk of a 'new international social class' or 'new global elites', Weenink identifies cosmo-politan capital in the following way:

> Cosmopolitan capital is, first of all, a propensity to engage in globalizing social arena . . . [it] comprises bodily and mental predispositions and competencies (savoir faire) which help to engage confidently in such arenas. Moreover it provides a competitive edge, a head start vis-à-vis competitors.

People accumulate, deploy and display cosmopolitan capital while living abroad for some time, visit and host friends from different nationalities, attend meetings frequently for an international audience, maintain a globally dispersed circle of friends or relatives, read books, magazines, and journals that reach a global audience and possess a near-native mastery of English and at least one other language.

(Weenink 2008: 1092)

This understanding or aspiration must be contextualised in a western political and economic situation where there is a struggle for privileged positions in the labour and educational markets for example, but it is arguably a concept that is not entirely out of place in other parts of the world. Rizvi (2008), however, expresses concern about the dominance of this understanding of cosmopolitanism in Western contexts, a type of liberal individualist cosmopolitanism entrenched within the global economy, when in fact there are alternative more reflective forms available more suitable for educational institutions.

Weenink (2008) draws upon the work of Szerszynski and Urry to usefully differentiate between three forms of cosmopolitanism that can in turn be used as: (a) different aspects or understandings of cosmopolitan capital; and (b) categories that facilitate the deconstruction of instrumentalist agendas in global citizenship education discourse. I have adapted, reinterpreted and simplified these here:

1) *Global knowledge*: 'an awareness of the current global socio-cultural condition', perceived and experienced either as a 'relatively autonomous force' shaping lives or as an increased awareness of 'everyday global connectedness' (Weenink 2008: 1092). A further differentiation might be between economic knowledge or learning for the global knowledge economy versus that relating more to global social justice, poverty alleviation, social development and social change.

2) *Global engagement*: a 'mode of orientation to the world' (2008: 1092), where the question is to what extent the aim is for young people to be aware, open-minded, interested or actively engaged in the global arena. A second question would be whether that particular level of engagement is in the global economic (e.g. aspiring to become a part of the global capitalist system) or global social justice arena (e.g. being outraged by social injustice) or both.

3) *Global competences*: a 'set of competences' or 'resources' that help young people 'make their way within other cultures and countries and/or that ... give ... a competitive edge in globalizing social arenas' (2008: 1092–3). These competences might also be seen in relation to an ability to engage in critical and reflective thought that exposes global stereotyping, media manipulation and selection, and historically or ideologically constructed positions. These competences might link to Rizvi's (2008)

key epistemic virtues of historicity, reflexivity, criticality and relationality
required in any effective cosmopolitan education curricula or form of what
he calls 'cosmopolitan learning'.

Two types of dominant cosmopolitan citizens are also identified in order to
differentiate the types of parent interviewed by Weenink: 'pragmatic
cosmopolitans' or those that regard international education as an instrument
for a later career or study and who prioritise, for example, the learning of
English; and 'dedicated cosmopolitans' who have a 'mental disposition about
taking the world as their horizon, daring to look and go beyond borders, and
be open to foreign cultures' (2008: 1095). This differentiation is arguably
fairly crude, and if one incorporated further understandings, for example
drawing upon Urry's (1998) multitude of global citizens and global citizenships one might arrive at a more nuanced and appropriate understanding of
how parents constructed themselves. Together, I argue that these notions
of cosmopolitan capital and multiple global citizenships can be used as tools
for critically engaging with calls for global citizenship education.

Understanding the underlying notion of 'the other' and applying a postcolonial critique

The idea of 'the global' and correspondingly 'global citizenship' has to be seen
as something that historically has been and continues to be politically and
socially constructed. Further tools and theories to aid critique of the socially
and historically constructed nature of 'the global', global citizenship, cosmopolitanism and/or the phenomena associated with globalisation can be found
in post-colonial theory. For example, Rizvi (2008) incorporates post-colonial
theory to engage with the idea of cosmopolitan learning and Andreotti (2006)
has developed an effective theoretical framework for engaging with indigenous
perspectives of global and development agendas in global citizenship education. Andreotti usefully draws upon the work of Andrew Dobson and Gayatri
Spivak to critique the dominant global constructs in global citizenship
education literature and discourse in the UK which Spivak, for example, might
see as reinforcing 'eurocentrism and triumphalism as people are encouraged
to think that they live in the centre of the world', that they have a responsibility
to 'help the rest' and that 'people from other parts of the world are not fully
global' (Andreotti 2006: 5).

The term 'global dimension' of education is more frequently found in
educational literature and policy in the UK than 'global citizenship education',
especially when used in relation to the school or national curriculum. In the
joint government and NGO recommendation for schools, *Developing the Global
Dimension in the School Curriculum* (DfES 2005), the global dimension is defined
in terms of the eight key concepts: global citizenship; social justice; conflict
resolution; sustainable development; values and perceptions; human rights;

interdependence; and diversity (DfES 2005). Global citizenship is defined as one of those concepts that a curriculum incorporating a global dimension should address. However, Andreotti has critiqued the literature and discourse of the global dimension in the UK from a post-colonial perspective for articulating the notion that 'different cultures' only have 'traditions, beliefs and values' while 'the West' has,

> (universal) knowledge (and even constructs knowledge about these cultures). The idea of a 'common history', which only acknowledges the contribution of other cultures to science and mathematics . . . projects the values, beliefs and traditions of the West as global and universal, while foreclosing the historical processes that led to this universalisation.
>
> (Andreotti 2006: 5)

Like Andreotti, Rizvi proposes the development of a more critical global imagination in global citizenship education, one that recognises that cultural differences are 'neither absolute nor necessarily antagonistic but deeply interconnected and relationally defined'. In the light of post-colonial critiques of certain forms of international and cosmopolitan education, Rizvi advocates a form of cosmopolitan learning that is,

> not concerned so much with imparting knowledge and developing attitudes and skills for understanding other cultures per se, but with helping students examine the ways in which global processes are creating conditions of economic and cultural exchange that are transforming our identities and communities, and that, unreflexively, we may be contributing the production and reproduction of those conditions through our uncritical acceptance of the dominant ways of thinking about global interconnectivity
>
> (Rizvi 2008, accessed online)

Both Andreotti and Rizvi emphasise the need for students to reflect upon their own situatedness, their own perspectives, their own critical and political presuppositions, their own global imaginaries and upon the way they create knowledge about 'others' and how they use this knowledge when they engage with them.

Understanding how 'knowledge' is being generated, selected and prioritised

Another set of theoretical tools for helping us to better understand global citizenship education drivers and practice can be found in sociological theory of knowledge and the curriculum. While the parameters of this chapter do not allow me to go into this body of theory in depth, it is useful to remind educationalists of some of the questions sociologists of education begun asking of the curriculum over thirty years ago. For example, Basil Bernstein was particularly concerned with the need to understand how knowledge is selected from fields of knowledge production and then rearranged, classified, framed and recontextualised to become educational knowledge (1975, 2000). A key question from a Bernsteinian perspective would be: what characterises the nature of these fields of knowledge production?

Michael Young's recent work helps us to re-engage with the role of knowledge in education and the need to distinguish between knowledge produced by specialists (e.g. in disciplines) and knowledge acquired by people through their experiences, families, communities and workplaces. He argues that

> questions of knowledge take us back to our most basic assumptions about what it is to be educated or to educate someone; they are in the broadest sense, philosophical and political questions about who we are and what we value.
>
> (Young 2008: xviii)

His particular concern is for educators to recognise the more dominant technical-instrumentalist and neo-conservative traditionalist views of knowledge, to always see knowledge as a social and historical product but to be careful not to 'slide into relativism and perspectivism' (2008: 19).

In this theoretical light, I argue that it is important to consider whether, and if so how, the drivers and agendas underlying global citizenship education initiatives are addressing the issue of knowledge. Some of those advocating global citizenship for global social justice (for example, those who might locate themselves within the tradition of development education or education for global citizenship and sustainable development), could be critiqued for not fully engaging with the knowledge base of what they are advocating. This collection of people and organisations tend to focus instead upon a particular interactive pedagogy and set of behaviours (Marshall 2005). In a slightly different way, those located more firmly within a technical-economic discourse can also be accused of not fully engaging with the knowledge question in that the notion of 'useful' knowledge can be entirely determined by the dictates of the global economy. This relationship can often go unrecognised and have enormous implications for more traditional or abstract forms of knowledge in schools. This economic discourse can also be accused of blurring the boundaries between articulations of 'skills' and 'knowledge'. Furthermore, some of the knowledge required by the advocates of global citizenship from a technical-economic instrumentalist agenda, can be advocating a form of interdisciplinary knowledge and learning when in fact schools maintain strong subject boundaries, and the concept of interdisciplinarity struggles to achieve a high status in a performance/exam-based curriculum and pedagogy (ironically, a practice also required by the technical-economic governmental agenda).

An important question for the relationship between knowledge and global citizenship education then relates to whether the required fluid and shifting knowledge of other cultures can be reconciled with traditional curriculum boundaries and static notions of the intellectual or disciplinary field. In other words, how can school subjects and subject boundaries remain when the global context appears to be calling for more fluid knowledge forms (Rizvi 2008)? A related question is whether contemporary knowledge structures in schools are serving to prop up existing, liberal-individualist conceptualisations of global citizenship located firmly within economic structures where the power of the critical and global imaginary is stifled? Conversely, one could also ask how can those advocating the deconstruction of traditional knowledge forms engage more realistically with the need for, and power of, established knowledge forms and truths?

To summarise, if we re-engage with the question of knowledge in global citizenship education and in relation to the instrumentalist agendas at play, we are invited to ask a number of significant questions. Sociological theory offers us one way to reconsider the role of knowledge in the curriculum 'without denying its fundamentally social and historical basis' (Young 2008: 19). Ultimately, a sociological lens encourages us to ask whether global citizenship education can ever be understood as an intellectual or disciplinary field, and whether, as suggested by Arnot (2008) and Rizvi (2008), it may require a whole new approach to schooling, curricula, pedagogy and educational knowledge.

Where the powers of instrumentalist agendas can be challenged

In this penultimate section I will briefly consider some of the ways in which the instrumentalist agendas and drivers for global citizenship education are being challenged or even halted. The first consideration relates to the essential role of, and perspectives of, teachers in relation to the delivery of any sort of global citizenship education. Second, I consider some of the obstacles faced by both governmental and non-governmental organisations in their quests to encourage schools to 'go global', no matter for what ends. Finally, the idea that children (and adults) rarely react well to being told how to think and act is considered.

Recognising the subjectivities of teachers

An interesting argument is put forward by Carson who argues that while there is much hope pinned on educational establishments to become engines of change (for example, in South Africa Curriculum 2005 has the intention of redressing 'past wrongs and to build a democratic, equitable, and multi-racial society' 2005: 3), little literature or research addresses the question of how the subjectivities of teachers will interact with the policies and circumstances to effect this change. Gender, class, cultural and racial differences and histories, for example, influence the way teachers engage in the teaching and learning of global citizenship education. It might be that some of the frustrations felt by those advocating a global citizenship agenda in schools (but coming up against resistance and/or obstacles) might be associated with the psycho-analytical argument that this new knowledge 'threatens familiar identities, unsettling the integrity of the self' (Carson 2005: 5).

In the NGO field it could be argued that the discourse of 'teacher development' is as dominant as, or even more dominant than that of 'curriculum implementation' or 'curriculum change' in the activities and policies of global citizenship education organisations. But it might be, as Carson argues, that some of the literature of teacher development neglects to fully engage with questions of identity and with 'a sense of the teacher as the subject who is changing' (2005: 7). The relationship between calls or policies for global citizenship education and the subjectivities, identities and practices of individual teachers, who may or may not support these initiatives, is something entirely under-researched.

Failing to recognise the realities of the current context

Another obstacle to the successful fulfilment of the instrumentalist agendas associated with global citizenship education, whether on the political left or the right, is a failure to realistically take stock of the current context in which schools, teachers and young people are working. Again, the empirical research for this argument is lacking, however, I am often concerned by the presumed 'starting points' of some global citizenship education initiatives.

Among those promoting education *for* global social justice, peace, inter-cultural understanding, sustainable development and so forth, there is much talk of the need to 'change' current practices, behaviours and viewpoints. Polls and studies (such as MORI 2008) suggest that (a) students lack sufficient global or development awareness or (b) they want to know more about the world. But beyond this the arguments are often anecdotal and entirely within the normative realm. The realities of parental attitudes and aspirations, as outlined by Weenink (2008) for example, or of the dominant technical-economic dis-courses rampant in schools, are often insufficiently acknowledged.

On the other hand, among those promoting education for technically literate, economically active, internationally mobile, worker global citizens, there is sometimes an absence of understanding that if global citizenship education activity exists in schools, it is often more likely to be *instigated* by an impassioned teacher or NGO with a more holistic, social-justice under-standing of the need for global education. There is an argument that governmental officials have rather hijacked the language of global citizen-ship education for their own ends, without taking into account how it has historically come to be in the educational arena (as outlined, for example, in Hicks 2003 and Marshall 2005).

Recognising that people do not like being told what to think, be and do

Another interesting challenge presented to advocates of different types of global citizenship education is the argument that people do not in fact like being told what to think, be or do. Vare and Scott (2007a, 2007b) remind their readers of this fairly obvious educational dilemma in their differentiation between 'education for sustainable development' (ESD1) and 'learning as sustainable development' (ESD2). They argue that this particular form of global citizenship education should be more about the learning process rather than working towards a set of predefined behaviours and the associated use of carrots and sticks. Not entirely unlike Rizvi's advocacy of a set of epistemic virtues, competences and skills, Vare and Scott argue that while ESD1 raises awareness, and 'provides a text' for reading the world (whilst also promoting certain behaviours), learning as sustainable development (ESD2) encourages young people to think more critically about what experts say, helping them to understand that text and develop the 'skills, self-confidence, knowledge and motivation to be effective learners' and giving them 'the wherewithal to take action' (2007a: 5).

A major criticism of any instrumentalist agenda in education is that it fails to recognise the complexity, uncertainty and risk of life on earth in an increasingly interconnected global environment – where doing the right thing is never simple. While a teacher, an NGO worker or an MP might believe that one thing, such as fair trade, learning another language or knowing about and being able to benefit from the global economy, might be an inalienably good thing, we must consider whether or not others would agree and whether in fact school is the place for this sort of communication. Both Fish (whose book (aimed at university and college lecturers) is aptly entitled *Save the World on Your Own Time*, 2008) and Vare and Scott articulate this very question, arguing:

> The challenge for any values-driven educator is not to force this process. If, as such a teacher, you think you know what the answer is (or ought to be), and feel it your role to convince your pupils of this, we would politely suggest you follow an alternative career in marketing
>
> (Vare and Scott 2007a: 5)

The focus of a less instrumentally driven global citizenship might therefore be less on our 'capacity to do the right thing now' and more on our 'capability to analyse, question alternatives and negotiate our decisions in the foreseeable future' (ibid.: 2).

Conclusion: saving the world in our own time and re-engaging with knowledge

This chapter has highlighted an important dilemma associated with all drivers for and manifestations of global citizenship education encapsulated in the question to what extent is it the job of teachers, schools and their curricula to help young people change or save the world? However, when asking this question we should simultaneously ask to what extent it is the job of teachers, schools and their curricula to recontextualise and reinforce the dominant technical-economic instrumentalist agendas so controlled by the global economy, a powerful trend of materialistic consumption and the ideology of liberal-individualism. Of course, there will be schools straddling the two instrumentalist agendas contrasted and considered throughout this chapter, and the challenge for those might be to reflect carefully upon their global citizenship education practice by using some of the theoretical tools outlined in this chapter.

To help with this educational task, which I would argue is imperative if schools are at all concerned about the nature of the future local, national and global societies of which their students will be part, it will be very important to recognise the sorts of global citizenships, cosmopolitanisms and global imaginaries that young people are already adopting. Rizvi suggests that it is possible to identify an *existing* strong contemporary form of global citizenship or cosmopolitanism, one set within a liberal individualist framework that rests upon the recognition that 'the world now consists of a single economic market, with free trade and minimal political involvement as its ideological mantras'. With this understanding, he argues that the key question then is how we should engage with the related dominant expressions of cosmopolitanism such as that related to the market-based practices of international education. For example:

> Within the framework of these practices, cosmopolitanism of international students consists of their participation in an economic exchange, in which they are less concerned with the moral and political dimensions of global interconnectivity than with education's strategic economic possibilities. As a result their cosmopolitan outlook is likely to be framed already by the role they believe international education might play in better positioning them within the changing structures of the global economy, which increasingly prizes the skills of interculturality and a cosmopolitan outlook.
>
> (Rizvi 2008: accessed online)

What is needed instead is for students to develop 'an alternative imaginary of global interconnectivity' which Rizvi goes on to argue is *not* informed by 'the universalising logic of the market, or by romanticised notions of global citizenship' but instead informed by 'our determination to develop a different conception of global relations, which views all of the world's diverse people and communities as part of the same moral universe' (ibid.). This call for a sense of moral responsibility links to the normative dimension of global citizenship education, which is of course a highly complex and sensitive dimension when one is concerned about exposing any instrumentalist agendas at play. Alternative calls for global citizenship education or cosmopolitan learning exist and, while they might still be labelled instrumentalist in some way, they may be preferable because they prize the ultimate goal of critical understanding and moral improvement, embracing both the empirical and the normative but without having an overtly ideological agenda. Of course, the underlying humanistic goal of such a call can still be situated within particular cultural and political frameworks, but such a goal *explicitly* acknowledges that forms of global interconnectivity and cosmopolitanism 'embody particular configurations of power that serve some interests, and ignore others' (Rizvi 2008). This understanding is crucial if educationalists are to help students discover the situatedness and historically constructed nature of different forms of knowledge particularly that which relates to notions of 'diversity' and the 'other'.

References

Andreotti, V. (2006) Soft versus critical global citizenship education, *Development Education Policy and Practice* Issue 3 Autumn: 83–98.

Arnot, M. (2008) *Educating the Gendered Citizen: Global Sociological Engagements with National and Global Agendas*, London: Routledge.

Banks, J. A. (2008) Diversity, global identity, and citizenship education in a global age, *Educational Researcher* 37(3): 129–39.

Beck, J. (1998) *Morality and Citizenship in Education*, London: Cassell.

Beck, U. (2006) *Cosmopolitan Vision*, Cambridge, UK: Polity Press.

Bernstein, B. (1975) *Class, Codes and Control Vol. 3: Towards a Theory of Educational Transmission*, London: Routledge.

Bernstein, B. (2000) *Pedagogy, Symbolic Control and Identity: Theory, Research, Critique* (revised edition), Lanham, Maryland: Rowman & Littlefield Publishers Inc.

Carson, T. (2005) Beyond instrumentalism: the significance of teacher identity in educational change, *Journal of the Canadian Association for Curriculum Studies* 3(2): 1–8.

DCELLS (2008) *Education For Sustainable Development and Global Citizenship: A Common Understanding for Schools*, Department for Children, Education, Lifelong Learning and Skills, Welsh Assembly.

DfES (2004) *Putting the World into World Class Education: An International Strategy for Education, Skills and Children's Services*, London: Department for Education and Skills, available online at: www.globalgateway.org.uk/Default.aspx?page=624 (accessed January 2009).

DfES (2005) *Developing the Global Dimension in the School Curriculum* (2nd edn), London: Department for Education and Skills, available online at: www.dfid.gov.uk/pubs/files/dev-global-dim.pdf (accessed July 2008).

DfES (2007) *Putting the World into World-Class Education: Action Plan*, London: Department for Education and Skills, available online at: www.globalgateway.org.uk/Default.aspx?page=624 (accessed January 2009).

Dobson, A. (2003) *Citizenship and the Environment*, Oxford: Oxford University Press.

Fish, S. (2008) *Save the World on Your Own Time*, Oxford: Oxford University Press.

Giddens, A. (2000) *The Third Way and Its Critics*, Cambridge: Polity Press.

Grenfell, M. (2007) *Pierre Bourdieu: Education and Training*, London: Continuum.

Held, D. (1995) *Democracy and the Global Order: From the Modern State to Cosmopolitan Governance*, London: Polity Press.

Hicks, D. (2003) Thirty years of global education: a reminder of key principles and precedents, *Educational Review* 55(3): 265–75.

Huckle, J. (2004) Citizenship education for sustainable development in initial teacher training, available online at: *Citized website*: www.citized.info/?r_menu=induction &strand=0 (accessed December 2008).

Kisby, B. (2006) Social capital and citizenship education in schools, *British Politics* 1(1) 151–60.

Lauder, H., Brown, P., Dillabough, J. and Halsey, A. (2006) *Education, Globalisation and Social Change*, Oxford: Oxford University Press.

Marshall, H. (2005) The sociology of global education: power, pedagogy and practice. Unpublished doctoral thesis, the University of Cambridge, UK.

Marshall, H. (2007) The global education terminology debate: exploring some of the issues in the UK. In M. Hayden, J. Levy and J. Thompson (eds) *A Handbook of Research in International Education*, London: Sage, pp. 38–50.

Marshall, H. (2009) Educating the European citizen in the global age: engaging with the post-national and identifying the research agenda, *Journal of Curriculum Studies* 41(1): 247–67.

MORI/DEA (2008) *Our Global Future: How Can Education Meet the Challenge of Change? Young People's Experiences of Global Learning: An Ipsos MORI Research Study on behalf of DEA*. Available online at: www.dea.org.uk (accessed July 2008).

Nussbaum, M. C. (2002) Patriotism and cosmopolitanism. In J. Cohen (ed.) *For love of Country*, Boston: Beacon, pp. 3–17.

O'Brien, S. and O Fathaigh, M. (2004) 'Bringing in Bourdieu's theory of social capital: renewing learning partnership approaches to social inclusion', paper presented at ESAI conference, NUI Maynooth, 1–3 April 2004, available online at: www.ucc.ie/en/ace/ Publications/DocumentFile,19907,en.pdf (accessed December 2008).

Oxfam (2006) *Education for Global Citizenship: A Guide for Schools* (2nd edition), Oxford: Oxfam Development Education.

Putnam, R. D. (2000) *Bowling Alone: The Collapse and Renewal of American Community*, New York: Simon and Schuster.

QCA (2007) Citizenship: Programme of study for key stages 3 and 4, London: Qualification and Curriculum Authority, available online at: http://curriculum.qca.org.uk (accessed July 2008).

Rizvi, F. (2008) Epistemic virtues and cosmopolitan learning, *Australian Educational Researcher* 35(1), available online at: www.articlearchives.com/labor-employment/worker-categories-migr:nt-workers/890870-1.html (accessed January 2009).

Roth, K. (2007) Cosmopolitan learning. In K. Roth and N. C. Burbules (eds) *Changing Notions of Citizenship Education in Contemporary Nation-States*, Rotterdam: Sense Publishers.

Urry, J. (1998) Globalisation and citizenship, unpublished paper, Department of Sociology, University of Lancaster, UK. Available online at: www.lancs.ac.uk/fass/sociology/ papers/urry-globalisation-and-citizenship.pdf (accessed January 2009).

Urry, J. (2000) *Sociology Beyond Societies: Mobilities for the Twenty-First Century*, London: Routledge.

Vare, P. and Scott, W. (2007a) Education for sustainable development: two sides and an edge, unpublished paper.

Vare, P. and Scott, W. (2007b) Learning for a change: Exploring the relationship between education and sustainable development *Journal of Education for Sustainable Development* 1(2): 191–8.

Weenink, D. (2008) Cosmopolitanism as a form of capital: parents preparing their children for a globalising world, *Sociology* 42(6): 1089–106.

Whitehead, K. (2005) 'Advertising advantage: the International Baccalaureate, social justice and the marketisation of schooling', paper presented to Australian Association for Research in Education Annual conference, Parramatta, 27 November–1December 2005, available online at: www.aare.edu.au/05pap/whi05426.pdf (accessed December 2008).

Young, M. (2008) *Bringing Knowledge Back In: From Social Constructivism to Social Realism in the Sociology of Education*, London: Routledge.

Name index

Achebe 29, 37
Achinstein 64, 75
ADAB 26, 37
Aga Khan 176, 180
Ainger 114, 115
Aitken 66, 78
Albright 143, 145
Allan 7, 18, 61, 75, 104, 115
Allen 72, 75, 87, 98
Alvesson 48, 56
Anderson 9, 18, 59, 61, 63, 67, 75, 76
Andersson 81
Andreotti 183, 185, 190, 191, 197
Archibold 117
Arnot 187, 193, 197
Arrighi 52, 56
Ashforth 64, 75
Ashton 41, 46, 54, 56, 57

Baker 15, 18, 110, 115
Balagangadhara 7, 106, 111, 113, 115
Baldridge 59, 75
Ball 59, 61–72, 75, 78, 129, 144
Banks 183, 197
Bartlett 107, 115
Bates 4, 9, 15, 18, 60, 76
Beach 64, 76
Beard 167, 177, 180
Beatty 69, 76
Beck 183, 186, 197
Bell 62, 76
Bennett 111, 115
Benveniste 158, 162
Bernstein 24–5, 37, 126–9, 134, 143–4, 149, 156, 162, 192, 197

Beveridge 27, 37
Bhanji 2, 11, 12, 13, 18
Bidwell 65, 76
Blackburn 107, 116
Blandford 64, 70, 76, 162
Blase 59, 61, 63, 65, 72, 76
Bloom 106, 116
Bochner 120
Bohler 16, 18
Boli 16, 18
Bonal 11, 20, 158, 159, 162
Bond 119
Bottery 68, 71, 76
Bourdieu 67, 71, 76
Bowe 78
Bradford 60, 79
Brain 81
Braslavsky 66, 76
Bray 9, 10, 18, 20
Brehony 60, 76, 77
Brenner 14
Brislin 102, 107, 116
Brooks 64, 82
Brown, P. 13, 18, 41, 46, 54, 56–7, 66, 76, 106, 116, 149–50, 162, 164, 198
Brown, R. 106, 116, 158, 163
Brummitt 1, 18, 42, 56, 86, 90, 98
Brundrett 60, 76
Bubb 65, 77
Bunnell 1, 18, 126, 144, 167, 171, 175, 177, 179, 180
Bush 60, 77
Busher 62, 67, 68, 72, 77
Butt 63, 81
Byram 42, 57

Cadell 10, 18
Caffyn 68, 70, 72, 73, 74, 77, 138, 144
Cairns 65, 77
Callinicos 39, 56
Cambridge 30, 36–7, 61, 65, 68, 71, 74,
    77, 85, 87, 98, 126, 131, 138, 142–3,
    144, 146, 160–1, 163, 166, 180
Cambridge International Examinations
    (CIE) 87, 98, 156
Canterford 42, 43, 56, 83, 90, 91, 97, 98
Carder 110, 116
Carlile 117
Carlson 64, 76
Carlyle 68, 82
Carson 193, 194, 197
Case 64, 77
Castells 22, 37
Clark 36, 37
Clarke 105, 116
Clegg 65, 77
Collier 110, 119
Comaroff 15, 18
Comerford Boyes 81
Connolly 80
Connor 171, 180
Corson 77
Coulby 9, 18
Crossley 132, 144

Dale 2, 11, 12, 14, 18, 20, 163
Danaher 65, 68, 77
Daniel 22, 37
Davies 64, 77, 144
Davis 107, 116
Day 68, 69, 77
DCELLS 187, 197
Deem 60, 76, 77
den Brok 120
Deveney 88, 98, 105, 108, 112, 116
DfES 185, 187, 190, 197
Dibb 91, 98
Dillabough 163, 198
Dimmock 96, 98
Dirlik 8, 9, 18
Dixon 94, 98
Dobson 186, 190, 198
Doeringer 91, 98
Doherty 126, 142, 143, 144, 166, 180
Donoghue 103, 120

Doyle 61, 77
Drennen 114, 116
Duckworth 105, 108, 116
Dunning 61, 69, 72, 73, 78, 80

Earley 77
Ecclestone 62, 78
ECIS 105, 152
Edexcel 87, 98
Elliott 80
Ellwood 61, 78, 107, 116, 138, 144, 158,
    163
Enever 151, 163
Enloe 120
ESL in the Mainstream 93, 98
European Council of International Schools
    163
Evans 23, 37, 64, 78, 144
Ezra 110, 112, 113, 116

Fail 6, 19, 107, 111, 116
Farahmandpur 13, 19
Fennes 103, 106, 116
Ferner 70, 78
Field 62, 78, 129
Findlay, 60, 78
Finegold 137, 144
Fineman 67, 78
Fish 185, 195, 198
Fitz 129, 141, 144
Flores 63, 78
Foucault 30, 62, 64, 66, 67, 68, 71, 78
Fowler 62, 78
Fox 43, 57, 114, 117, 166, 180
Frank 76
Fraser 4, 19
Friedman 87, 98
Fry 113, 117
Fukuyama 3, 19
Furnham 120

Gabriel 72, 74, 78
Gardner 125, 144
Garton 85, 91, 92, 98
Geertz 104, 107, 117
Gerner 111, 117
Gewirtz 60, 64, 65, 78
Giddens 188, 198
Gold 71, 74, 78

Goldfrank 168, 180
Goodman 113, 117
Goodson 63, 64, 79
Gray 3, 4, 19, 88
Green 65, 78
Grenfell 188, 198
Grimshaw 91, 98
Gunesch 111, 117
Gunew 28, 38
Guy 138, 144, 145, 158, 161, 163

Hahn 126, 143, 145
Halicioglu 55, 57
Hall 64, 80, 106, 109, 117, 119
Halsey 163, 198
Hammick 64, 78
Hampden-Turner 106, 109, 120
Handy 66, 78
Hapgood 103, 106, 116
Hardman 70, 78, 84, 85, 86, 99, 126,
  145
Hargreaves 60–4, 66, 69–70, 72, 74, 78,
  79
Harris 61, 72, 77, 80, 117, 168, 181
Hastings 89, 99
Hatcher 65, 79
Hawley 97, 99
Hayden 42, 44, 57, 61, 70, 72, 75, 79,
  83, 88, 94, 96, 98, 99, 100, 101, 112,
  114, 117, 118, 119, 131, 140, 145,
  146, 157, 163
Haywood 70, 79
He Quinglian 48, 57
Held 183, 198
Henderson 54, 57
Herr 60, 68, 79
Hey 60, 79
Heyward 61, 79, 99, 110, 117
Hicks 195, 198
Hill 5, 19, 43, 57, 101, 114, 117, 140,
  145, 165–6, 180
Hinton 102, 104, 112, 117
Hirst 133, 145
Hobsbawm 14, 19
Hobson 55, 57
Hofstede 102–6, 108–9, 112, 117, 126,
  145, 158, 163
Holliday 102, 103, 106, 117
Howes 68, 79

Hoy 67, 79
Hoyle 59, 61, 62, 64, 65, 69, 70, 72,
  79
Huckle 186, 188, 198
Huckman 64, 82
Huntington 3, 19
Hymer 168, 180

Inglehart 107, 117
Inglis 103, 117
International Baccalaureate (IB) 32, 87,
  99, 114, 125–8, 138, 145, 153, 163,
  165–7, 176, 178, 180
International Primary Curriculum (IPC)
  87, 99, 175
International School of Nice 35, 38
International Schools Services (ISS) 83,
  99
International Teacher Certificate (ITC) 95,
  99

Jackson 7, 19
Jalaluddin 7, 19
James 61, 62, 69, 71, 72, 74, 78, 80
Johnson 63, 80
Jones 67, 78
Jonietz 101, 117
Jordan 105, 117
Joslin 83, 99

Kağitçibaşi 119
Kaldor 15, 19
Kaplan 68, 79
Kardinia International College 33, 38
Keck 16, 19
Keep 144
Kerr 139, 146
Kilham 46, 57
Kisby 188, 198
Kluckhohn 103, 118
Knapp 126, 145
Knight 103, 106, 117
Kocka 15, 19
Kohls 103, 106, 117
Kotrc 107, 118
Krathwohl 106, 116
Krober 103, 118
Kugler 143, 145
Kusuma-Powell 110, 118

Labaree 122, 145
Langford 46, 57, 94, 108, 110, 111, 118
Lauder 2, 19, 39, 41, 46, 51, 54, 56, 57,
  66, 76, 150, 151, 163, 187, 198
Lautrette 7, 19
Lave 66, 69, 72, 74, 80, 132, 145
Leach 101, 118, 148, 151, 163
Lee 107, 118
Leggate 97, 99
Leitch 68, 69, 77
Leney 136, 147
Lenski 66, 80
Levy 116, 117, 145, 163
Lewis 7, 16, 19, 159
Lingard 66, 81
Lips 1, 19
Litfin 23, 38
Littleford 64, 70, 80
Louden 72, 82
Lowe 87, 99, 151, 163
Lukes 60, 80

McCaig 110, 118
McCaughtry 82
MacClelland 159, 160, 163
McCleneghan 19
McDaniel 104, 105, 106, 109, 119
MacDonald 1, 19, 42, 57, 64, 80, 82, 87
McGee 173, 180
McInnes 77
MacKenzie 88, 99, 113, 118
McKillop-Ostrom 94, 99
McLaren 13, 19
McNay 60, 80
Magalhaes 148, 149, 163
Marshall 182, 184, 192, 195, 198
Maslen 1, 19
Mattern 107, 118
Matthews 16–17, 19, 71, 80, 95, 99,
  101, 118, 161, 163, 174, 180
Mead 103, 118
Medgyes 91, 100
Mejia 112, 118
Miliband 144
Millican 90, 100
Minoura 120
Morgan 74, 80
MORI/DEA 198
Morley 80

Morris 66, 80
Moscovici 102, 118
Moselle 117
Mu 166, 180
Muijs 61, 80
Mundy 16, 19
Munro 109, 114, 118
Murphy 16, 19, 110, 114, 118
Murray 119

Nelson 97, 100
Newton 60, 78
Nias 63 80
Nilsson Linström 81
Nisbett 109, 118
Norhaidah 105, 119
Nussbaum 183, 198

O Fathaigh 188, 198
O'Brien 188, 198
Oden 159, 163
Odland 92, 100
Oldroyd 64, 80
Olssen 4, 19
Oplatka 64, 80
Osler 142, 145
Oxfam 183, 186, 198

Pak-Sang Lai 42, 57
Paris 114, 118, 163
Parkin 48, 57
Pasternak 113, 118
Pearce 7, 19, 61, 65, 69, 80, 101, 111,
  118, 119
Pennycook 74, 80
Perry 117
Perryman 65, 81
Persson 72, 81
Peters 133, 145
Peterson 41, 101, 119, 136, 145, 166,
  180
Phenix 133, 146
Phillips 65, 71, 81
Pieterse 4, 20, 31, 38
Pinnington 61, 81
Piore 91, 98
Pollock 110, 111, 119
Ponisch 101, 119
Poore 7, 8, 20

Porter 104, 105, 106, 109, 119
Potter 88, 100, 113, 119
Poulantzas 65, 67, 81
Power 60, 65, 66, 67, 68, 77, 81
Price 126, 146
Prickarts 55, 57
Putnam 198

QCA 188, 198
Qian 119
Quicke 68, 71, 81
Quintanilla 70, 78
Quiroz 76
Quist 30, 31, 38

Rader 118
Raffe 144
Rajan 69, 81
Ramalho 152, 163
Rambla 158, 159, 162
Ramesh 55, 57
Rancic 61, 79
Rawlings 131, 146
Reich 50, 51, 57, 148
Reid 64, 81
Reimers 138, 146
Renaud 6, 20, 141, 146
Retallick 63, 81
Richards 72, 81
Rischard 87, 100, 174
Rizvi 28, 38, 64, 66, 68, 81, 183, 185,
    189, 190–1, 193, 195–6, 198
Roberts 16, 20, 63, 71, 77, 81
Robertson 2, 11, 12, 14, 18, 20, 65, 70,
    81, 163
Robinson 40, 48, 49, 54, 57, 168, 181
Robottom 105, 119
Röhrs 126, 146
Ross 110, 119
Roth 183, 198
Rothkopf 57
Rousseau 115, 119
Rowntree 125, 146
Rugus 100
Ruzicka 92, 100

Sachs 64, 67, 81
Said 23, 30, 38
Saks 64, 75

Samovar 104, 105, 106, 109, 119
Sapir 110, 119
Sato 9, 20
Schagen 139, 146
Schirato 77
Schubert 122, 123, 124, 143, 146
Schwartz 107, 119
Scott 41, 124, 125, 126, 127, 130, 133,
    146, 195, 199
Sears 110, 118, 119
Seefried 166, 174, 177, 181
Selvester 64, 77
Sen 3, 4, 20, 172, 181
Shaw 64, 70, 76, 81, 96, 100, 162
Shield 166, 180
Sidhu 12, 16, 17, 19, 20, 71, 80, 161,
    163
Sikkink 16, 19
Simkin 91, 98
Singh 129, 143, 146
Siskin 128, 146
Skinner 105, 119
Sklair 6, 20, 36, 38, 49, 57, 65, 66, 71,
    74, 81, 87, 100
Smith 29, 38, 102, 106, 109, 119, 137,
    146
Snowball 93, 100, 105, 119
Sobulis 165, 181
Spencer-Oatey 109, 119
Spours 144
Stack 117
Starkey 142, 145
Stenhouse 125, 126, 146
Sternberg 105, 119
Stirzaker 93, 95, 100
Stobie 113, 114, 119, 139, 140, 141, 146
Stoer 148, 149, 163
Stuart 46, 57
Sutcliffe 6, 20, 83
Sylvester 2, 20, 41, 57, 126, 146

Tamatea 2, 20
Tao 105, 119
Terwilliger 101, 119
Thaman 30, 38
Theresa 161, 163
Thiong'o 29
Thomas 16, 18, 88, 100, 110, 119, 126,
    146

Thompson 6, 19, 42, 44, 57, 61, 65,
  68, 70, 71, 72, 77, 79, 83, 89, 96, 97,
  99, 100, 113, 116, 117, 118, 120, 131,
  132–4, 136–8, 142–3, 144, 145, 146,
  163
Thrupp 60, 81
Tomlinson 65, 81
Tooley 12, 20
Torrance 158, 164
Totterdell 77
Touraine 15, 20
Tourish 61, 81
Troman 60, 63, 82
Trompenaars 106, 109, 120
Tsolidis 109, 120

Urry 183, 184, 189, 190, 198
Useem 43, 46, 58, 103, 120

Van Oord 7, 8, 20, 102–3, 106, 108,
  112, 120, 126, 147, 158, 164, 165,
  181
Van Reken 110, 111, 119
Vare 195, 199
Vidovich 60, 82
Vryonides 65, 78
Vygotsky 105, 120

Walford 134, 147
Walker 6, 19, 96, 98, 104, 107, 114,
  116, 117, 120, 163, 170, 176,
  181
Wallace 61, 64, 82
Walsh 91, 100

Walters 175, 181
Ward 110, 120
Watson 59, 67, 68, 72, 82
Webb 60, 77, 82
Weenink 65, 183, 185, 187, 188, 189,
  190, 194, 199
Whitehead 64, 82, 126, 143, 147, 185,
  199
Whitty 64, 65, 81
Wigford 90, 92, 100
Wildy 72, 82
Wilkinson 41, 44, 45, 58, 126, 147
Willis 113, 120
Willmott 60, 81
Winters 52, 58
Wood 40, 54, 58, 82
World Bank 1, 20
Wright 60, 71, 82
Wrigley 60, 68, 82
Wylie 2, 20, 27, 28, 33, 38, 134, 135,
  147

Yamamoto 18, 20
Young 64, 82, 136, 144, 147, 148–9,
  164, 184–6, 192–3, 199
Yuan 119
Yusuf 52, 58

Zambeta 9, 18
Zaretsky 60, 65, 82
Zembylas 69, 82
Zilber 6, 20, 65, 82
Zsebik 64, 70, 82
Zuo 119

Subject index

A level (GCE Advanced level) 87, 136, 137

Advanced Placement (AP) 136, 152, 157

Africa 1, 12, 23, 25, 166, 169, 171–2, 174, 176, 177, 179, 185

Aga Khan Academies 176

Alliance for International Education 174, 175

America see USA

AQA (Assessment and Qualifications Alliance) 175

Argentina 33, 175

ASEAN 8

Asia 1, 12, 174, 176,

attitudes 5, 6, 8, 16, 45, 64, 103, 104, 106, 107, 108, 110, 128, 142, 153, 186–7, 191, 194

Australia 1, 12, 16, 26, 28, 32–3, 83, 89, 149, 152, 155, 165, 166, 169, 170, 171, 172, 173, 175, 196

Australian Council for Educational Research (ACER) 160

benchmarks 159

Bislama 26

border artistry 166,

boundaries 4, 73–4, 89, 127, 133–4, 137, 141, 153–4, 184, 192–3

Brazil 172

British Council 172

Cambridge: Advanced International Certificate of Education 132, 136; AICE 132; ESOL Examinations 156; International Examinations (CIE) 87, 95, 136, 156, 157, 161; International

General Certificate of Secondary Education (IGCSE) 26–7, 87, 132, 138–9, 152, 156–8; International Primary Programme 175; University of Cambridge Local Examinations Syndicate (UCLES) 156

Canada 1, 35, 83, 152, 165, 171, 175

China 1, 25, 33, 41, 47–8, 51–4, 57, 58, 87, 169, 171–2

Chinese students 9

citizenship, 13, 15–16, 40, 44, 46, 55, 56, 131, 138, 142–3, 182–4, 186–8, 190, 192–7

civil society 14, 15, 33, 134, 135, 188

classification 127, 128, 134, 137–8, 141

Cold War 3

collection code 128, 134, 156

College Board 157, 161

colonialism 2, 9, 23, 24, 28–9, 33, 37, 80, 134–5

constructivism 105

continuity 113, 116, 122, 131, 139–40

contract of employment 85

cosmopolitan citizenship 142, 183

cosmopolitanism 4, 142, 182–3, 185, 187–91, 196, 197

Council of International Schools (CIS) 21, 92

cross-phase liaison 139, 142

cultural identity 6, 15, 27, 31, 111

Curriculum, Evaluation and Management Centre (CEMC) 160

Dubai 176

Earth Charter 177
Ecuador 171, 175
elites 2, 16, 29, 35–6, 37, 39, 41–5,
    47–50, 54–6, 65–6, 68, 70–1, 88, 143,
    150–51, 165, 166–71, 175, 178–9,
    188
emotions 65, 68–9, 72–5, 104
English, native speakers 7, 83–4, 88, 91
English medium education 10, 83, 86–8,
    94, 101, 104
English as a Second Language (ESL) 93,
    98
English for Speakers of Other Languages
    (ESOL) 156
epistemology 29, 125
essentialism 102–4, 106–8, 110–11, 114
Eurocentrism 9, 29
Europe 1, 8, 35, 47, 151, 157, 174
European Baccalaureate 132, 136
European Schools 132
European Union (EU) 12, 132, 185
expatriates 6, 7, 9, 33, 37, 42, 44, 72–4,
    84–8, 90, 132, 143
experiential learning 89, 126

Fieldwork Education Ltd 175
Fiji 27
framing 128, 134, 141
France 26, 32, 33, 37, 167, 172
franchising 160–1,
French Baccalaureate 27

Gabbitas 92
GATS (General Agreement over Trade in
    Services) 12–3
gender 4, 5, 9, 22, 36, 63, 109, 124
Germany 49, 171
global capitalism 8, 25
global citizenship 2, 16–17, 46, 71,
    142–3, 162, 182–97
global civil society, 2, 10, 15–6, 25,
    33–4, 36–7, 134–35
global corporate social engagement
    11
global culture 4, 7, 9
global labour market 42, 46, 50–1,
    53
global markets 2, 10, 16, 34, 40, 71
global nomads 46

Hahn, Kurt 2, 5, 126, 168
hidden curriculum 113, 133
Hong Kong 10, 45

imperialism 28–31, 36, 56, 107, 132,
    134
independent schools 11, 131
India 25, 41, 44, 45, 47, 49, 51–4, 90,
    169, 171–2, 175
individualism 108, 189, 193, 196
Indonesia 61
Information and Communications
    Technology (ICT) 2, 22–3, 25, 33, 36,
    156
instrumentalist 124, 127, 182–7, 189,
    192–7
integrated code 128, 134, 156
intercultural education 5, 6
International Association for the
    Evaluation of Educational Achievement
    (IAEEA) 158
International Baccalaureate: Creativity,
    Action, Service (CAS) 35, 138, 154;
    Diploma Programme (DP) 32, 43,
    54–5, 135, 138, 140–1, 151–3, 155–7,
    162, 165, 168–75, 177–9; Extended
    Essay 138; Jeff Thompson Research
    Fellowships 95; Learner Profile 126,
    128, 167, 173; Middle Years
    Programme (MYP) 138–41, 152–3,
    155, 157, 158, 165, 171–2; Online
    Curriculum Centre (OCC) 154;
    organization 6, 17, 21, 27, 32–6, 39,
    45, 87, 95, 114, 125–9, 131–3, 136,
    138, 140, 142–4, 152, 165, 167, 174,
    185–6; Peterson Lecture 176; Primary
    Years Programme (PYP) 33–4, 126,
    138, 152–3, 155, 165, 172, 175;
    Teacher Award 95; Theory of
    Knowledge (TOK) 138, 154
International Baccalaureate Schools and
    Colleges Association (IBSCA) 174
international competitiveness 159
international curriculum 17, 44, 87, 114,
    121–2, 125, 128, 131, 133, 135, 139,
    142, 144
International Labour Office (ILO) 167
international mindedness 71, 89, 131,
    134, 153, 158–9, 161–2

International Monetary Fund 13
International Primary Curriculum (IPC) 87, 175
international qualifications 41, 151, 156
International School of Moshi 35
International Schools Assessment (ACER) 160, 162
International Schools Association (ISA) 6
International Schools Services (ISS) 83, 91, 92
International Teacher Certificate (ITC) 95
international understanding 2, 140
international values 7, 134
internationalism 5, 16, 26, 32, 66, 68, 71, 74, 132, 183
interstitial learning 133
Ireland 83
ISC Research 176
Italy 169, 172

Japan 12, 33, 93, 113, 152, 172

knowledge society 148
knowledge workers 149
Korea 33, 47, 55

leadership 7, 47, 59, 61, 63–6, 69–71, 96–7, 177
League of Nations 167
liberal democracy 3, 142
liberal individualism 15, 196

Mexico 171, 175
middle class 1, 12, 22, 31, 43, 50, 65, 141, 143, 148, 183
Middle East 171, 172, 174, 176, 179
migration 6
minorities 4, 5, 30
mobility 6, 10, 41, 44, 94, 114, 122, 131, 135, 152
multicultural 5, 46, 88, 90, 94, 101, 105–6, 130, 142, 159

national identity 13, 45, 55, 142
Nauru 33
neo-liberalism 2, 31, 40, 49
Nepal 10
Netherlands 55, 134, 183
New Labour 188

New Zealand 12, 27, 33, 83, 152, 172
Nigeria 172
North America 43, 174; *see also* Canada, USA

OECD 12, 22, 158, 160
Oxfam 183, 186, 187

Pacific Islands 30
Pacific Senior Secondary Certificate 27
pedagogised society 148
pedagogy 2, 21, 23–5, 30, 33, 36, 37, 59, 75, 88–90, 94, 104, 124, 126, 128, 132, 134–5, 141, 144, 153, 158, 160, 162, 192–3, 197, 198
PIRLS 158
PISA (Programme for International Student Assessment) 13, 158, 160
positional advantage 43, 150, 159, 162
positional competition 36, 39, 43, 56, 122, 131, 142, 151
post-colonialism 2, 31, 34
post-welfare 61, 63, 65
private sector 11, 13, 43
progression 129, 139
psychodynamics 61, 62, 69, 72–5

Qatar 176
qualifications frameworks 149

racism 162
recruitment fairs 92
Russia 172

salary scales 126
SAT (Scholastic Achievement Test) 152, 157
Saudi Arabia 176
Save the Children 187
Search Associates 92
Shanghai 9
Singapore 87, 156, 174
social class 5, 39, 40, 103, 127, 168, 188
South Africa 83, 193
Spain 171, 175
standards 27, 43, 123, 131, 156, 159–60, 168, 173, 185
Subject Tests Preparation Center 157
sustainability 183, 186

Sweden 171
symbolic analysts 50–1, 148

Tanzania 35, 169
Teachers International Consultancy 92
textbook industry 11
Thailand 33, 87, 112,
third culture kid (TCK); *see also* global
    nomad 46–7, 51, 110–11, 114
TIMSS 158
totalitarianism 15
trade liberalisation 12
trailing spouse 85
transnational advocacy networks 16
transnational capitalist class (TCC) 6, 8,
    35, 36, 65, 87, 168
transnational corporations (TNCs) 11–13,
    16, 36, 41, 46–51, 53, 54, 56, 66
Turkey 54

UNESCO 167, 177
UNICEF 187
United Kingdom 1, 25, 33, 35, 47, 83,
    89, 91, 114, 133, 152, 171, 175,
    182–5, 187–8, 190, 194; Britain 43,
    50, 165, 173; England 134, 136–7,
    139, 165, 170, 171, 174, 175, 179,
    188; Wales 136–7, 168, 188

United Nations 126, 166, 167
United World Colleges (UWC) 5, 6, 20,
    45, 101, 113, 120, 126, 146, 168
Universal Primary Education 12
USA 1, 8, 12, 22, 25, 33, 34–5, 42,
    43, 47, 49, 53, 64, 83, 89, 91, 105,
    110, 113–14, 133, 143, 152, 157,
    161, 165, 167, 170, 171, 172, 174–5,
    177–9

values 3, 6, 7, 9, 15, 16, 25, 30, 33, 36,
    42, 45, 47, 55, 59, 61, 65, 67, 71, 89,
    94, 103–4, 106–7, 113–14, 126, 128,
    131, 133–4, 139–40, 143, 158, 168,
    176, 183, 185–6, 190–1, 195
Vanuatu 26, 27, 28, 32, 37
Vietnam 33

Welsh Assembly 187, 197
World Bank 1, 13, 174
world citizenship 140
World Class Learning Schools and
    Systems Group 175
World Economic Forum 13
World Trade Organisation (WTO) 12,
    14, 49

Zimbabwe 7